The
Changing Countryside
in Victorian and Edwardian
England and Wales

'By the rivers of Babylon, there we sat down, yea,
we wept, when we remembered Zion.'   Psalm 137, v.1

The
Changing Countryside
in Victorian and Edwardian
England and Wales

Pamela Horn

THE ATHLONE PRESS
LONDON

FAIRLEIGH DICKINSON UNIVERSITY PRESS
RUTHERFORD · MADISON · TEANECK

First published 1984 by The Athlone Press Ltd
44 Bedford Row, London WC1R 4LY
and Associated University Presses,
440 Forsgate Drive, Cranbury
New Jersey 08512 USA

British Library Cataloguing in Publication Data

Horn, Pamela
The changing countryside in Victorian and Edwardian England and Wales
1. England – Rural conditions – 19th century
2. England – Rural conditions – 20th century
I. Title
942′.00973′4   HN398.E5
ISBN 0-485-11235-3

Library of Congress Cataloging in Publication Data

Horn, Pamela.
The changing countryside, 1870–1918.
Bibliography: p.
1. England – Rural conditions. 2. Wales – Rural conditions.
3. England – Economic conditions. 4. Wales – Economic conditions.
I. Title.
HN398.E5H67 1984   307.7′2′0942   84-4025
ISBN 0-8386-3232-7

Printed in Great Britain by
Nene Litho, Earls Barton, Northants
Bound by Woolnough Bookbinding,
Wellingborough, Northants

Contents

Illustrations

Tables

Acknowledgements

I should like to thank all those who have helped in the preparation of this book. My thanks are due, in particular, to Mrs Crispin Gascoigne for permission to quote from the Harcourt manuscripts at the Bodleian Library, Oxford; to Miss Dorothy B. Dew, for allowing me to use the diaries of her father, Mr George James Dew; and to the Duke of Bedford and the Trustees of the Bedford Settled Estate for permission to quote from records at the Bedford Estate Office in London.

I have received much help from the staff at the Libraries and Record Offices in which I have worked or who have provided me with information. These include the Bodleian Library, Oxford; the British Library; the British Library Newspaper Library, Colindale; the Imperial War Museum; the Museum of English Rural Life, Reading; Reading University Library; Christ Church, Oxford; the Public Record Office; the Library of the National Union of Teachers; the National Library of Wales; and the county record offices of Buckinghamshire, Essex, Hampshire, Northamptonshire, Oxfordshire, and Pembrokeshire in the county of Dyfed.

As always, I owe a great debt to my famiily for their help and support. My mother has provided personal reminiscences of country life before and during the First World War and my husband has, as always, helped in many ways. Without his assistance this book could not have been written.

Pamela Horn
April 1983

Notes on the System of References
The reference numbers in the text refer the reader to the corresponding entry in the Bibliography section at the end of the book.

Conversion Table

Shillings and pence and some illustrative decimal coinage
equivalents

1d	½p	1s 7d	8p
2d		1s 8d	8½p
3d	1p	1s 9d	
4d	1½p	1s 10d	9p
5d	2p	1s 11d	9½p
6d	2½p	2s	10p
7d	3p	2s 6d	12½p
8d	3½p	2s 9d	
9d		2s 10d	14p
10d	4p	3s	15p
11d	4½p	5s	25p
1s	5p	7s 6d	37½p
1s 1d	5½p	10s	50p
1s 2d		12s 6d	62½p
1s 3d	6p	13s 6d	67½p
1s 4d	6½p	15s 0d	75p
1s 5d	7p	18s 0d	90p
1s 6d	7½p	20s 0d	100p i.e. £1
		£1 5s 0d	£1.25

Introduction

In discussing the nature of change within the countryside of England and Wales between 1870 and 1918, there is a danger that the historian will be tempted to make sweeping assertions or to draw broad conclusions, which are not justified by the evidence. This is particularly true where efforts are made to advance a particular unifying thesis about the processes of change, for real life often obstinately refuses to be fitted into a neat theoretical framework. Throughout the period there were wide divergences of experience not only between arable and pastoral districts, and between highland and lowland regions, but within those areas and even within individual parishes. Access to capital, and variations in farming ability, size of holding, or the nature of the land itself might call forth different responses, even within a relatively limited geographical district. As the Farnham wheelwright George Sturt put it, 'the art and crafts of farming vary, with every variation of soil'. Equally, the way of life of the large landowner and the substantial tenant farmer was very different from that of the small cultivator, carefully tilling a few acres with the help of members of his family and with little reward beyond a sense of pride in his precarious independence.

Such differences survived the buffetings of agricultural depression in the final quarter of the nineteenth century, as cheap imports of food, particularly from Australasia and the Americas, undermined the competitive position of the British farmer and led to sharp price falls. In the early years these difficulties were reinforced by the effects of bad harvests at home, which cut crop yields and added to farming costs. Initially it was the grain producers who were the principal sufferers from these developments, but by the mid-1890s imports of frozen meat and dairy produce were undermining the position of the livestock men as well. Not until the early twentieth century was there a slowing down in the inflow, and a modest recovery in prices.

Yet, with these limitations on the scale and scope of rural

1

change, it is still possible to trace an overall pattern in the way society developed. Transport improvements, better educational provision, and the growing availability of cheap newspapers opened up village life to outside influences, and encouraged the migration of many people – especially the young – to the towns or even overseas, where opportunities for economic and social advance seemed more promising. Employment in agriculture, forestry and fishing, which had absorbed about 15.1 per cent of the British labour force in 1871, had dropped to only 8.7 per cent of the total thirty years later, while the respective figures for manufacturing industry and mining were 43.1 per cent and 46.3 per cent, with the position changing little thereafter up to the time of the First World War. National income statistics underline these trends. As late as 1871 agriculture, forestry and fishing contributed perhaps 14.2 per cent of the British national income; this had fallen to 6.1 per cent by 1901. By contrast the share of manufactures, mining and building had grown from 38.1 per cent of national income in 1871 to 40.2 per cent thirty years later.[147]

The extension of mass-production techniques and technological change to manufacturing industry also undermined the prosperity of country craftsmen and the workers in cottage industries. Some were able to adapt to the new conditions, like the blacksmiths who concentrated on the repair of machinery and upon their work as farriers, or the wheelwrights who took on the tasks of ordinary carpenters, but many were forced to move out. For farmers and landowners, too, in much of England and Wales, the effects of cheap food imports from the 1870s brought about changes in husbandry methods and cropping techniques, as well as leading to falling rentals and some reduction in living standards. But the transforming powers of adverse circumstances should not be exaggerated. Even in 1908 the historian of Hertfordshire agriculture could assert that English farming was 'still largely a matter of use and tradition – a social form as much as a business', adding gloomily that '[William] Ellis's account of how it was practised in Hertfordshire in 1732 may still, with a few additions, be taken as a very fair picture of what it is to-day'.[224]

Yet, as the economic importance of agriculture and of rural trades and crafts dwindled in the face of growing industrialisation and foreign competition, and as the migration of agricultural workers and their families proceeded apace, among the newly prosperous urban middle classes there was, paradoxically, a yearning to return to what were seen as the simpler verities of village life. During the last years of the nineteenth century, rural parishes on the fringes of many towns were swallowed up into suburbs and there were doubtless large numbers of country people who shared George Sturt's resentment at this alien invasion. In March 1898, Sturt wrote sourly in his journal of the 'abominable villas' which were being built in his part of Surrey. This intrusion of the outside world was to become yet more pervasive during the First World War, with its need for the construction of army camps, aerodromes and munitions factories in erstwhile rural areas and its insatiable demand for men and horses.

This book seeks to trace the course of change within the country community during what was, in many respects, a watershed in the nation's history. Already by 1851 a majority of English men and women had ceased to dwell in rural areas. But it was between 1870 and 1918 that the centuries-old predominance of country life and attitudes was finally swept aside by industrialisation and by war. It was in these years that the economic, social and political subordination of the agricultural interest to manufacturing industry and the service sector was irrevocably established.

Nowadays there is a tendency to look back with nostalgia to Victorian and Edwardian village life, to an existence which seems more secure and peaceful than the world we know today. But a closer investigation reveals that this stability was more apparent than real. The anxieties of agricultural recession, the declining influence of the landed classes, the diminishing support for religious institutions and the disruption of many traditional aspects of rural life were also widely experienced. They are indicative of powerful underlying stresses and tensions. As early as 1856 the novelist George Eliot had warned against the tendency to romanticize rural life, when she wrote scornfully of painters who depicted 'idyllic ploughmen' driving their teams merrily to the field and 'idyllic shepherds' making 'bashful love under hawthorn bushes'. As she drily observed, 'selfish instincts are not subdued by the sight of buttercups . . . To make men moral something more is requisite than to turn them out to grass'. When we examine the process of change and decline in much of country life between 1870 and 1918, it is as well to recall George Eliot's cynical comments.

1
The Mid-Victorian Countryside

At the beginning of the 1870s the English countryside had probably never looked more prosperous. Despite occasional black spots, the general picture was one of well-tilled fields, neatly laid hedges and comfortable farmhouses, with gates and fences in good repair. The overall impression was of order and stability, of good management, and of the availability of a plentiful supply of skilled labour which took pride in a job well carried out.

Community ties remained strong, especially in the south, the midlands and rural Wales, where there was little inward migration to upset the established pattern of local society. At the 1871 census of population, 70 per cent or more of the agricultural labourers in parishes as far apart as Yetminster in Dorset, Milton-under Wychwood in Oxfordshire and Wilburton in Cambridgeshire were working in the place of their birth. Inevitably this meant that people grew up knowing their neighbours as the fathers, mothers, brothers and sisters of school friends, and appreciating how they fitted into the general kinship network. Given the small scale of society, they were also inescapably involved in one another's affairs, and if an individual offended against the traditional values of that society, he or she was likely to be made aware of it in no uncertain terms. At Harpenden in Hertfordshire, Edwin Grey described one fairly common response when he noted that if any 'glaring case of immorality' occurred, the offending parties would be treated to what was termed 'rough music': 'at the appointed time one might have seen a very mixed-up gang, composed of men, youths, and women, gathered outside the offenders' house, each member of the gang carrying some sort of article whereby he or she could make discordant noises; old kettles with stones inside, old tea-trays and sticks, bells, whistles, clackers . . . At a given signal all would get in procession and march to and fro past the house, rattling the kettles, banging the tea-trays . . . making a most terrific and earsplitting din, for about an hour or so, and this for three successive nights sometimes.'[172] In that way, communal

5

disapproval was made clearly manifest, and the offending parties given an opportunity to mend their ways.

The close-knit character of rural life was underlined by the fact that few labouring people travelled beyond the nearest market town, which they could visit on foot or in a carrier's cart. Only the most venturesome took advantage of railway excursions in the mid-Victorian years, and thereby came into contact with the wider world.

Yet, these impressions of continuity and well-being were deceptive. Already the processes of decline had set in which were to topple agriculture from its erstwhile dominance of the nation's affairs. In the century which followed the advent of steam power and its application to manufacturing production, in the 1780s and beyond, the British economy had been slowly weaned from a dependence on farming and its associated trades to a reliance on industrial development. During those years it was the major manufacturing towns and the coalmining areas of the north which gained most markedly in population and importance. Now the prosperity of England and Wales had come to rest on its exports of coal, manufactured goods, and services and on its earnings from overseas investment, while, in return, it purchased increasing quantities of food and raw materials from abroad.

In social matters, too, the half-century which separated mid-Victorian England from the outbreak of the First World War was of great importance. In 1871, well over a third of the population was still living in rural areas; by 1911 that proportion had fallen to little more than a fifth. There were frequent complaints that the younger and more active men and women, impatient with the limited opportunities and narrow prospects of village life, were leaving the countryside for better-paid employment in the towns or the coal mines. As one Oxfordshire schoolmaster put it, in his parish 'three-quarters of the young men and all the young women left the village at nineteen or twenty years of age, only the dullest staying at home.'[177] Politicians, in their concern to stem the outflow, promoted legislation during the 1880s and 1890s to provide allotments and smallholdings, so as to give the labourer a modest stake in the soil. But their efforts had little effect and the exodus continued to the end of the century. At the same time the total of male farm labourers, shepherds and farm servants of all ages employed in England and Wales fell from more than 920,000 in 1871 to just over 600,000 thirty years later.

In this process of urbanization and industrial growth, the nature of the rural community itself altered considerably. Whilst many villages shrank in size as a result of the outward migration, others were transformed into industrial centres, like D. H. Lawrence's childhood home of Eastwood on the Nottinghamshire/Derbyshire border, which lost its rural character as the coal mines expanded, or Wolverton in Buckinghamshire, which developed as a railway town and increased its population by 25 per cent during the 1890s alone. In other cases, towards the end of the century, communities on the fringes of large cities were transformed into suburbs or commuter belts. The middle-class, town-bred people who moved to them had little sympathy with the old way of life. Instead, as George Sturt wrote bitterly of his own Surrey hamlet, they were preoccupied with their card and tennis parties and with having 'nicer neighbours, of our own sort'.[261]

In the early 1870s much of this gloomy future for agriculture was still hidden and farmers and landowners, if not their labourers, could look back on a 'golden age' which had lasted for more than a decade. Despite the fears which had been expressed when the Corn Laws were repealed in 1846 and the home food market opened to unrestricted foreign competition, agrriculture had remained largely prosperous. Partly this was because the European countries, thanks to their own growing populations, had no large stocks of food to hand for shipment to Britain. American production, too, was still in its infancy, although over the period 1854–66 the USA did supply 35 per cent of wheat imports, as opposed to Germany's 20 per cent and Russia's 17 per cent.[134] Another cause for optimism lay in the high investment and seemingly favourable returns available to both landlord and tenant so long as they kept a judicious eye on market trends and adjusted their output accordingly. More than one farmer would have agreed with the West Country yeoman who described the early 1870s as 'the glorious Victorian peak of the last lap of really prosperous agriculture' in the nineteenth century.[201]

Already there was an effective railway network within the country which had increased the choice of distribution outlets. With this improvement in communications, graziers, market gardeners and livestock breeders from the 1840s and 1850s could despatch their produce and animals to the towns without arranging laborious journeys by road and canal. Producers could choose the optimum moment at which to sell, and the long-distance drover and his noisy cavalcade of cattle and sheep no longer plodded from Wales and Scotland to the English markets. Apart from the central area of Wales and perhaps the border country in the north, there were few farms which in the 1870s were unable to get their cattle or their carts to a railway station within a day.

Agriculturists gained, too, from their access to bigger markets. As the *Welshman* declared in 1871, the 'Manchester and Milford railway [had] done as much good to Cardiganshire as if an immense town had sprung up in the midst, with thousands of population requiring to be fed'.[191] Even traditional fairs and marketing centres were affected by the growth of weekly or monthly auction sales held on or near the railroads, while it became common for travelling dealers to buy grain and livestock *in situ* on the farm. Although fairs survived more vigorously in Wales than in England as a means of transferring animals from scattered rearing grounds to the grazing districts near to towns and cities, there were changes here, too. The Llanbadarn fairs, for example, were merged with those of Aberystwyth, and Bridgend increased its importance as a marketing centre at the expense of Cowbridge.

The building of the railways had arguably an even greater impact in undermining the social isolation of rural life. Coal, once regarded as a luxury for the poor in areas remote from the coalfields, began to replace wood, turf and furze on cottage fires. Shops in country towns had a wider range of goods for sale, and although farm workers may rarely have travelled by train themselves, they became aware of events in the world outside their own village as a result of the wider distribution of newspapers and of improvements in the postal service which the railways helped to achieve. In Wales it was estimated in 1870 that farm wages had risen by between a third and a half as a result of the construction of the railways, since men could now more easily move to better-paid employment in the mines and ironworks of Monmouth and Glamorgan. As a result the bargaining position of those who remained behind was enhanced, and they were able to secure better pay.[61]

In a minor way the rail companies continued to provide jobs for country workers, too. Although the great days of building contractors and 'navvies' were now at an end, almost five-and-a-half thousand miles of new track were constructed between 1875 and 1910. In addition, posts were available as linesmen, porters, booking clerks and signalmen for a minority of villagers. But their contribution should not be exaggerated; as the census returns show, many villages even in 1871 had no railway workers at all.

By the 1870s, therefore, the innovatory impact of railway building had largely ended. But its role in social and economic relationships was still clearly apparent. Much the same was true of another, older source of community change, the enclosure movement. Only in a few places was this still a live issue, although vast tracts of upland waste remained unenclosed, particularly in Wales. In 1894 the principality's 'cultivated' land was put at only 59.8 per cent of its total area, while in England it amounted to 76.4 per cent. But the high cost of enclosing such marginal territory made it unattractive, particularly in Wales, where agricultural capital was in notoriously short supply. Significantly, too, when attempts were made to enclose land in the Roe area of Carnarvonshire during the 1850s and 1860s, they were met with sustained resistance from the local people on a scale reminiscent of an earlier, more violent age. As Home Office correspondence reveals, walls were torn down during the night by gangs of armed men, and in the spring of 1870 the chief constable was forced to arm some of his own men, who were 'employed at night on the hills, to prevent them being drawn off & killed'.

In the New Forest in Hampshire, enclosure also continued to arouse feeling, forming the subject of anxious debate into the 1870s. As the commoners and their friends warned a Select Committee in 1868, if they lost their rights of grazing it would 'be simply ruin'. It was pointed out that cottagers, too, benefited from being allowed to cut turfs and to collect wood, or to turn out pigs to eat the acorns and beech mast during the pannage season. The cutting of furze and heath faggots likewise provided fuel for firing the local pottery kilns, as well as supplying the raw material for broom-making, which was another local industry, along with charcoal-burning and the making of wooden shovels. The land issue here was bitterly contested for almost a decade, until the commoners emerged victorious in 1877, with a guarantee that no more of the forest would be enclosed.

But in most areas these questions of territorial boundaries had been settled many years before, and it was enclosure's role in emphasizing the tripartite divisions of British agriculture into landowners, farmers and labourers which was now significant. Over much of the country it was the larger landowners and the bigger tenant farmers who emerged, in the long run, as the major beneficiaries from such developments, and this was reflected in the increasing lavishness of their personal expenditure.

It was with these events in mind that the historian of English farming, Rowland Prothero (later Lord Ernle), wrote enthusiastically of the prosperity of the mid-Victorian countryside:

> During the 'Sixties', while the Continent and America were at war, England enjoyed peace. The seasons were uniformly favourable; harvests, except that of 1860, were good, fair, or abundant; . . . imports of corn, meat, and dairy produce supplemented, without displacing, home supplies. Even the removal of the shilling duty on corn in 1869 produced little effect. Counteracted as it was by the demand for grain from France in 1870–71, it failed to help foreign growers to force down the price of British corn. . . . Even when corn began to decline in value, meat and dairy produce maintained their price or even advanced. . . . Rentals rose rapidly; yet still farmers made money.[154]

Boosted by increasing rents, landowners, too, were encouraged to build or extend their own houses and to improve their estates. Over the period 1847–78, the Duke of Northumberland laid out £992,000 in draining, building and other improvements to his estate, while during the same period other major landowners, like the Duke of Cleveland, the Marquess of Bath and Lord Sidmouth were spending around £7 10s. per acre on improvements to their properties.[266] Between 1856 and 1875 the Duke of Bedford spent £566,558 on his estate in Cambridgeshire and no less than £832,274 on that in Bedfordshire and Buckinghamshire. Although some of the outlay covered general running expenses or charitable payments, £142,553 was spent on 'new works and permanent improvements' on the former estate and £203,833 on the latter, during these years. On both properties the sum far exceeded amounts spent on similar projects during either the preceding twenty years or those which followed.[131] In several instances, too, as with the Earl of Scarborough's estate at Sandbeck in Yorkshire, effort was concentrated on building up a compact property by purchase or by land exchanges with other owners. An additional motive here was anxiety to protect shooting rights: 'An effort was always made to buy land which might go to urban purchasers who wanted it for its proximity to estate game preserves.'[129]

In some cases landowners took advantage of the £4m. Exchequer loans offered under the Public Money Drainage Act of 1846, or of sums made available by the various land improvement companies which were set up between 1846 and 1870 with funds largely provided by the insurance companies. The cost of loans was met by rent-charges imposed for a specified number of years upon the improved property. Elsewhere, cash was advanced for the building of new farm houses or, more frequently, for the construction of farm buildings and labourers' cottages. Unfortunately, it was later found that despite the higher rents secured under the various schemes, much of this spending was misplaced, even before the onset of the 'difficult' years, since the return on capital invested was rarely more than 2 per cent to the landowner himself. In commercial life a return of at least 4 per cent would have been expected. Indeed, on Lord Pembroke's estate at Wilton in Wiltshire between 1862 and 1871, the outcome was so unsatisfactory that whilst improvement charges increased by £5,000 a year, rents rose by only £3,100. The Marquess of Bath, too, became so concerned about his expenditure that in 1867 he brought in an outside agent to report on the estate's finances.[142]

On the positive side, many acres of quagmire, reeds, rushes and buttercups were transformed by these endeavours into dry sweet pastureland or converted to tillage. But improvement was patchy, with progress slowest in the north of England. In 1870 an official inquiry discovered that in eleven out of forty-two English counties drainage operations had been negligible; in a mere six were they completed or not required.

The building and remodelling of country houses was another absorbing preoccupation of the landed classes during the mid-Victorian years, and an examination of construction dates for five hundred such properties erected or altered between 1835 and 1889 shows them reaching a peak of seventy-four between 1870 and 1874. After that the total fell sharply. Indoor domestic staffs matched the opulence of these new edifices, with fifty or more servants employed in the largest houses, like Eaton Hall in Cheshire or Thoresby Hall in Nottinghamshire. At Holkham Hall in Norfolk, the Earl of Leicester had a resident staff of thirty at the time of the 1871 population census, and in addition a coachman, three stable helpers, and a gamekeeper who resided in a bothy attached to the stables. There was also a butler who was married and lived out. Anything eligible for the title of a country house was unlikely to have fewer than eight resident domestics.

Social gradations within these households were carefully observed. Each person had his or her established niche, be it that of the most highly regarded guest or member of the family, or the least considered scullery maid. Even the staircases and the entrances of the houses reflected the hierarchical arrangements. As Mark Girouard has written, a country house could easily have six staircases, including men and women's staircases in the servants' wing, the main staircase, 'the back staircase (it was, of course, inconceivable that servants could go up the main staircase, except to clean it); a family staircase leading from outside the boudoir up to the master-bedroom suite and on up to the nurseries; and a bachelors' staircase'.[167]

The larger farmers shared some of their landlords' affluence and, often enough, aped their life-style. As had been the case during the Napoleonic Wars more than half a century before, contemporaries commented critically on their pretensions. James Cornish, son of the vicar of Debenham in Suffolk, recalled that in his parish, the landowner, the Duke of Hamilton, had to prohibit his tenant farmers from giving luncheon to the 'field' when his harriers met at a farmhouse because 'the hospitality of the farmers was so lavish that it entailed great expense on them and, of course, was not beneficial to the hunting in the afternoon.'[140] In the years of prosperity a mistaken view gained ground that farming was an easy task. As one MP put it in 1875, even 'retired tinkers and tailors' from the towns sold their businesses and 'settled down as farmers'. Later the extravagant and the unskilled among them were to learn by bitter experience the error of their ways.

The new generation of farmers were impatient with the narrow, self-sufficient attitudes of their predecessors, content with growing most of their own food and brewing their own beer. They demanded instead silk dresses for their wives, a piano, claret, a well-bred hunter and a governess for their children. Some, like S. G. Kendall's father, who farmed 700 acres on the Wiltshire/ Somerset border, sent their sons to boarding school, where they could mix with 'boys drawn from a higher class'. It was in these circumstances that a member of the prosperous Stratton family of Kingston Deverill in Wiltshire recalled taking over a farm in 1864 on which his predecessor had required the groom 'to take his hat off when he brought his horse to the door'. As Stratton ironically added: 'One of Mr Simonds' legacies was a great supply of rats.'[9] Whilst the good times lasted, the dangers of this self-indulgent approach to farming were not apparent, but when conditions became difficult, many were slow to appreciate the need to adapt to the new circumstances.

During the 'golden' years only the labourers had little cause for rejoicing. Admittedly wages moved upwards in many parts of the country, but in certain of the more remote areas they barely kept pace with price increases. In 1860, the average basic weekly wage in Dorset and Norfolk was put at 9s. 4d. and 10s. 7d., respectively; by 1869–70, these figures were virtually unchanged at 9s. 4d. and 10s. 5d., even though the retail price index was around 2 per cent higher.[181] Only in the north of England and the industrial mid-lands, where alternative employment was available in urban factories and the mines, or on the fringes of London, where demand for labour was also heavy, were wage rates high and a measure of prosperity assured, with day labourers in Northumberland, the North and West Ridings of Yorkshire, and Cumberland receiving almost 16s a week at the end of the 1860s. But on average, agricultural wage rates were little more than half the average industrial rate at that date.[215]

Some men enjoyed perquisites, like free fuel, cheap milk and other foodstuffs, or a free cottage, which could supplement basic cash earnings, or the opportunity to carry out piecework tasks at the busy seasons, such as spring hoeing or the hay and corn harvests. But these benefits were often counterbalanced by their being laid off during the winter when work was in short supply. A Kentish witness claimed in 1881 that workers in his area lost an average of eighty-five days a year due to inclement weather.[283] Many more men lost at least thirty to forty days per annum.

The labour of women and children provided a more worthwhile supplement to family income, especially in the arable counties, although only in Northumberland, where the 'bondager' system flourished, was there a large permanent female labour force on the land. Under this arrangement a male farm worker was required by his employer to supply a female assistant. She was hired by the labourer, 'fed and housed by him, and paid wages', which in the 1860s averaged about £12 a year. A bondager 'is strictly a servant in husbandry', wrote a contemporary, 'she is hired to do outdoor work, and that only'.[187] In Northumberland as a whole there were 3,894 women working full-time on the land in 1871 (out of just over 58,000 female labourers and farm servants for the whole of England and Wales in that year). At that date about one in fifteen of all girls aged fifteen to nineteen in the county was engaged in agriculture. Elsewhere it was more usual for women to help only at the busy seasons and to stay at home at other times. As with the men, their wage rates varied widely – from the 4s. per week allowed in parts of East Anglia and Dorset to the 6s. per week secured in Kent, Surrey and Sussex, and as much as 9s. a week paid in parts of Cheshire, Lancashire and the West Riding of Yorkshire, where the textile mills offered a formidable rival for female employment.[67]

Child labour was most exploited in the arable eastern counties, where the public gang system operated, particularly on newly settled fenland or in thinly populated districts like the northern Wolds or the Heaths of Lincolnshire. Here there was insufficient cottage accommodation to cater for resident workers, and, given the labour-intensive methods in vogue in corn growing districts, the demand for seasonal labour could be met only by using gangs of women, young people and children who moved round from farm to farm under the direction of an overseer. About half of the agricultural gangs consisted of children and young people aged between six and eighteen. In many, the sexes were mixed and there were frequent allegations both of immorality and of the ill-treatment of the youngest children by ruthless overseers. The gangs were engaged in hoeing, stonepicking, weeding, manure spreading, setting potatoes, harvesting, potato picking and turnip pulling. In the mid-1860s one Norfolk mother who had three children in a gang, the youngest a girl of nine, admitted that they had to walk five or six miles to their work on many occasions. 'The big ones help the little ones on; that is how they have to get home. If so be there isn't a big one to help, the men won't take the little ones, and they won't take them till they can earn 6d. My little girl could hardly get home last night.'[65] The children rose soon after 5 a.m. and were lucky to reach home before seven or eight in the evening. It was also customary for the gangmasters to carry a stick with them, and they did not hesitate to use it on those youngsters who were lagging in their work. Much of that work was exhausting, and during wet and frosty weather, the hands of the children became swollen and sore.

One girl who began work at the age of eight in a gang in the Lincolnshire fens, along with forty or fifty other children, recalled that during the four years she laboured in the fields, she 'never worked one hour under cover of a barn. . . . The cold east wind . . . the sleet and snow which came every now and then in showers seemed almost to cut us to pieces'.[145]

It may be asked why parents allowed their offspring to be used in this fashion. The answer lay partly in family poverty and partly, no doubt, in an unthinking acceptance of the need for juvenile labour. The view of the child as a small adult who must begin to earn his or her living as early as possible was slow to die in Victorian England.

In 1867, disclosures concerning child labour in the gangs were published in the *Sixth Report of the Children's Commission*. They so aroused public and parliamentary concern that later in the year the Agricultural Gangs Act was passed. This prohibited the employment of any child in a public gang below the age of eight (a limit raised to ten in 1875); made gangs of mixed sex illegal; and required all overseers to be licensed by magistrates. A licence to act as gangmaster was not to be granted to innkeepers or others licensed to sell alcohol. In this way it was hoped that the worst abuses would be eliminated. But, of course, the Act did not regulate working conditions for children who were recruited privately by farmers; nor did it give much protection to youngsters in the public gangs once they had reached the age of eight. And in households where the annual income of an adult male labourer might be as little as £30, the extra £4 or £5 a year which a child could bring in was a matter of significance. The same was true of the offspring of smallholders, for the contribution made by a boy or girl might be just sufficient to obviate the need to employ an outsider, to whom a wage would have to be paid. One critic claimed that in the hilly parts of Glamorgan and throughout much of Brecon, where small occupiers abounded, the children of agricultural workers were better placed than those of the farmers. The latter were 'too poor to pay for any labour', and so as soon as their children could do any work at all they were kept at home: 'these hand-to-mouth farmers . . . rear their children in ignorance'.[61]

It was against this background of endemic poverty, and at a time when average retail prices rose by around 6 per cent in a year, between 1871 and 1872, that farm workers in southern and midland England turned to trade unionism, in an effort to force male wage levels upwards and compel employers to improve working conditions. As will be seen in Chapter 4, their endeavours had some short-term success, but in the long run the onset of unfavourable seasons and of agricultural recession eventually brought about the unions' demise.

This, then, was the external picture of rural life in the 1860s and early 1870s – one of apparent prosperity for landlords and the larger farmers, coupled with continuing hardship for many of their workers. Only on closer examination does such a view seem oversimplistic. For even during the 'golden' years, there ware many underlying stresses within the agricultural community. Apart from such short-term disasters as the outbreak of cattle plague (rinderpest) in 1865/66, which decimated many herds, there was a steady growth of food imports even in these years. By the 1860s about 40 per cent of the nation's wheat consumption was being met from imported grain, while about one-ninth of the meat and between one-quarter and one-fifth of the butter and cheese consumed were also supplied from abroad. Thanks to improving living standards and increasing population in the towns, the demand for meat and dairy produce more than kept pace with the supplies of these commodities and prices continued to rise. But for wheat the position was one of price stability, until the brief frantic upsurge which occurred during the boom conditions of the early 1870s.

Already by the mid-Victorian years there were signs that within mixed farming systems it was the livestock side which was replacing grain as the most profitable element. Even in 1864, the Scottish agricultural writer and MP James Caird pointed out that with the rising price of meat and dairy produce it was inevitable that there would be a 'diminished growth of corn and an increased growth of those articles which were more remunerative to the farmer'.[90] In

16

other cases, the rise in the horse population used both for pleasure and for haulage in the towns provided the more perceptive agriculturists with opportunities to sell forage crops. Well before the onset of depression, therefore, profits from livestock rather than grain had become a major factor in agricultural prosperity. Unfortunately, many large cereal producers in the eastern counties failed to see just how far the balance had swung against their traditional approach to farming. In counties like Bedfordshire and Essex, as late as 1870, 20.7 and 23.1 per cent, respectively, of the cultivated land was still devoted to wheat growing. To large arable men the humbler occupations (as they saw it) of cow-keeping and laying down land to grass in order to sell hay and straw were 'distasteful violations of the canon' of husbandry, and so they went on blindly to disaster.

Table 1   The Gross Output of English Agriculture: 1867–71 and 1894–98

	1867–71 £m	1894–98 £m
Wheat	28.44	7.64
Barley	12.62	7.54
Oats	4.28	4.23
Potatoes	3.00	3.00
Hay, Straw, Fruit and Vegetables	14.00	17.00
Other crops	3.09	2.06
ARABLE	65.43	41.47
Beef	14.59	16.02
Mutton	14.60	12.59
Pig meat	9.59	10.52
Horses	1.00	2.00
Milk	15.40	20.29
Wool	5.62	2.36
Poultry and Eggs	3.50	7.00
LIVESTOCK	64.30	70.78

From T. W. Fletcher, 'The Great Depression of English Agriculture, 1873–96' in *British Agriculture 1875–1914*, ed. P. J. Perry (1973), 54.

Table 1 shows the gross output of the various agricultural crops in England at the end of the 'golden era'. Comparisons with earlier periods are not possible, as it was only in 1866 that the first national census of agricultural output was taken in this country. But the figures show that already the sale of meat more than equalled that of wheat, while milk, too, had become a major source of cash. In the years ahead both trends were to intensify and, for purposes of comparison, figures for the latter part of the century are also included.

These underlying problems of the 'golden' years were not the only factors which precluded the drawing of any simple uniform picture of rural England during the period. Pre-eminent among other influences at work were the important regional diversities in settlement and occupational patterns. To the north and west of a dividing line drawn along the western boundary of the East Riding of Yorkshire to the eastern edge of Dorset, the land was primarily devoted to pastoral farming. To the south and east of that line were the arable counties, which had more than twice as much land under the plough as in permanent pasture. But even within that broad division, there were variations according to soil, climate or proximity to urban markets. Wiltshire alternated between corn and sheep farming on its chalky downlands and dairying in other districts. In Kent, the areas within easy reach of London concentrated on dairy and garden produce, green forage crops, and hay and straw for that market, while hops thrived around the Medway valley and its tributaries and on the rich loams of east Kent. A parish like Brenchley could have as much as 16 per cent of its total cultivated acreage in 1870 under hops.[5] Thanet was famous for arable crops, especially barley, while the Romney Marsh provided excellent summer grazing for sheep. Fruit growing was another speciality of the county.

Equally significant differences applied to employment prospects and to the pattern of landownership between one part of the country and another. Although farmers and agricultural workers provided the bulk of the male labour force in most villages, even quite small communities had a substantial minority of craftsmen as well. In many areas, too, cottage industries survived and exerted a major influence on occupational structures. Already by the early 1870s a number of these were under pressure from foreign competition or from the output of the expanding factories and workshops of urban England, but others survived into the final quarter of the nineteenth century. They included straw plaiting for the hat and bonnet trade in the south midlands; shoemaking in Northamptonshire; glovemaking in Worcestershire, Herefordshire, Dorset, West Oxfordshire and Somerset; pillow lacemaking in the south midlands and Devon; the making of 'slops' or cheap clothing around Abingdon in Berkshire; and netmaking on the Dorset, Cornish, and Norfolk coast.

Apart from these categories, there were other groups who earned a living indirectly from the land. They included blacksmiths, wheelwrights, hurdle-makers and millers, who provided agriculturists with the specialized skills and services they needed, and the large class of domestic servants and estate workers upon whom much of the smooth running of any major property depended. Most professional men and retail traders in the country towns also found in the land their chief means of livelihood:

> The processer of agricultural produce who was in a large way of business, the brewer, distiller, tanner, miller, or clothier, probably ranked as a member of a separate interest in spite of his close links with the land. But his brethren who catered only for local needs from a base in the market town were . . . under the wing of the landed interest . . . as were most of those engaged in the marketing of foodstuffs.[266]

Even in the 1860s and 1870s some landowners preferred to engage a solicitor from a nearby market town to act as their agent, rather than a full-time professional. Sir Roger Gresley of Drakelowe, Derbyshire, employed his family lawyer, Mr Mousley, in this fashion to administer an estate of about 3,000 acres. Mousley was expected to collect the rents, maintain the accounts and supervise the work of the bailiff. Other opportunities for lucrative employment were provided for such men by the drawing up of tenancy agreements, leases and similar contracts.

The character of community life was, of course, much affected by the type of farming followed in a locality. The daily round in a cattle breeding and dairying county like Devon, or a market gardening centre like the Vale of Evesham, was very different from that in the arable areas of East Anglia. The small, mainly family farms of Devon and Wales produced narrower economic and social divisions between farmers and labourers than applied in Norfolk, Essex and Suffolk, where despite the survival of a number of farms under 100 acres, there were many large holdings with labour forces to match. This was especially true up to the 1870s, when the 'high farming' methods used in grain growing districts led to the recruitment of substantial numbers of workers, many with specialist skills. In mid-nineteenth-century Norfolk at least eighteen farmers claimed to employ more than sixty men, as did eight of those in Suffolk. By contrast, in the pastoral North Riding of Yorkshire, an area of small farms, no agriculturalist employed even thirty-five men, and around two-fifths of the holdings reported the recruitment of no outsiders at all. Family labour alone sufficed. At the end of the century it was still possible for a man and wife to start on a smallholding in that area with £20 as capital. If they began on a sixty-acre farm with £200 they were condidered quite well off.

These are examples for the extremes of husbandry, but within individual parishes labour forces varied widely according to the size of holding or the methods of tillage followed. Thus in two representative communities – the township of Ivinghoe in Buckinghamshire and the parish of Helmingham in Suffolk – where in each case approximately two-thirds of the land was under crops and one-third under permanent grass, the pattern shown in Table 2 emerges.

The wages paid to each man naturally varied with age, individual skill and the duties to be performed. Normally those workers connected with stock – the shepherds and head horsemen – were paid the highest rates, while the general men not only earned less but were more likely to be laid off during bad weather. The daily routine on carefully regulated larger holdings (like the majority of those in Ivinghoe in 1871) therefore established clear distinctions not only between master and man but between the different classes of workers.

The situation was very different on the small farms of Wales or the North Riding of Yorkshire, where farmers worked in the fields alongside their men. In Wales, indeed, labourers often achieved their ambition of becoming tenants in their own right, since the small Welsh holdings, like those in North Yorkshire, could be taken with very little capital. Frequently the first stage in the process was for a labourer, whilst still working as an agricultural

Table 2   Farmers and their Labour Forces: Ivinghoe and Helmingham in 1871

Ivinghoe		Helmingham	
Total no. of farmers (holding 1755 acres)	5	Total no. of farmers (holding 1772 acres)	11

	No. of workers they employed		No. of workers they employed
1 with 679 acres	20 men and 4 boys	1 (also a landowner)	
1 with 670 acres	15 men and 6 boys	with 322 acres	15 men and 3 boys
1 with 191 acres	8 men and 4 boys	1 with 236 acres	11 men and 3 boys
1 with 170 acres	8 men and 2 boys	1 with 233 acres	8 men and 1 boy
1 (also a licensed		1 with 203 acres	8 men and 1 boy
victualler) with		1 with 198 acres	7 men and 1 boy
45 acres	1 man and 1 boy	1 with 190 acres	7 men and 3 boys
		1 with 124 acres	5 men and 1 boy
		1 with 114 acres	5 men and 2 boys
		1 with 86 acres	3 men and 2 boys
		1 with 54 acres	3 men and 1 boy
		1 with 12 acres	No workers

From 1871 Census of Population: returns at Public Record Office, R.G.10.1564 for Ivinghoe and R.G.10.1743 for Helmingham. Information on cropping patterns from the annual agricultural retrun for 1870 at the Public Record Office MAF.68.231 for Buckinghamshire and MAF.68.260 for Suffolk. Both Helmingham and Ivinghoe formed part of a large estate, with one major landowner in each.

wage earner, to acquire a smallholding on which to commence farming operations.

The sense of community to which this gave rise is illustrated by North Yorkshire, where it was the custom for farmer, family and servants to sit down to their meals together, and perhaps to spend some of their leisure hours in one another's company. As a contemporary wrote:

They sit down to the same table and partake of the same dish. At least, with one exception: the mistress prepares the food . . . sets it on the table, and in one word 'waits', getting her own meal afterwards. When the labours of the day are over, all gather in the same room, kitchen, or house, or whatever other term may be used; and in a truer sense than as the word is customarily used, they are all 'one family'.

Nay, in ninety-nine cases out of the hundred the masters and the mistresses, the male servants on the farm, and the female workers in the house, the dairy, the fields, all went to the same school and imbibed the same amount of the three R's at the lips of the same teacher.[124]

Here, as elsewhere in the pastoral North of England and Wales, where livestock farming was the prime consideration, it was usual for workers to 'live in' with their employers, or at least to be provided with free lodgings. By contrast, in the arable southern and eastern counties, 'outdoor' labourers were the order of the day.

A further variation on the agrarian theme was provided in Dorset and parts of Wiltshire by the practice of large farmers 'letting' their cows to a specialist dairyman, for a rent. In return the dairyman and his wife would make butter and cheese and raise pigs. From the sale of this produce they made their own profit. To substantial arable farmers, the time-consuming skills of dairying were felt to be beneath their dignity. As S. G. Kendall recalled of his family's 700-acre holding in Wiltshire: 'our large corn farms with considerable flocks of sheep were . . . *our first consideration*'.[201] In their case, the dairyman was provided with a rent-free house, pigsties and poultry, while the farmer supplied the cattle, replacing any loss by death or disease, and found some of the workers needed to milk a large dairy. 'One quarter of the rental of the dairy was paid in advance by our . . . tenant to make the owner's position fairly secure.'

In areas devoted to market gardening or in large parishes where landownership was widely spread, the number of people cultivating the soil could be considerable. At Epworth in Lincolnshire in 1871 more than one in five of all the families were farmers, the vast majority of them cultivating holdings of fifty acres or less. Many of them were concerned with market gardening, while a number, in order to make ends meet, took casual work whenever they could spare the time from their own holding.

Still greater differences in community structure arose on the northern hillsides and fells, where sheep grazed on huge farms or on common land. They included places like the township of Kidland in Northumberland, where the whole settlement in 1871 comprised eight farms. All were tenanted by shepherds who had been born and bred locally. So remote were these communities, and yet so imbued were their inhabitants with a respect for education, that they hired a schoolmaster of their own and provided him with board and lodgings. Frank Dodds of Linbriggs in the north of Northumberland, one of the teachers thus employed, noted that in the late 1860s his school was maintained by three shepherds and a farmer. Not only did they pay his salary, but one of the shepherds supplied the schoolroom. The pupils remained at school until the age of twelve and the master obtained his board and lodging by staying '14 days for each scholar' with the four families who had hired him.[61]

Westmorland shared many of these characteristics. In 1870, only about 42 per cent of the country's total acreage was even under cultivation (as compared to three-quarters or more in the eastern counties of Bedfordshire, Cambridgeshire, Essex, Suffolk and Norfolk, or of Oxfordshire and Leicestershire in the midlands). In Westmorland, corn growing was virtually non-existent, with wheat covering a mere 1 per cent of the cultivated area in the early 1870s. It was sheep which were all-important, with communities like Langdale and Kentmere owning flocks numbering more than 8,900 and 5,700, respectively, in 1880.[5] The shepherding of these animals on the rough fells provided a major occupation for the inhabitants and their skilled sheepdogs.

Alongside the differences in community character attributable to agricultural or geographical factors, there were those created by the wide range of other employments which were followed within the countryside. Even small villages had some specialist craftsmen, while in larger communities, such as Milton-under-Wychwood in Oxfordshire (population 962 in 1871), the range could be formidable. Milton in 1871 boasted five tailors, five grocers, three blacksmiths, two butchers, two carriers and nine carpenters as well as other crafts and professions, including two hurdle-makers, three hawkers, a medical practitioner and a veterinary surgeon. Some men even combined two occupations, so that one of the Milton grocers was also a builder, and a tailor doubled up as a draper. To have more than one string to one's occupational bow was a useful insurance when faced with the vagaries of agrarian life and the problems of seasonal unemployment or underemployment.

Where cottage industries survived they, too, exerted a powerful influence on employment patterns, particularly for women and children. In mid-Victorian Bedfordshire, nearly one in three of all girls aged between ten and fifteen worked as plaiters, while about one in nine of the girls in Buckinghamshire in the same age group worked as lacemakers. The problems and the benefits to which these cottage industries gave rise will be examined in more detail in a later chapter.

Finally, in considering the variations in village society, there remains the important question of landownership. Where this was concentrated in the hands of one or two proprietors only – in the so-called 'close' parishes – social stratification tended to be most obvious. At the head of affairs stood the principal landowner, followed by other gentry living within the parish, and then by the Anglican clergyman, the substantial farmers, the rural craftsmen, the shopkeepers, and the smallholders. At the bottom of the scale came the agricultural labourers and their families, the new categories of railway employees and postal workers, and the various 'catch' workers, who carried out a whole variety of jobs as opportunity offered. These could range from sweeping chimneys to helping on the farms at the busy seasons of the year, thatching, catching vermin, and similar tasks. Fishermen, too, might spend the summer and autumn at sea and then supplement their income by working on the land for the remainder of the year. Needless to say, if all else failed many of these 'catch' workers fell back on poaching.

The incidence of 'close' parishes varied considerably from county to county. This was attributable partly to historical reasons and partly to topography, for it was in the cultivated country of 'champion' England, which extended from the midlands to parts of the south and east, that the system of large estates was likely to be found. In districts of later settlement, where pastoral and woodland activities were more important and the population less concentrated, a system of hamlets and small family-based farms tended to prevail, as it did in most of Wales. The proximity of a county to London or to a major industrial town, where the cost of land was likely to be high, also had a role to play, as did the residual effects of enclosure. Thus whilst around one-third to one-half of all the villages in Norfolk, Rutland, Leicestershire and the East Riding of Yorkshire and one-quarter of those in Bedfordshire fell into the 'close' category, in Essex, Cambridgeshire and Hertfordshire the proportion was little more than one-twentieth. In the country as a whole, 'close' parishes accounted for perhaps a fifth of the total in rural areas.

Where they existed, such communities were often firmly regulated by the squire and his agent, with owners like Lord Tollemache at Helmingham, Suffolk, not only insisting that farm workers attend church on Sunday but evicting families from their cottages if a daughter transgressed by having an illegitimate child, or a son was convicted of poaching. Other men, like Lord Bolton on the Hackwood estate in Hampshire, adopted their own unofficial methods of enforcing law and order, rather as some of their late-eighteenth-century predecessors had done. At Hackwood during the 1860s wrongdoers were required to sign an undertaking not to repeat the offence. By so doing they avoided the danger of possible imprisonment in the county gaol at Winchester. Although it would be misleading to imply that all squires imposed such conditions as these, the fact remains that where they owned all the property in a parish they could exercise dictatorial powers should they choose to do so.

But for those willing to conform, there were benefits. Lord Tollemache let cottages at moderate rents on the understanding that the tenants' children attended school regularly up to the age of eleven. He also spent £16,092 over the period 1852–81 on rebuilding fifty-two cottages and erecting ninety-one new ones. Similarly, Sir Edward Kerrison personally supervised the careers of the young people on his estate near Eye, also in Suffolk. He helped with clothing and travelling expenses where necessary and, at his express wish, girls were not employed in agricultural gangs.[264] On the Hackwood estate it was customary to offer pensions to long-serving estate workers and their widows. Among those benefiting in this way in the mid-1860s was Matthew Paice, aged seventy-two, who had formerly worked in the stables and had served the estate for forty years. He was paid 5s. per week and also acted as lodgekeeper, for which he was provided with a rent-free cottage and free fuel.[12]

'Close' parishes normally had smaller populations – perhaps fifty to three hundred persons only – than less restricted communities. One reason for this was the desire of property owners to maintain the 'select' character of the locality in which they lived. Where a squire was non-resident this motive was obviously less pressing. Another reason was that under Poor Law regulations, prior to the passage of the Union Chargeability Act of 1865, each parish had to support its own paupers. Consequently, it was in the interests of the landowner, as a major ratepayer in his own estate village, to keep the number of inhabitants down to a minimum so as to reduce the level of poor rate expenditure. Even labourers working in estate villages could not always obtain cottages in them, but were obliged to walk to work each day from homes in neighbouring parishes. At Helmingham, the eleven farmers resident in 1871 employed seventy-two adult male labourers and eighteen boys, though only fifty-eight labourers and five farm boys were recorded as living in the village by the census. The rest evidently came in from outside. Tollemache frankly expressed his own philosophy when he declared that he wanted 'only two sorts of people in the parish: the rich and the poor. He didn't want any in between'.[161] He seems to have achieved his ambition, for Helmingham had few tradespeople. Two blacksmiths, two carpenters, two wheelwrights and a shoemaker were the only ones reported in 1871.

This approach was firmly condemned by the Revd James Fraser in his report to the Royal Commission on the Employment of Children, Young Persons and Women in Agriculture, published at the end of the 1860s: 'anything more selfish and, I will venture to say, wicked than the motive which led to the creation of [close] parishes it is difficult to conceive', he declared. 'They arose from a desire to rid one's self of a just share of a burden which is only tolerable when borne by all equally. Mixed with this was a desire to get rid of an eyesore and of a nuisance; of people intruding upon the squire's privacy or disturbing his game.'[61]

Nevertheless despite such strictures, as we have seen, the vast majority of villages were *not* of the 'close' kind. Apart from the irrelevance of such a concept in the scattered communities of the pastoral far north of England, even in the rest of the country a majority of parishes were 'open', with ownership widely dispersed. In them the parson was perhaps the only 'gentleman' in the community, though in village affairs the larger farmers would also take a lead. Overall, social divisions were less rigid, controls fewer, and the population 'mix' wider. Unfortunately, open parishes also became sadly overcrowded, acting as dumping grounds for the unwanted inhabitants of estate villages and as places of refuge for those who could obtain a roof nowhere else. Housing was frequently jerry-built and was let at comparatively high rents by small tradesmen, builders and other speculators anxious to make a profit. Many lacked even the basic amenity of an oven. As late as the 1890s, at Blakeney in Norfolk, one woman recalled seeing housewives carrying their joints of meat to the bakeries to be cooked in the large ovens because they had no facilities of their own with which to roast a joint. Other critics commented on the inadequate water supply, which made even personal hygiene difficult, while the laundering of clothes was a still greater problem. In Norfolk, water was 'nearly all drawn from surface wells, occasionally from ditches, and in one instance, according to the medical officer of the Privy Council, from "a bright green pond, dangerous of access". There was always the danger of pollution from a leaking cesspit, and a great many labouring folk must have owed their lives to the fact that the men drank beer and the women and children tea, which was made from boiled water.'[255] In years of drought, water had to be purchased at 1d or 1½d a pail by those whose own supply had dried up. Food storage was equally unsatisfactory, with 'a cupboard in the living room, or . . . a damp and unwholesome cellar' commonly used for this purpose.[118]

From 1865 the accommodation problem was slightly eased by the passage of the Union Chargeability Act. Under this, the cost of maintaining the poor was no longer confined to a single parish but was spread equally throughout the area of a Poor Law union of perhaps thirty parishes. The incentive to a landowner to keep down expenditure in his own estate village was thus lost, since he was now responsible for paying his share of the costs of nearby 'open' parishes. As a result, the number of new cottages built on many estates increased during the 1860s and 1870s. But the effect should not be exaggerated. In some cases, as with the Rothschild family in Buckinghamshire or the Tollemaches in Suffolk, an owner's pride in the appearance of his village had more to do with rebuilding programmes than mere changes in legislation. Elsewhere improvement might be hampered because owners lacked the necessary capital or will to carry out such a programme. Absentee landlords or institutional owners of property, like the Oxford and Cambridge colleges, attracted particular criticism on this score.

It was in these circumstances that an assistant commissioner with the Royal Commission on the Employment of Children, etc., in Agriculture noted in 1868 that in Lincolnshire there was 'a strong feeling' that 'Government should give assistance in providing cottages for the labouring class'. It was a theme to which social reformers returned over the years, though without much success. Not until 1924 did a Housing Act provide specific and adequate subsidies to encourage the building of local authority houses in country districts.

From the late 1870s and beyond, estate housing policies were inevitably affected by the onset of agricultural depression. Landlords, facing a decline in farm rentals, cut back on expenditure and the upsurge of interest in cottage building of the mid-Victorian period faded away. Admittedly, this was partly counterbalanced by the sharp fall in rural population which also occurred during the late nineteenth century and which helped to relieve the pressure on accommodation. But the parishes where housing problems were most acute were not necessarily those which lost population. As late as 1900 commentators could write of the dilapidated and insanitary dwellings 'bought up by village tradesmen and others . . . as a paying speculation . . . knowing that owing to the scarcity of cottages there will always be a supply of tenants, these owners can demand a comparatively high rent, and spend nothing, or almost nothing, upon repairs'.[95]

Contrary to popular myth, the estate village with its resident squire was never the norm in the Victorian countryside. But it is true to say that where large magnates resided – men such as the Dukes of Bedford and Northumberland – their influence was felt over a wide area, in 'open' and 'close' parishes alike. The number of such major owners differed markedly from county to county, and as the so-called 'New Domesday' survey of 1873 revealed, there were still parts of the country where large estates did not dominate the scene. Thus, whilst in England as a whole 53.5 per cent of all cultivated land was held in estates of 1,000 acres or more, in Cumberland only 41 per cent of the land was so owned, in Essex 43 per cent, and in Middlesex, where proximity to the capital had forced up land values, a mere 21 per cent. The influence of London also made itself apparent in other Home Counties, like Kent and Surrey, where the heavy demand for land made it both impossible and undesirable to build up and retain very large estates. In Northumberland, on the other hand, 85 per cent of the land was held in estates of 1,000 acres or more, and in Dorset, 71 per cent. In the former, the property of the Duke of

Northumberland predominated, covering 14 per cent of the whole county. Alnwick, the 'heartland' of that estate, formed a compact block of some 25,000 acres. In Wales, the counties of Carnarvon (78 per cent) and Merioneth (70 per cent) were also heavily concentrated into estates of 1,000 acres or more. Indeed, 50 per cent of Carnarvon's territory was held in properties of over *10,000* acres, while in Merioneth the corresponding figure was 40 per cent, most of it consisting of vast sheepwalks. Half the land in the former county (excluding waste) was held by six men.[191] Distance from London played a part in explaining this dominance by a few landlords, together with climatic and topographical disadvantages. In Northumberland historical factors also intervened, given the county's strategic position between Scotland and England.

Overall, the 'New Domesday' survey showed that four-fifths of the land in the United Kingdom was owned by fewer than 7,000 people, with the really major estates of 30,000 acres and above probably covering about one-seventh of the total area of England and Wales. As the *Scotsman* sourly noted: 'the Peerage of the United Kingdom, about 600 in number possess among them rather more than a fifth of all the land, and between a tenth and an eleventh of its annual income.'[135] Meredith Townsend, editor of the *Spectator*, made the same point in the mid-1860s: 'The English "aristocracy" is . . . only another word for the greater owners of land. It has little to do with office . . . Still less . . . with pedigree . . . the "aristocratic" element of the English constitution is, in fact, simply the class which owns the soil.'

In the succeeding half-century this position changed little. Admittedly, there was a movement into landownership by some former industrialists, anxious to enjoy the status which possession of an estate could bestow. But that had been going on well before 1870, with the very high prices in the land market boom of the late 1860s and early 1870s partly attributed to this attempt by the 'new rich' to spend part of their large personal fortunes in acquiring a country estate. For land carried with it a prestige which no other form of property could equal. As the *Economist* of 16 July 1870 pointed out, a man who held his fortune in paper shares had little to show for it, while 'everybody can tell the value of so many acres'. Consequently, 'it would "pay" a millionaire in England to sink half his fortune in buying 10,000 acres of land to return a shilling per cent, and live upon the remainder, rather than live upon the whole without the land.' By so doing 'he would be a greater person in the eyes of more people'. Bagehot, too, remarked on the eagerness of 'new wealth . . . to worship old wealth, if old wealth will only let it. . . . Rank probably in no country whatever has so much "market" value as it has in England just now.'[125] At the same time he commented upon the reverence accorded the 'old squire', which a new man could never hope to match. It was just this ability to inspire deference in the 'rude classes at the bottom' of the social scale which made the position of landowner so attractive to a substantial number of the *nouveaux riches*. But as W. D. Rubinstein has shown, that did not necessarily mean the purchase of a *large* estate of, say, 2,000 acres or more. Smaller properties or even rented land satisfied the aspirations of many wealthy business and professional men during the mid-Victorian years.[247]

It is to an examination of the way of life of the leaders of Victorian landed society that we must now turn, to see how far their position changed during the difficult late nineteenth century, as the optimism of the 1860s and 1870s gave way to doubts and even despair over much of rural England and Wales.

2
The Leaders of Rural Society

Despite the challenge of commerce and industry to the power of the landed classes on the national scene, within the countryside they continued to exert much of their traditional authority until the end of the nineteenth century. But for many owners the final quarter of that century was a time of economic difficulty, as agricultural prosperity and rentals dwindled in the face of competition from cheaper imported food. In arable areas this was aggravated by the effects of a damaging change in consumption patterns among better-off industrial workers. No longer were they satisfied with a diet of bread, potatoes and bacon, but demanded instead fresh meat, eggs, dairy produce and green vegetables. Slowly farm outputs were adjusted to meet the new conditions, but in the interim, the profits of most agriculturists fell sharply.

In such circumstances, landlords had little option but to assist tenants by reducing rents, though certain of the more optimistic, or the more desperate, embarked upon a programme of capital expenditure, in an attempt to maintain existing returns, or to retain tenants otherwise anxious to quit their holdings (see Appendix (a)). Thus the Duke of Cleveland, cushioned by a comfortable non-agricultural income, spent heavily in re-equipping his Northamptonshire property for livestock farming, while the Duke of Northumberland paid £3 an acre for inferior arable land 'laid down to permanent grass, as well as providing suitable buildings for the new type of farming'.[266] Northumberland was a major beneficiary from mineral royalties derived from the extensive collieries on his estate.

But those owners without access to outside capital, or whose property, because of inferior soil, climate or location, proved unsuitable for such changes, could only cut rent levels and, ultimately, their own personal expenditure. It was during these years that the financial gap between the very richest landowners and the minor aristocracy and gentry widened, for it was 'the super-rich, particularly those with lucrative non-landed sources of wealth, who could best weather the storms of the years following the start of the Agricultural Depression in 1879'.[247] Especially hard-hit were those with land mortgaged by a predecessor, who faced the burden of interest payments, or who had to meet heavy family settlements. Among these unfortunates was the Marquess of Ailesbury, whose Savernake estate by 1895 not only carried interest charges of £3,500 on inherited debt, but a further sum of £5,000 for jointures; the total income was just over £23,000 per annum. Small wonder the agent bemoaned these 'terrible jointures' and predicted that there would be no financial relief 'until the Dowagers die'. In the meantime, the Marquess had to move into a small house on the estate, leaving Tottenham Park empty. Until 1911, he relied on bank overdrafts to keep the estate going.

Another owner with heavy family responsibilities was the third Lord Hatherton, who complained sadly in 1891: 'what a dreadful thing it is to inherit a debt'.[93]

But most landlords found the situation sufficiently serious without these added complications. In Suffolk, the rental drawn from Lord Stradbroke's estate in 1895 was a mere one-third of that secured in 1877, while on the Duke of Bedford's Buckinghamshire and Bedfordshire estate and that of the Duke of Richmond at Goodwood, net income per acre had dropped by almost a quarter between 1872–74 and 1890–92.[229] Further reductions followed, and by 1895 the 10th Duke of Bedford estimated that the total rent of his Bedfordshire and Buckinghamshire property had fallen to £20,063, compared to £43,975 received in 1878. In addition, £132,222 had been granted in rent remissions over the same period, while certain charges formerly borne by the tenants had been taken over by the landlord. These included maintaining boundary fences and insuring the farmhouses and buildings. But insulated by a large income from London ground rents, which by the later 1880s were worth perhaps £100,000 a year, the Duke could afford to be generous.[131]

In parts of Essex, where the soil was high-cost, heavy clay, and yields were low, many landlords proved still more vulnerable. Even in August 1876 Sir George Brooke-Pechell of Alton, Hampshire, non-resident owner of a small Essex estate, was writing anxiously to his agent about the difficulty in letting Hazeleigh Hall Farm, which had been in hand for some months:

Could we not let off the pastures – and let the rest run up to grass? Is tithe & property tax payable on uncultivated and unprofitable land? Can the property, by throwing the arable into grass or out of cultivation be made to pay its expences so that the year will give me no loss even if it gives no profit. . . . I have done what I can here to reduce expences. I have reduced my stable estab$^{t\cdot}$ to one horse & a boy & my coachman & my house servant are under notice, as it is pretty clear that the Hazeleigh income is getting small by degrees and . . . our childrens education expences are getting large by degrees.[22]

Six months later, with the farm still unlet, he was again pressing the agent:

Have you heard of any applicants for tenacy. I really think . . . if you have not that we must seek the intervention of some London farm letting agent with a bribe to push it . . . the . . . advertising in local papers seems to be ineffectual & its being without a tenant is so ruinous I can't stand it.

During 1878 Sir George visited Scotland to seek out potential tenants for his unwanted Essex holdings, and between May and August a number of Scottish farmers made enquiries about Hazeleigh Hall. But in the end, 'no fish rose to the bait'. Eventually the agent himself took over the renting of the farm, but the skirmishes over the disposal of this property led to an ending of the landlord/agent relationship in 1879, under conditions of some acrimony.

A second sufferer was the Earl of Harrowby, with estates in Staffordshire, Gloucestershire, and Lincolnshire. Between the mid-1880s and the mid-1890s, less than three-quarters of the nominal rent due on his Gloucestershire property was met by actual payments. And despite the granting of regular abatements, by the end of the century tenants' arrears had inexorably mounted. In 1900 they reached £5,805 on the Gloucestershire property, against an estimated gross rental for that year of £5,878. On the estate in Staffordshire, which was centred around Sandon, they amounted to £2,957, as against a gross rental of £9,549.[296] Not surprisingly, in February 1885 Harrowby wrote to his agent, stressing the need for economy:

I am further reducing household and horses from the present small establishment, but if I had not your assurance that from

January, 1885, there is being a complete change as to this large and increasing expenditure, I should probably have been obliged to let our house in London, break up the Garden Establishment at Sandon, and settle abroad or elsewhere.[296]

Eight years later, when asked to contribute towards the building of a school near to his Lincolnshire property, he couched his refusal in similar terms: 'The loss of income on my moderate Harrowby Estate has been great, having much increased again lately: elsewhere things have now become rapidly worse; I have farms paying no rent at all, others making extremely reduced returns; we are therefore reducing our household in all directions and are letting our London house.' By the time of his death in 1900, he had not only let his London residence but had sharply cut expenditure on the gardens and grounds at his seats in Staffordshire and Gloucestershire, as well as relinquishing the game rights in Staffordshire, and generally curtailing his personal outgoings. Management expenses were reduced by employing only one agent to oversee both the Gloucestershire and Staffordshire properties. Yet, with all this, arrears had mounted, and his successor had little choice but to write off almost £5,000 of these when he inherited the estate, in order to give his tenants a fresh start.

In such circumstances, rent audit dinners became gloomy affairs. All too often, as at Lincoln College, Oxford, in 1880, 'the tenants came to dine but not to pay'.[222] And agents were driven to various stratagems to recover arrears. In November 1883 Frederick Mair, steward on the Harcourt estate at Nuneham Courtenay, Oxfordshire, even approached a corn dealer who was handling grain belonging to a non-paying tenant, to persuade him to hand over cash to cover rent due the previous Michaelmas.[13]

Far more precariously placed were those landowners unable to secure tenants at all. As the agent of Christ Church, Oxford, frankly admitted in 1883: 'in letting land, at the present time, its intrinsic value does not by any means decide the amount of rent which can be got for it. It is notorious that the number of Farms vacant far exceeds the number of Tenants with sufficient capital who are able and willing to take them, and the rental, if the Landlord is determined to let, will be fixed by what a Tenant can be found to give, rather than by what ought to be obtained.'[4] Four years later, when a tenant was offered an extra 15 per cent rebate by the Dean and Chapter, he was warned that it was 'conditional' on his 'remaining in the farm'. It is clear that the threat to leave was used by some farmers purely to obtain rent reductions, since they knew that few landowners relished the prospect of finding the working capital needed to cultivate their own land.

The heavy costs involved when property was 'in hand' can be illustrated from the Petre estate in Essex. In 1884 seven farms, covering about 2,000 acres, were cultivated by the owner. According to his agent, this meant a loss of rental of about £1,800 per annum, while the landlord now had to pay all tithes, land tax and insurances, as well as meeting the running costs of the farms. In these circumstances, he decided to advertise for tenants in Scottish newspapers, since demand for land was well maintained among dairy and stock farmers north of the border. Eventually he managed to let all of the holdings, and by 1895 the tenants included fourteen Scotsmen, renting farms with an acreage of about 3,840, with three Devon men and two from Northumberland.[23] Rentals had been cut, in some cases by between a third and a half, and money spent on building additional cow houses, connecting fresh water supplies, and making other provisions to cater for the dairying needs of the new tenants. But that was considered preferable to having the property in hand.

Smaller squires, with estates up to 3,000 acres or so, were especially affected by the economic pressures, since they had few resources to fall back upon. Among them were men like Joseph Jones of Worcestershire, whose 3,519-acre estate produced a gross return of £4,860 a year, upon which he was forced to make a 20 per cent abatement. In Wales, with its multiplicity of small owners, not even the persistent land hunger of the peasantry could prevent similar problems from arising. From the mid-1880s rent remissions were being granted in the principality, too. As one Welsh squire, whose family owned about 600 acres near Cardigan, bitterly observed, 'the real crime of the smaller Welsh gentry was their poverty'. Between 1885 and 1894 he estimated that approximately £2,000 had been spent on his estate for buildings, repairs, and general improvements, while the total rental in 1894 amounted to a mere £341 per annum. Overall, 'nearly six years' rental out of nine was . . . spent for the benefit of the estate'.[274]

Only those owners whose land lay in areas traditionally devoted to dairying overcame the problems with comparative ease, with the dairy producers of Lancashire and Cheshire benefiting, in particular, from their concentration on milk sales and ready access to urban markets. On the Earl of Derby's Fylde estate in Lancashire rentals rose by 18 per cent over the 'depression' years, while an estate of 16,110 acres in Cheshire quoted by the Royal Commission on Agricultural Depression, 1894–97, did even better, with rents increasing by more than 26 per cent between the early 1870s and the early 1890s. Few landlords outside this favoured area, and not all within it, shared their good fortune, though there were some, like the Marquess of Bath's Longleat, where severe depression was felt on part of the property only. Here difficulties were experienced on about one-third of the estate, which lay in the Wiltshire chalk country, with its sheep and corn farming. The remainder, lying in the dairying districts of Wiltshire and Somerset, suffered little, and rents were well maintained (see Appendix (b) for further examples of the differing regional impact of the 'depression' on landlords' incomes).

Yet, despite the setbacks faced by many proprietors in economic affairs, within the rural community itself their influence remained formidable. The estate of the Duke of Portland at Welbeck Abbey was described by a contemporary as 'more like a principality than anything else. . . . Within the borders of Welbeck Abbey, His Grace the Duke of Portland, wielded an almost feudal indisputable power.'[190] In the 1890s the Duke of Westminster, then one of the richest men in England, employed more than three hundred servants (including ground staff) at the family seat at Eaton in Cheshire. Each employee was allocated to an appropriate departmental head. The senior forester alone had seventy men under his jurisdiction; the clerk of works, forty tradesmen; while the head gardener presided over forty underlings, plus a cook and a cleaner for the bothy, where the unmarried men lodged. Because the nearest railway station to Eaton was three miles away, in 1896 the Duke even completed his own light railway to run to the Hall, with branch lines serving the estate timber yard and brickworks. There was also a private fire brigade equipped with uniforms and fire appliances.

On a more modest level were properties like that at Middle-Hill on the Worcestershire/Gloucestershire border, about six miles from Evesham. In 1878, when it was advertised for sale, it boasted

2,782 acres of land, with a rental of about £4,400 per annum. It included thirteen farms, about twenty-four cottages, a mill, and just over seventeen acres of allotment ground. There was also a school, and the purchaser had the right of presentation to the rectory of Buckland, which lay within the ambit of the estate.

On these properties, large and small, the squire was expected not merely to concern himself with the prosperity and good management of his estate, but to take account of the welfare of those who lived within its borders. At Compton Verney, Lord Willoughby de Broke prided himself on the way that the estate workers had 'the certainty of employment for as long as they chose to work. They were looked after when they were sick. They were pensioned when they could work no more. . . . And above all, there was a mutual bond of affection that had existed for many generations between their families and the family of their employer.'[282] Local tradespeople, too, were much dependent on the goodwill and patronage of the 'big house', and, particularly on political questions, were unwilling to oppose the views of the squire.

Unfortunately, as the depression deepened, a number of workers discovered that whatever Lord Willoughby de Broke might say, landlords were not always able or willing to conform to this idea of a miniature welfare state. With the bankruptcy of an owner, the much-vaunted 'security' of the estate employee counted for little.

On a more sentimental level, the pre-eminence of landowners in parish affairs was underlined by the way in which major events in their lives and those of their families were translated into objects of widespread public joy or sympathy. A birth, the coming of age of an heir, his marriage, even a death, were all turned into matters of communal concern. Thus the return from honeymoon of the 7th Baron Rodney and his bride in May 1891 led to the declaration of a general holiday in the small market town of Leominster, where their seat, Berrington Hall, was situated. They were greeted by a detachment of the Yeomanry Cavalry, and were then escorted to the Town Hall, where addresses of welcome were presented to them by the mayor and corporation and the inhabitants.[45] If necessary, the squire's agent would give guidance to the tenantry on the way these ceremonies were to be conducted.

More common was the holding of celebratory dinners or teas,

when the tenants could drink the squire's health in plentiful supplies of alcohol. One such event occurred in 1882, when Lord Cottesloe celebrated the wedding of a younger daughter by holding a dinner for about 120 guests at his home at Swanbourne. The notes of his speech on that occasion indicate the spirit in which such events were conducted:

> Glad to see so many friends responding to my invitation. Not much to offer beyond a hearty welcome & good wishes.
> Not a political gathering – shall not make a political speech.
> I thank you once more for your kindness & liberality to my daughter on her marriage.
> Let me assure you of the interest which I take in the welfare of all belonging to Swanbourne.
> Interests of Landlord and tenant intimately connected not only in a pecuniary sense, but as friends & neighbours. . . . Lived among you for 84 years for 3 generations always treated with kindness & respect. Hope I have not got an Enemy in Swanbourne. Say the same for my father & mother, who first came to live among you at the end of the last century . . . it is a pleasure to me to see you in this House & to collect my tenants & friends around me.[10]

Yet, however well-intentioned these gatherings may have been, they inevitably carried with them an element of social control – a hint of the iron fist inside the velvet glove for those tenants who did not wish to conform. As such they were regarded with suspicion by certain of the more self-reliant farmers.

Alongside these social responsibilities, owners were also expected to maintain the physical fabric of their parishes in good order. That included the rebuilding and repair of cottages, the construction of new schools, the restoration and enlargement of churches, and the erection of parish clubrooms. In the case of the largest landowners, this might involve expenditure in several villages. Needless to say, not all landlords had either the means or the inclination to meet those high standards, and one recent writer has applauded this fact, arguing that the slothful landlord was more likely to allow the villagers a degree of social freedom than his conscientious counterpart.[216] Whether this was adequate compensation for the lower standard of accommodation provided must be left to individual judgement.

Certainly in some communities the efforts of the squire to carry out reforms and improvements were greeted with covert hostility by more independent-minded villagers, like the agricultural trade union leader Joseph Arch, who declared bitterly:

> We labourers had no lack of lords and masters. There were the parson and his wife at the rectory. There was the squire, with his hand of iron overshadowing us all. . . . At the sight of the squire the people trembled. He lorded it right feudally over his tenants, the farmers; the farmers in their turn tyrannised over the labourers.[120]

Yet, despite this ill-feeling on the part of some country people, it was only in rural Wales that a sustained challenge to the influence of the landed interest developed. Here the persistent land hunger of the peasantry combined with the growing strength of Liberal nonconformity and a revival of nationalism to undermine the authority of the landlords, with their traditional links to Anglicanism and the Conservative Party. Dissenting ministers were actively engaged in weakening the power of proprietors in the political sphere; or, as a witness put it in the late 1860s, it was a case of 'landlord influence as against minister influence' at elections.[82] The vernacular press in the principality played a particularly active role in this campaign, notably the *Baner* newspaper. In its issue of 2 November 1887 it declared fiercely:

> The landowners of our country are, in general, cruel, unreasonable, unfeeling, and unpitying men. It does not matter to them who gets drowned so long as they are allowed to be in the lifeboat; it does not matter to them who suffer the mortal pangs of poverty and hunger, if they have plenty of luxuries. Many of them have been about the most presumptious thieves that have ever breathed.[276]

And on 25 April 1888, it accused the principality's landlords of living in England, while 'the poor Welsh, through the sweat of their brows are collecting every halfpenny in the neighbourhood for them to have the pleasure of spending them in England or on the Continent'. Despite these outbursts, events in Wales never developed along the bitter lines of those in Ireland, and attempts to set up a Land League on the Irish model failed completely in the principality.

*   *   *

So far, in considering the 'leaders' of rural society, attention has been confined to the nobility and gentry. Although they formed the core of that select band, they were by no means its only members. Lord Willoughby de Broke neatly defined that broader grouping, whom he called 'the County', when he listed them in order of precedence:

The lord-lieutenant
The master of fox hounds
The agricultural landlords
The bishop
The chairman of quarter sessions
The Colonel of the Yeomanry
The Member of Parliament
The dean
The archdeacons
The justices of the peace
The lesser clergy
The larger farmers.

Save for the farmers, these categories were restricted almost entirely to the landed proprietors and the clergy of the Established Church, who were themselves often the younger sons of gentry families. And in parishes where there was no resident squire, or where landownership was too widely dispersed to permit of one man exercising a predominant influence, the Anglican clergyman often took the lead. Many clerics were also landowners in their own right, as well as being justices of the peace, with about half of all magistrates in mid-Victorian England clergymen. Thereafter their numbers dwindled, from the thousand or so recorded in the 1860s.

Augustus Jessopp was one cleric who assumed this 'leadership' role when he became curate of an East Anglian parish where landownership was widely spread and farms small and ill-cultivated. There was much drunkenness, 'sometimes a fight, now and then a case of wife-beating: the village doctor lived seven miles off, though there was always fever, ague, and English cholera hanging about the place'. In these circumstances it was the curate who dealt with the problems that arose. Not only did he dispense medicine, 'with an audacity . . . such as now makes me shudder to remember', but he advised farmers on their tenancy agreements and gave assistance on a whole range of legal and social matters: 'my experience ranged from writing a letter to making a Will, and from setting a bone to stopping a suicide'.[198] Similarly, at Clyro in Radnorshire, the diaries of the curate, Francis Kilvert, reveal that he was regarded as a friend and mentor by many of the villagers. When he left the parish there was much lamentation, and one old woman told him: 'If gold would keep you with us . . . we would gather a weight of gold.' As Kilvert sadly wrote: 'What am I that these people should so care for me?'[232]

Where an incumbent or a curate was married, his wife would also be expected to play her part, visiting the poorer families, organizing the distribution of charity, holding mothers' meetings, and ensuring that food was sent from the parsonage kitchen to the sick and needy. As with the landowners, these services were continued during the 'depression' years, despite the fact that many clerical livings were hard-hit by the collapse of grain prices. For not only did that mean that their income from tithe rent-charges was reduced, since this was calculated on the basis of corn prices, but where they had glebe land to let, they frequently found great difficulty in securing tenants for it. In Berkshire, clergymen whose tithe income had been about £100 in 1882 found by 1897 that it had dwindled to under £70. But those parishes in which the endowment was in land rather than tithes were still worse off. At Letcombe Basset, Berkshire, it was virtually impossible to find an incumbent willing to take a 'living' which comprised 'a large and almost useless farm', the buildings of which he was expected to keep in repair.[140] The financial problems of the clergy will be examined in more detail in Chapter 6, when their pastoral role is considered.

Meanwhile, on the larger estates, the squire and the parson were joined in the exercise of authority by the agents of the major owners. Although their power was derived from the position of their employer, normally they were given considerable discretion to act as they thought best to promote his interests. This included the selection of tenants, the preparation of tenancy agreements, the keeping of accounts, the supervision of the farming activities of the tenants to ensure that husbandry covenants were not neglec-ted, the hiring and firing of estate workers, and often the exercise of a close control over the lives of the cottagers. At Mentmore, in

Buckinghamshire, Lord Rosebery agreed to his agent's request in September 1912 that a family should be evicted from one of the lodges, primarily because the wife persisted in walking in the woods without permission, thereby disturbing the pheasants. In the agent's view, this would be 'a good example & they are very unsatisfactory'.[16]

Even the most trivial matters might be taken up by some stewards, such as the chopping down of a tree in a cottage garden without permission, or the querying of prices charged for bundles of brooms purchased for the estate. Inevitably such detailed supervision often made an agent unpopular with the tenants, though where he failed to take a sufficient interest in the holding this could arouse equal ill-feeling. The frustration of Cornelius Stovin, who farmed 600 acres in the Lincolnshire wolds, is made very clear in a letter he wrote to his landlord in 1874, complaining that his efforts to persuade the agent to build additional cottages on his holding and to rebuild the farmhouse itself had met with no success:

> I have received no expressions of approval or disapproval. Any request I might make has been heard in a gentlemanly manner with a promise to come over but with no performance. I have been quietly ignored in every shape except when the rents were due, and then I am recognised as a tenant.[256]

On a broader plane, the agent's duties could also extend to political questions. In Wales there were widespread complaints that landowners allowed their stewards to issue directives to tenants which they would have been unwilling to promulgate themselves. At Woodstock in 1880 Lord Randolph Churchill, though the chosen candidate of the Duke of Marlborough, found that his personal popularity had been undermined by the high-handed and unsympathetic attitude of an agent employed by the Duke to run his estates during his absence as Viceroy of Ireland. And in Cheshire, a witness claimed in the late 1860s that although landlords were unwilling to persuade tenants to vote along a particular electoral line, they were quite prepared to allow the agent to do so on their behalf:

> He allows his agent to go to the tenant . . . and give hints that if the tenant does not vote as his landlord wishes, all sorts of petty

indulgences, in the shape of small repairs, additional gates, and perhaps a little time to pay his rent, will be withdrawn, and the landlord, except in very few instances, has not the straightforwardness to say, 'You may vote as you please.' He stands by and lets the agent hint all those things.[82]

With the passage of the Secret Ballot Act in 1872 this particular pressure became more difficult to apply, as the agent now had no foolproof way of knowing just how a tenant *had* voted.

Overall, though, most owners probably shared the view of Lord Willoughby de Broke that it was better to allow the agent to deal with questions of estate management and husbandry practice rather than to come into direct contact with the tenants themselves. As Willoughby de Broke put it, it was preferable to keep as a buffer between landlord and tenant 'that mysterious institution called the Estate Office'.

Some stewards achieved considerable eminence in their own right, like Hugh Taylor, who was the Duke of Northumberland's principal agent from 1847 to 1865 and a 'greatly respected and authoritative figure in his county'. Still more notable was Rowland Prothero (1851–1937), who acted as chief agent to the Duke of Bedford from 1898 to 1918 and as President of the Board of Agriculture from 1916 to 1919, during the vital later stages of the First World War. As chief agent, Prothero enjoyed a generous salary and free occupancy of a country house which was staffed at the Duke's expense with three indoor and seven outdoor servants. Game, garden produce, cream, milk and butter as well as whisky and port were free allowances. He also enjoyed as an additional perquisite the facilities of another country house, Thorney in Cambridgeshire, on the same terms.

The largest agents often managed, in general supervisory terms, many different estates, rather than being tied to one owner. Thus Messrs Rawlence & Squarey had under their aegis during the 1890s about a quarter of a million acres in twenty-four counties.[52] Elsewhere, on the major estates, there might be a complicated hierarchy of offices, with a central office in London which co-ordinated the diverse estates. This applied, for example, to the Bedford properties.

Not surprisingly, under the pressure of agricultural depression and financial retrenchment, more and more landowners began to insist that their agents should receive specialist training. No longer was it sufficient to employ a local solicitor or farmer or ex-army officer in that capacity, or to regard as a steward's prime qualification the 'possession of a genial manner and the ability to wear riding breeches at any hour of the day with distinction', as had allegedly once been the case.[212] From 1881 the Chartered Surveyors began to hold examinations which included land agency as part of their programme. And in 1896, the Royal Commission on the Land of Wales and Monmouthshire laid down what it saw as the proper training of a land agent. Although a majority of men working on estates at that date had still not followed such a course, it is clear that the days when a steward picked up his knowledge without the aid of much formal instruction were on the wane:

> We think [declared the Commissioners] that such [an] agent should be one who in addition to a sound preliminary, general and scientific education has received a special theoretical training in agriculture and land surveying, and in the sciences (such as mathematics, chemistry etc.) upon which the practice of these arts depends, as well as practical experience in an estate office and on a farm. To put the matter in another way, we think a young man, intending to become a land agent should, in addition to acquiring the average degree of culture and knowledge of a university man, attend courses of study at an agricultural college or a college giving technical instruction in the practical arts, and then pass some time gaining practical and actual experience in an office or on a farm. In short, we would have him prepare himself professionally in a manner analogous to that in which the physician qualifies himself to practice the art of medicine, or a solicitor that of the law.

It was against this background that in 1902 the Land Agents' Society was formed, to bestow upon the occupation an acceptable professional status. By the time of its first annual meeting in October 1903, it had recruited 508 full members and 128 associates, who together administered something like one half of the large estates of England and Wales. The Society's first president was a former agent of the Earl of Sefton, while its vice-president was E. G. Wheler, Commissioner to the Duke of Northumberland.

From the landowner's point of view, the use of specialist agents had the merit both of improving estate administration at a time of financial stringency and of leaving him free to pursue his own private interests, be they those of the fox-hunter, as with Lord Willoughby de Broke, or of the statesman, as with the Marquess of Salisbury. Admittedly some proprietors, like Lord Wantage and Lord Rayleigh, turned their attention to the management and improvement of their own estates, while others followed the example of the 9th Duke of Bedford, and kept a supervisory eye upon the husbandry standards of the tenants. If a farm were given up in bad order, it was said that the Duke would not let it to a new tenant at a reduced rent, 'for that he considered a premium on bad farming'. Instead the farm would be taken in hand, returned to good order, and re-let at an appropriate valuation. But the commitment of landowners to the cause of 'agricultural improvement', which had been so apparent at the end of the eighteenth century and again in the middle years of the nineteenth, was less in evidence after 1875. There was also a withdrawal of aristocratic leadership from scientific societies. Only in the twentieth century did a few members of noble families take up the earlier tradition of aristocrat–scientist, including Bertrand Russell and the Hon. Charles S. Shelley-Rolls, who was a co-founder of Rolls-Royce.

Many more preferred to follow the congenial country pursuits of hunting, shooting and fishing, interrupted by three-monthly migrations to London on or about the first of May, for the Season. Late Victorian and Edwardian England was, indeed, the era of the sporting landlord, with men like Lord Willoughby de Broke devoting four days a week for seven months of the year to riding to hounds. It is significant that in his list of 'the County', Willoughby de Broke placed the master of fox hounds second only in importance to the lord-lieutenant himself. Siegfried Sassoon, in his autobiographical novel, *The Memoirs of a Fox-Hunting Man*, illustrates the enthusiasm with which the sport was followed, and the way in which a good 'run' was savoured long after it had been completed. It is significant that most of the best hunting country in the midland shires, Northampton, Leicester and Nottingham, had a low level of game preservation, 'because foxes and pheasants were not compatible, and enthusiasm for the one tended to exclude the other'.[216] Fox-hunters were, indeed, sometimes warned off by shooting landlords. But with falling rentals, a growing number of landlords found it harder to meet the costs of a hunt on their own. They were forced either to economize or to accept subscriptions. In 1895 Lord Yarborough, whose family had supported the Brocklesbury hunt since the eighteenth century, was forced to sell his dog pack, retaining only the bitches. Even the Duke of Rutland had to cut back hunting to four days a week at the end of the century.

Still more popular than riding to hounds was game preservation. Large beats were organized and shooting developed a mystique of its own, with special rituals and ceremonies. The size of bags increased enormously, and estates enthusiastically vied with one another in their efforts to produce the biggest 'kill'. In December 1913 seven guns (including the King, George V, and the Prince of Wales) shot 3,937 pheasants, three partridges, four rabbits and what is described as one 'various' in a single day's shooting on the Burtley beat at Beaconsfield. Even the architecture of houses was affected, since it was from the 1870s that the gun room became a characteristic feature of country mansions, with its walls adorned by cases of stuffed game and fish, and its racks of firearms.[64] The total of gamekeepers also increased sharply, growing from 12,429 in 1871 to 16,677 thirty years later. By 1911, as F. M. L. Thompson points out, there were more than twice as many gamekeepers as there were country policemen in the rural districts.[216]

Admittedly, financial problems meant that on some estates, economies had to be made even in this sphere by the end of the century. On the eve of the First World War, the *Estates Gazette* observed that a number of those who had once gone shooting were now taking up the less costly alternative of golf, or were spending the winter abroad, where living expenses were much lower. But their place was taken by others, especially from the thrusting ranks of the *nouveaux riches*, who prized the status which the purchase or renting of an estate could bestow, or who needed the dignity of landed property to support their aspirations to a peerage. Often, when estates were offered for sale, mention was made of their 'excellent shooting'. The sale catalogue of the Middle-Hill property stressed the fact that with 'only ordinary care the large extent of woodland would enable any amount of game to be preserved, while Buckland Wood is believed to be one of the best fox covers in the kingdom . . . The North Cotswold Hounds are located in the village of Broadway, and the Cotswold, Heythrop, Warwickshire, Lord Coventry's, and Worcestershire Hounds meet in the neighbourhood.' Overall, the sporting facilities here were described enthusiastically as 'almost unrivalled'.

Newcomers who acquired properties under these conditions rarely paid much attention to the agricultural prospects of the land and its occupiers. Farmers in Lancashire complained of 'cotton capitalists who had bought estates for the sport and knew nothing about farming and cared less'. The game damaged their crops and when shoots were held, the land was trampled over and their gates left open.[252] A further source of trouble and annoyance was provided by the gamekeepers, 'who were for ever suspecting and accusing them of keeping poaching dogs'. Rider Haggard had similar problems in mind when he wrote in 1901/2 that Lord Iveagh's estate in Suffolk had become 'a game property where bona-fide agricultural conditions did not prevail. Indeed, there existed a general tendency to turn many of the estates in this part of Suffolk to pleasure rather than to agricultural purposes'.[177] Two out of every three country seats in Suffolk were let for game and, with ten gamekeepers per 10,000 acres of land, the county was in 1911 the most densely keepered in the land. Over the border, the partridge was ironically described as 'the salvation of Norfolk farming', while in Cambridgeshire, where between a half and two-thirds of owners' income had been allegedly lost through the depression, a number of the traditional landowning families had been driven into bankruptcy: 'almost all the old Cambridgeshire landed aristocracy had departed', wrote Haggard, 'and . . . their ancestral homes have passed into the hands of rich racing or shooting men, who hold them for amusement, and are not animated by the same objects and ideas as the class which they dispossessed.'

Not surprisingly, these 'incomers' failed to win the respect of the villagers in the way their predecessors had done. Thus, although the tenant of Lofts Hall, Elmdon, in Essex, between 1905 and 1910 presented the parish with a reading room, organized fêtes at which garden produce was exhibited, and provided broth and free gifts for the children, he was never seen as the 'head' of local society. That privilege was reserved for the 'old' squire, who now lived in one of the farms on the estate. It was to him that the local people deferred and his changed fortunes seemingly made no difference to the respect in which he was held.[239]

The contrast between the Victorian hey-day of the old landed families and the life led by their Edwardian counterparts, when new men, such as the South African diamond and gold millionaires, had risen to the fore, was commented upon by Lady Dorothy Nevill. Even the scale of expenditure had changed out of all recognition, under the influence of the newcomers:

Half a century ago . . . [she wrote in about 1906] a landed proprietor . . . was quite content to live the greater part of the year on his estate, where he amused himself with the sport which satisfied the moderate taste of those days. If he had not a house in town, he hired one for three months or so, when he would bring up his wife and daughters for the season. Entertainments were certainly given – entertainments the comparative modesty of which would to-day provoke a contemptuous smile – and the season over, the family would once more return to the country, there to remain until the following year. This mode of life was in some cases varied by a voyage . . . abroad.

Country-house parties were few, but lasted longer than at present, when people go hundreds of miles to stay a day. Life, in short, was slow, rather solemn, inexpensive, not undignified, but, according to modern ideas, dull.

What is the life of the rich man of to-day? . . . Paris, Monte Carlo, big-game shooting in Africa, fishing in Norway, dashes to Egypt, trips to Japan. . . . At the proper time he goes to the country to shoot, more often than not entertaining a large party, who disperse the moment the last shot has been fired and the last pheasant killed. . . . Such individuals have changed the whole standard of living, and imported the bustle of the Stock Exchange into the drawing-rooms of Mayfair.[219]

It was these altered circumstances which caused the Dowager Countess Cowper to write sourly: 'Certainly *money* is a vulgar thing, and money is what rules us now. I quite agree with Weigall who, talking of Barons Grant, Sturrs, Oppenheim, Boutil and Co. said, "What right have such people to force themselves into our society?"'[167] But force themselves they did, and as the old landed families recognized the threat to their traditional position which this offered, the more astute of them started to adjust to the changed conditions. A number took directorships, or secured membership of the boards of companies for their impecunious younger sons. As early as 1874/75, Anthony Trollope was examining the more unsavoury aspects of this in his novel *The Way We Live Now*, while according to Lady Dorothy Nevill, a number of landowners displayed 'nearly as much shrewdness in driving bargains . . . as a South African millionaire himself'.

The new attitude came to the fore particularly during the 1890s, and by 1896 more than a quarter of the peerage (i.e. 167 noblemen) held directorships, most of them in more than one company. Among them was the 3rd Earl of Verulam, who by 1913 had become a director of thirteen companies, nine of them involving mining enterprises overseas. At this stage he derived more than one-third of his total income from directors' fees and from dividends. It was during the nineties, too, that landowners sought to spread their assets by investing in stock exchange securities. Both the Earl of Durham and Earl Fitzwilliam undertook large-scale conversions of their assets into stocks and bonds. Others, including the Earl of Leicester and the Duke of Portland, invested in a whole range of enterprises, from breweries and bank stock to collieries and stores, South African gold mines and foreign railways. Likewise the Duke of Devonshire, after disposing of land in Ireland and in Derbyshire, used the proceeds to pay off debts amounting to around £1½m. and also to purchase a variety of British, Colonial and United States government bonds and overseas railway shares. Holdings were acquired in Vickers, the naval construction and armaments company, and by the First World War these different enterprises were providing the Duke with nearly a third of his income.[94]

Other magnates, including the Dukes of Marlborough, sought to restore family fortunes by marrying heiresses and by selling off surplus possessions or property. In the 1870s and 1880s paintings, books, porcelain, and other items to the value of between £400,000 and £500,000 were sold, while an estate at Waddesdon in Buckinghamshire was disposed of for almost a quarter of a million. Some of the proceeds were used to pay off debts, with £20,000 handed over to the Sun Fire Office in 1877 to discharge a loan which had been contracted in 1816. Part of the remainder was expended on estate improvement, while purchases of urban land were also made.

Town land was, of course, a major source of income for owners like the Dukes of Bedford and Westminster, while a few, including the Duke of Devonshire, with Eastbourne, and the Earl of

Scarborough, with Skegness, began to develop their own seaside resorts. Unfortunately for both of them, the projects proved to be long and costly.

A further possibility was to exploit the mineral resources of an estate, with mining royalties providing 40 per cent of the Duke of Northumberland's gross income by 1914. The Marquess of Bute, too, enjoyed a burgeoning income from the Glamorgan coalfields as well as from Cardiff docks, and was able to undertake an extensive house-building programme in consequence. But not all of these industrial ventures proved successful. The Duke of Devonshire found his heavy investment in Barrow-in-Furness sadly misplaced when the steel industry went into recession in the 1870s. In his case, his large agricultural fortune was used to subsidize his industrial enterprises.

Harder-pressed owners, especially the smaller men, resorted to the traditional solution of trying to mortgage their property but, given the unpromising state of the land market at the end of the nineteenth century, this proved easier said than done. With the depression, the capital value of land fell everywhere by around 30 per cent, 'thereby wiping out the margin which was customarily left between the size of the first mortgage and the assessed value of the land to be used as collateral'.[93] With this uncertainty in predicting land values, loans were difficult to secure. It took the solicitors of the young Sir Edwin Dashwood several months to arrange a mortgage of £10,000 on his estate at West Wycombe in Buckinghamshire and on a property in London. The land already carried mortgages amounting to £24,000 at 4 per cent interest, and it was intended to raise the new loan at a lower rate of interest and also to exchange the existing mortgages for cheaper ones, following the general fall in interest rates. Eventually the Prudential Assurance agreed to take over the entire mortgage at a rate of 3¼ per cent, and the deal was concluded in July 1890. However, as the negotiating solicitor admitted, the rentals from the 'agricultural lands' were only about half what they had been, though he added hopefully: 'they are therefore more likely to rise than fall in value, while [a] portion of them are about to be developed for building purposes, which will considerably enhance the value of the property'.[6] In other cases, old loans were carefully scrutinized, as anxious mortgagees demanded either more collateral or an immediate paying off of part of the loan. As the *Economist* gloomily noted in 1897, no security had ever been relied upon with more implicit faith than English land, and 'few have lately been found more sadly wanting'.

Finally, for those who had tried every other expedient for raising cash, the sale of land might have to be contemplated, providing a purchaser could be found. The Lisburnes, for example, began the large-scale selling of their estates in the 1880s. As Appendix (b) confirms, over the period 1878–92 there were also reductions in the size of the Goodwood estate in Sussex, the Earl of Ancaster's property in Lincolnshire and Rutland, and the Orwell estate in Suffolk, among others. But at the height of the 'depression' even land sales were difficult to arrange, despite the passage of the 1882 Settled Land Act, which made it easier for holders of entailed property to sell. Under it, declared the Duke of Marlborough in 1885, 'were there any effective demand for the purchase of land, half the land of England would be in the market tomorrow'. Two years later the *Times* commented on the tendency of 'sport capitalists' to rent rather than buy property, since they mistrusted 'for purposes of investment . . . the security which land offers in present circumstances'. Among estates offered for sale but unable to find buyers in these years were the Marquess of Cholmondeley's Houghton Hall property in Norfolk, Lord Saye and Sele's estate in Lincolnshire, Lord Rodney's Berrington estate in Hereford, and the Charlton family's 20,000 acres in Northumberland.[266] Sometimes, as with an estate of 477 acres at Great Thurlow, Suffolk, in 1891, not a single offer was made for the property concerned.[45] Not until the early twentieth century, when improved agricultural prospects induced a more optimistic spirit, were many landowners at last able to dispose of unwanted estates.

There were, of course, exceptions to this gloomy picture. Some upland areas on the flanks of growing industrial towns were acquired for reservoirs in the last decades of the nineteenth century, and by 1904 the gathering grounds (mostly moorland) held by local authorities in England amounted to at least 82,050 acres and in Wales to 6,350 acres. Elsewhere, a few fortunate landlords were able to sell infertile tracts of land for military barracks and training grounds, but this was essentially a localized and specialist development, which affected a tiny minority of owners only.[144]

Tax burdens, too, added to the worries of these years, for at a time when their incomes were under pressure landlords found the calls upon their purses for rates, taxes and other expenses increasing. For example, the 1883 Agricultural Holdings Act, and subsequent amending legislation, sought to meet one long-standing grievance of farmers by making it compulsory for landlords to compensate outgoing tenants for the unexhausted value of any improvements they may have made to the rented property. This was particularly serious for landowners who were unable immediately to find a new tenant for a vacant farm, since they could easily be compelled to pay heavy sums by way of compensation to the former tenant, only to find that when the incomer arrived, he refused to reimburse the landlord for these improvements.[222] Again, under the 1891 tithe legislation, responsibility for the payment of tithes was placed unequivocally upon the landlord, who could no longer use his tenant as an agent on his behalf, though he could, of course, increase the rental by the relevant amount. Most serious of all was the change in policy towards death duties under the Finance Act of 1894. This imposed a new duty upon all settled estates, while the rates at which duties were levied on other inherited property were increased. Sir William Harcourt, the Chancellor of the Exchequer, estimated that under the new arrangements, a man owning £1m. in land would have to pay about £60,000 more for succession and estate duty than hitherto; in the case of a more modest property, valued at £100,000, the extra duty would be £3,500 (or £5,500 as against some £2,000 under the old system).[13] Stocks and shares could easily be sold to pay death duties, but with land, especially in the depression years, the story was very different. Although it was possible to deal with the problem by taking out special insurance policies – an approach which Harcourt himself recommended – there must have been many landowners who would have agreed with Lady Bracknell when she declared: 'What between the duties expected of one during one's lifetime, and the duties exacted from one after one's death, land has ceased to be either a profit or a pleasure. It gives one position and prevents one from keeping it up. That's all that can be said about land.' It was a sign of the times that after 1880 landowners ceased to comprise the majority of very rich men.

A few, nevertheless, reacted to the gloom of the late Victorian years not by repining or allowing their property to be turned into mere game preserves, but by taking unwanted farms in hand and cultivating them efficiently from their own resources. Although the heavy capital outlay this involved made it unattractive to most, a minority saw it as an opportunity to use their skill and ingenuity. Among them was Lord Wantage, whose 26,000-acre estate on the Berkshire downs was especially vulnerable to the effects of the recession because of its concentration on corn production and the raising of sheep. Both were hit by foreign competition, with the price of wool collapsing even before that of grain. By the mid-1890s around 13,000 acres were in hand and were being farmed as a single unit. At this stage Lord Wantage claimed to be 'the largest farmer, probably, in England'. He was able to afford to spend lavishly thanks to his wife's banking fortune, with the estate acquiring the best and newest steam ploughs, and the most modern mowing and reaping machines. Subsequently he described his methods:

> You get a superior sort of agriculturalist to manage the land, a better man in knowledge, both theoretical and practical, in training and in capacity, than the neighbouring farmers, so that he can set an example to the whole country round; farmers see the work better done, and the labourers are not slow to find it out. I employ one head bailiff only for all the land I have in hand. He buys everything and sells everything, and under him are only ordinary working foremen. In farming on a large scale there is great economy; you can use machinery more advantageously, and you can diminish the number both of labourers and horses.[278]

Water was supplied to the downland by the use of pumps, to reinforce the existing dewponds, and a reservoir was constructed on a high point on the estate. As a result of these initiatives, a cattle 'ranch' was developed on the downs, where formerly only sheep had grazed. In addition, a stud of Shire horses was established which, at the time of his death in 1901, was valued at £15,211. Alongside this, more than a hundred men were employed as mechanics, carpenters, bricklayers, etc., in the estate workshops, while during the winter months Lord Wantage would undertake a programme of roadmaking, tree planting, ditch cleaning and the like to give work to labourers who would otherwise have been unemployed.

At Terling in Essex Lord Rayleigh and his brother, Edward

Strutt, embarked on a different policy. Over the depression period the amount of land in hand rose from 854 acres in 1876 to 4,315 acres twenty years later, while estate income dropped by around two-thirds in the eleven years 1882 to 1893 alone. In these circumstances, Strutt decided to take advantage of the nearby London market by switching to intensive milk production. Calving was concentrated in the autumn in order to secure high winter milk prices; large areas of roots were grown to provide winter fodder and to prepare the land for wheat; pasture was reduced to a minimum and the rest of the land was ploughed up for corn. Milk sales rose sharply, from a value of £5,738 in 1886–87 to £9.734 in 1895–96, and in 1900 came the establishment of Lord Rayleigh's Dairies Ltd, to enter the London retail trade. By 1914, the company was operating about a dozen shops and depots. In addition, on the farm itself, efforts were made to produce cleaner milk, and a laboratory was opened in 1910 at which samples from each of the herds were tested regularly for fats and solids-not-fat.[166] Adjoining Hatfield Peverel Station a collecting depot was constructed, and to this the milk from the surrounding farms was delivered. It was then cooled to a lower temperature than was possible on the farm itself, before it was loaded on to the train. As a result of the efficient manner in which the enterprise was conducted, the Rayleigh estate emerged from the buffetings of the eighties and nineties ready to embark upon a programme of expansion in the new century. By 1914 the acreage in hand had risen to 5,925 and the gross profit had jumped from an average of £2,352 per annum for the ten years 1887–96 to £6,364 for the eighteen years 1897–1914. For the last two years before the War it was over £9,000 per annum. In addition, potato growing was introduced as another cash crop, while Edward Strutt himself acted as adviser to a number of other estates in the area.

Such whole-hearted responses as these to the depression were, admittedly, rare, especially in the hard-hit eastern counties, but they indicated what could be done by determined landowner.

It is against this background of social and economic change that we must chart the daily round of life in the country house. For most landed families it remained a subtle mixture of freedom and restraint, of pleasure and duty. For, as Thompson has pointed out, despite the authority which the head of the household wielded, in practice he was restricted by the demands imposed upon him by his position and 'subject to the discipline of his own butler, valet and household timetable'.[266]

From an early age the children, at least in theory, were taught to appreciate the responsibilities as well as the privileges of their position. At Hatfield House, the young Cecils learned that 'wealth was a trust' and that in addition to the public service demanded by their position in life, they must give at least one-seventh of their income to charity.[241] Often, too, in their early years the children of the squire would mix with the offspring of estate workers. In this way bonds of friendship were early forged.

Education, in the case of the boys, normally meant attendance at a public school, though for the youngest children and the girls a tutor or governess was customary. By the end of the century some girls were also being sent to private schools, where the main emphasis lay on the acquisition of 'accomplishments' rather than on academic attainments.

For their sons, the wealthiest county families still chose the older public schools (especially Eton). The limited curriculum, with its bias towards the classics and its general neglect of science, in no way worried them. After all, they did not expect their children to earn a living in the hurly-burly of the industrial arena, but in the armed forces, the church, the civil service, or perhaps the world of finance. In the later Victorian years the administration of Empire also exerted a growing attraction for impecunious younger sons.

The public schools, for their part, concentrated on fostering qualities of leadership among their pupils, and stressing the merits of organized team games – what some cynics have labelled 'muscular Christianity'. According to two of their masters, writing in 1909, they sought to produce a race of 'well-bodied, well-mannered, well-meaning boys, keen at games, devoted to their schools, ignorant of life, contemptuous of all outside the pale of their own caste, uninterested in work, neither desiring nor revering knowledge'. They were of a type 'admirably fitted for maintaining a static political and social system and for building an Empire'.[220] But some pupils may have seen things differently. The young Cecils complained dismally of dampness, rheumatism, an uninspiring routine and tedious teaching, when they wrote home from Eton. As one of them later declared: 'I should not grudge all the time I spent on classics, if in learning, or rather not learning, them I had learnt how to work; but that is just what we were not taught. At best we were taught how to cram but never how to extract knowledge and pack it neatly away in the mind for future reference.'[241]

Within the household itself most children spent little time with their parents, but were confined to the nursery and the school-room, where their closest companions were the servants. For the older boys there was, of course, the need to learn the country pursuits which would form so significant a part of the later life of many of them. Lord Willoughby de Broke recalled the especial debt he owed to the head gamekeeper at Compton Verney: 'It was with him that I saw my first fox killed; it was with him that I killed my first pheasant, partridge, duck, hare, rabbit and rook; also my first fish. He showed me my first rat hunt, and escorted me on my first expedition in quest of birds' nests . . . No wonder that I was attached to him.'[282]

After school came Oxford or Cambridge, which for most of the young men was merely an opportunity to pursue their private leisure interests in company with others of a like mind, rather than to follow any formal scholastic routine. Lord Randolph Churchill, in his first year at Merton College, Oxford, founded the 'Blenheim Harriers', and spent much of the following two years training the pack and hunting it successfully over the Oxfordshire country-side. He also became a founder member of the Myrmidons, a dining club formed by Merton men, plus a few selected guests, whose feastings became notorious within the University. For Lord Willoughby de Broke, who was at Christ Church, Oxford meant fox-hunting, racing, cricket, 'and no end of good dinners in the company of the best fellows in the world'. Later some of these youngsters would move into politics, as Lord Randolph Churchill did, or into court circles. Others took over the reins of an estate, with the responsibilities that this entailed, but without the specialized training which later generations have deemed necessary. The cult of the amateur, at this level of society, still reigned supreme.

For the smaller country gentlemen, that is those owning up to 3,000 acres or so, life probably much resembled that attributed by Richard Jefferies to his fictional Squire Filbard. Filbard began the day by interviewing the steward or gamekeeper or gardener in his study, in order to discuss with them the running of the estate. One day a week he would devote to visiting the nearby market town; on another he took his place on the petty sessional bench; and on Sundays he attended church with unfailing regularity. Perhaps, like Lord Tollemache, the strictness of his Sabbath observance would preclude even the serving of hot meals on that day, in order that the servants might attend church. Tollemache's son recalled that when there were large house-parties at Helmingham, the guests on Sunday were 'not only deprived of hot meat, but also given chablis instead of champagne'.[271] In many families, too, each day commenced with pre-breakfast prayers, at which the whole household was expected to be present, and over which the *paterfamilias* would preside.

For the rest, as Jefferies wrote of his archetypal country gentleman, he 'could not account for his time. He sometimes, indeed, in the hunting season, rode to the meet. . . . He went out shooting, but not in regular trim. He would carry his gun across to the Home Farm, and knock over a rabbit on the way, then spend two hours looking at the Alderney cow, the roof of the pigsty, and the poultry, and presently stroll across a corner of the wood, and shoot a pheasant'. Later there would be a visit to London for the Season, perhaps followed by a trip to the seaside, 'and then home in the autumn to peddle about the estate'.[196] Neighbours would be entertained to lengthy dinners, followed by cards, and probably there would be croquet and archery parties, like those attended by the Revd Francis Kilvert in Radnorshire. Dancing and singing similarly took their place in the entertainment. 'I danced the first quadrille', wrote Kilvert on one occasion, '. . . and made innumerable mistakes, once or twice running quite wild through the figure like a runaway horse. . . . Between the dances there were songs and negro minstrelsy.'[232]

The female members of county families, meanwhile, occupied themselves with needlework, sketching, music, reading, and visiting 'the poor'. They would dispense charity to deserving villagers, while some of the more energetic would become expert horsewomen, and from time to time the younger girls would teach at the local Sunday school. Their mother would oversee the smooth running of the household, although naturally she carried out no domestic chores herself. Those were reserved for the servants.

With the financial pressures of the late nineteenth century, some landowners were forced to economize on their domestic staff, but in most cases a large number of indoor servants continued to be employed. As Lady Cynthia Asquith declared, there was never 'any virtue other than economy, in keeping only one instead of several servants'.[257] Even in these years anything aspiring to the title of a country house would have at least eight resident domestics, and the grander mansions might have as many as fifty. At Longleat in the 1880s and 1890s there were forty-three, ranging from the house steward, the butler and the chef at the head of the male staff, down to the pantry boys, a lamp boy and two 'oddmen'. The female side was headed by the housekeeper, the nurse, and two lady's maids, while at the lower end of the scale came two kitchen maids, a vegetable maid, a scullery maid, two still-room maids, and six laundry maids. Fourteen other servants were employed in the stables. They included a coachman, a second coachman, a carriage groom, 'a steel boy (whose task was to burnish the bits and the metal parts of the harness) and a "tiger", a small boy in livery who sat upright on the box of the carriage, his arms folded stiffly across his chest. . . . The "tiger's" other duty was to lead the ponies of the children of the house when they went out riding.'[127]

Domestic life in these large establishments was carefully structured, with each department under the control of the relevant head servant. A number of servants were also kept to wait upon these senior colleagues. One landowner estimated that out of a domestic staff of twenty-three employed in his household, fifteen waited on the family and eight on the fifteen![216] General supervision of the men was undertaken by the house steward or the butler, while the housekeeper was responsible for the women, and the kitchen staff would be under the jurisdiction of the chef or cook. Each member of staff had his or her specific duties to perform. At Longleat, the Marchioness of Bath recalled that the butler was 'far too grand a figure to roll up his sleeves and work in his own pantry; and in the dining room he would serve only the wine and the more imposing dishes. Even the house steward would always knock at the pantry door out of respect for the butler.' In more modest establishments this division of labour was less rigid, especially among the males. For to have a footman in livery to open the front door to callers or ride behind the carriage was the main objective, even if that footman was at other times found mucking out the stable.

Often senior members of staff would be recruited from a distance away, so that a wider choice of candidates could be secured. Only the juniors, the scullery and kitchen maids or the pantry boys, came from the immediate locality. Even at Compton Verney, despite the avowed attachment of Lord Willoughby de Broke to his estate dependants, the butler, under-butler, housekeeper, nurse and lady's maid employed in the early 1870s all came from outside Warwickshire.

Nor was every employer anxious to engage even *junior* staff from the immediate vicinity of his mansion, perhaps on the grounds that they would betray household secrets or that they would be always running home. In 1871 Lord Camoys, an Oxfordshire landowner, had only one Oxfordshire-born servant among his resident staff of twenty-three, while the Harcourts of Nuneham Courtenay had only two Oxfordshire-born servants out of a staff of twenty-one. Neither came from the vicinity of Nuneham.[190] In the Harcourt household, like that of many other Anglican landed families, all the servants had to be members of the Church of England, and this applied even to estate workers, like gamekeepers or carpenters.[13]

A notable contrast to such attitudes was provided by the Yorke family of Erddig, near Wrexham, whose indoor domestics in 1887 numbered fourteen. Not only did they recruit their servants locally, but they also seem to have treated them almost as friends. Matilda Bolter, the first housemaid, would even be invited from time to time to play her violin in accompaniment to Mrs Yorke's father, who played the cello. The women servants were also provided with a comfortable workroom, and often before they retired to bed for the night there would be time for a game or two of whist. So interested were the family in their servants that they composed poems about them. In 1887 the following verses were penned about two of the maids:

Two servants of the name of Trevor
United here in one endeavour
Each working for the general good
In Laundry, and preparing food.

Born and brought up within our ground
(The Parents here their work had found)
These sisters now within our Town
Are married well, and settled down.

Needless to say, few country house owner displayed such a high degree of concern for their servants as this, but in many households warm feelings grew up between old retainers and their employers. The single-minded devotion which Sir Winston Churchill accorded his nurse, Mrs Everest, amply demonstrates this. For twenty years, until her death in 1895, she was 'destined to be the principal confidante of his joys. his troubles, and his hopes'. For years after she died he paid an annual sum to a local florist for the upkeep of her grave.

Finally, it must be remembered that servants were employed not merely to carry out domestic duties but, by their number and, in the case of the men, their liveries, to impress friends and neighbours with their employer's standing in the world. They were an essential part of the ceremonial of country life, although often an expensive luxury as well. Lord Rosebery's agent was not alone when in 1912 he vainly sought to curb the extravagances of his employer's chef and steward. He pointed out to the Earl that, between 1909 and 1911, expenditure on the household and the kitchens had increased by around £1,000, although staff numbers were about the same and the price of food had not changed appreciably. His employer shared this concern, but when a suggestion was made that a less prestigious cook should be substituted for the chef, with an outside chef specially hired for important dinners in London, Lord Rosebery rejected the idea out of hand: 'hired chefs', he firmly declared, 'are simply appalling'. So things continued as before, with the agent vainly striving to bring the household finances under control.[16]

For many members of the landed classes, the final quarter of the nineteenth century was a time of anxiety and, often enough, of financial retrenchment. Only those with access to outside sources of capital from industry, the City, or foreign investment, or who also owned remunerative urban land, were able to weather the economic storm with ease. Socially and politically, too, there were increasing pressures from the thrusting ranks of newly enriched manufacturers and financiers who sought to enjoy the trappings of life on a landed estate, but lacked any real commitment to its traditions. The self-confident serenity displayed in so many photographs of late Victorian landed families often enough hid an inward turmoil of doubt and anguish as they saw much of their old standing in the world inexorably sliding away from them.

3
The Farmers

If the final quarter of the nineteenth century proved a time of difficulty for many landowners, the hardships faced by the farmers were still more severe. For in their case, failure meant not merely a loss of income and a cutting back upon personal expenditure, but perhaps the disappearance of their entire livelihood. As might be expected, those in the arable eastern counties were the worst affected by the depression. From Suffolk, it was reported in the mid-1890s that tenant farmers had 'seen the great bulk of their savings, or their fathers' savings, swept away, and with all their industry and pinching and care they were unable to preserve themselves' from a 'very near approach to bankruptcy'.[54] The typical Norfolk farmer was likewise described as 'a harassed and hard-working man, with little time to devote to anything but the struggle to make both ends meet'. Even on the well-run Holkham estate, holdings were difficult to let by the 1890s, with six farms changing hands in 1895–96 alone. For the first time the estate had to resort to advertising rather than personal recommendation to secure new tenants. And the largest farmers, for their part, were no longer bringing up their sons to work on the land. As Rider Haggard declared: 'for £1,000 a man could be put into a profession whereas to farm he needed £3,000 which he stood a good chance of losing'.[177]

Even in Lancashire, although the impact of depression was here relatively light, there were complaints by 1893 of shortage of cash and of an unwillingness on the part of landowners to carry out necessary capital expenditure. The combined effects of imports of meat and dairy produce, drought, and outbreaks of pleuro-pneumonia among cattle had all taken their toll. Thomas Armistead, auctioneer for the Lancaster Auction Mart Company, and agent for a manure company, claimed that whereas three years before he would conduct nine out of ten auction sales of farmers' stock on three months' credit, from the autumn of 1893 he had set himself 'entirely against credit sales, as we had so much difficulty in getting the money in . . . I also find, . . . as agent for a manure company, that the farmers are buying much less manure, quite 25 per cent less, and we have the greatest difficulty in getting paid. . . . It is all hand-to-mouth farming now, just what will show the quickest return.'[54]

Exactly what this change of fortune could mean in personal terms was shown by Richard Jefferies. In 1880 he described the bitterness and heartbreak faced by one man who was forced to give up a good-sized farm to become a bailiff in the same locality, for a wage of 15s. a week. The author wrote from some personal experience, for in 1878 his own father had been forced to sell up a small farm he owned near Swindon and had moved to Bath, where he became an odd-job gardener. Advertisements in the agricultural press confirm that this was no isolated incident. Typical of many was the appeal inserted in the *Mark Lane Express* in February 1891, by a 'respectable Farmer', seeking a position as a bailiff, 'Stock farm preferred; wife good dairywoman'.

In Jefferies' view, it was the slowness of the process of decline which was hardest to bear:

> [The farmer] cannot, like the bankrupt tradesman, . . . put up his shutters at once and retire from view. Even at the end, after the notice, six months at least elapse before all is over – before the farm is surrendered, and the sale of household furniture and effects take place. . . . So far as his neighbours are concerned he is in public view for years previously. He has to rise in the morning and meet them in the fields. He sees them in the road; he passes through groups of them in the market-place. As he goes by they look after him, and perhaps audibly wonder how long he will last. . . . The labourers in the field know it, and by their manner show that they know it.[196]

His family, too, was forced to share the disgrace. His wife was no longer invited to social gatherings, the neighbours' wives did not call, and 'their well-dressed daughters, as they rattle by to the town in basket-carriage or dog-cart, look askance at the shabby figure walking slowly on the path beside the road'. It was the all-embracing nature of financial disaster which lent such an edge to farmers' anxieties during the 'depression' years.

Yet, once the initial impact of the recession had been faced, the total of occupiers remained surprisingly stable compared to that of their workers. Between 1871 and 1891 the number of farmers and graziers in England and Wales dropped from 249,907 to 223,610, a decline of about 10.5 per cent in twenty years. Then in the rather more prosperous later 1890s they slightly increased, to reach 224,299 by 1901. Only in a few of the hardest-hit counties was the fall in the farming population significant. In Essex the number of farmers and graziers dropped by about 17.4 per cent between 1871 and 1891, while in Berkshire, with its concentration on sheep and corn farming, the decline was around 20.4 per cent. Much of the land in both counties had to be taken in hand by its owners because tenants could not be found, and in parts of Essex it was allowed to tumble down to grass and was then let in largish blocks as rough grazing, at a nominal rental.[54]

By this date most farmers were tenants, who relied upon their landlord to provide fixed capital for buildings, drainage, and similar matters. Only in a minority of counties, like Devon, with its dairying preoccupations, and Westmorland and Cumberland, with their well-established tradition of small owners or 'statesmen', was the role of the small owners significant. In Cumberland, they held about 38 per cent of the acreage; in Westmorland, 34 per cent; and in Devon, 33 per cent. Middlesex and Surrey, where proximity to London and the consequent high cost of land discouraged the building up of large estates, also had a substantial body of small owner-occupiers, who possessed around a third of the total acreage in each case.[266] During the depression years these owner-occupiers were particularly vulnerable to the adverse conditions, for they had no resources but their own to fall back upon. By the late 1880s 82 per cent of all occupiers of agricultural holdings were tenants, as opposed to 14 per cent who owned the whole of their land, and 4 per cent who owned part of it.[64] At this stage only 15 per cent of the total cultivated acreage was owned by its occupiers; in 1908 that proportion had fallen to 12 per cent, and by 1914 to 11 per cent. Not until the short-lived agricultural boom in the immediate aftermath of World War I did the total of owner-occupiers show a revival.

The daily round of the farmers naturally varied as greatly as did the size and character of the holdings they occupied. On some larger estates especially in the eastern counties, owners like Lord Monson or the Earl of Yarborough provided a whole range of different-sized farms, to allow for upward mobility among the tenants. At the top of the scale came men and women cultivating 300 acres or more, an estimated 15,579 in England and 527 in Wales by the mid-1870s. Although they accounted for only a tiny proportion of all occupiers (a mere 4 per cent of those in England and 1 per cent of those in Wales), the acreage they held was a substantial 29 per cent of the cultivated acreage in the former country and 9 per cent in the latter. By contrast, 293,469 holdings in England and 40,161 in Wales were of 50 acres of less. In each case they comprised about 70 per cent of the total, though the area they covered amounted to only 15 per cent of the cultivated area in England and 23 per cent of that in Wales. This included accommodation land rented by tradesmen for a few animals, paddocks attached to larger houses, and a whole range of market gardens and cow pastures, as well as traditional small farms. By the mid-1880s the median holding in the pastoral west of Britain was 65 acres; in the arable and stock-feeding districts of the east and south-east, it was 120 acres.

As we saw in Chapter 1, during the mid-Victorian years many of the larger farmers had enjoyed an extremely comfortable standard of living and had occupied a position of authority within their home parishes commensurate with it. Not only did they play a major role as cultivators of the soil and employers of labour, but some, like the Holkham tenant farmer, John Hudson, kept a permanent wheelwright, carpenter and blacksmith, as well as farm workers, upon their staff. They expected to go hunting or shooting two or three days a week during the appropriate seasons and to drive about on business in some style, in a carriage and pair.

The working capital requirements of such men were considerable. When the Hudsons gave up one of their holdings on the Holkham estate in 1878, the farm sale indicated the value of the livestock and equipment they had kept. Among the former were twenty-four cart horses, five riding and carriage horses, seventy-four cattle (including dairy cows), and more than a thousand sheep. The wide selection of farm implements included about thirty ploughs, and the same number of harrows, as well as scarifiers, cultivators and rollers. For harvesting there was a reaping machine, a threshing drum, and two elevators with horse gearing. Turnip cutters, fifteen waggons, eleven tumbrils, and a nine-horsepower portable steam engine for use in the fields were

among other items offered for sale. Altogether this tenant farmer
had perhaps £4,000 to £5,000 tied up in stock and implements.
Seed, manure, and cattle feed would constitute additional expenses upon his approximately 800-acre farm.[208]

Alongside their farming activities, these larger occupiers also
acted as administrators of local charities, organizers of parish
welfare schemes, and Poor Law guardians. On outlying parts of
the Holkham estate, it was the big tenant farmers rather than the
landlord who initiated schemes for the restoration of the parish
church, the building of a school, and the improvement of roads
and bridges. The wives of these men helped to administer parish
clothing-clubs, to manage the village school, and to run the choir,
in association with the clergyman. Should they desire to do so,
farmers of this class were 'able to help their own labourers in case
of sickness or accident in a way which, to the man of fifty acres,
would be impossible'.[200] Thus, on a large farm in the Bromyard
area of Herefordshire, labourers were provided with a coat,
trousers, a blanket and flannel by their employer every other
Christmas; in addition, some of the men were given help with their
children's clothes.[80]

Within the farmhouse, two or three female servants would
normally be employed to carry out the roughest work, while the
mistress confined herself to supervisory duties and the lighter
tasks. Perhaps, like the farmer's wife encountered by the French-
man, Taine, in the early 1860s, she would merely go to the kitchen
every morning to give her orders, supervise what was done, and
'sometimes [make] a little pastry herself'.

The labour force employed on these major holdings was substantial. On the big downland farms, or those in Norfolk and the
Lincolnshire wolds, perhaps fifty or sixty men might be employed.
Within such enterprises the farmer assumed the role of manager
and overseer, relying on a bailiff or foreman to cope with the day-
to-day problems of running the holding. Even Cornelius Stovin,
with a 600-acre farm on the Lincolnshire wolds and a labour force
of only ten men and three boys, delegated most of the running of
his farm during the 1870s to a foreman, unwisely as it turned out.
He himself spent considerable time at the numerous markets and
fairs of the district, 'assessing prices and comparing yields, if not
buying or selling himself'. His own labour on the farm was
peripheral, although he still enjoyed helping with threshing,

harvesting, turnip-dragging and similar tasks. He also took an active interest in the introduction of new machinery.[256] In other cases, as at Cottisford in Oxfordshire, a large farmer might employ a bailiff to discipline the men and do his dirty work for him, while he rode round his land in a high dogcart, jolly and affable.[268]

It was against this background that criticisms began to mount concerning the new breed of large farmers who seemed to have pretensions above their station and who were unwilling to carry out the hard physical labour necessary to make a success of their holdings. Lord Burghley, for one, sourly observed in 1879 that farmers' wives and daughters should give up the piano and French lessons and 'put their shoulders to the wheel', while twelve years later T. E. Kebbel condemned the system of 'farming-pupils', whereby young gentlemen from well-to-do backgrounds were sent to learn practical agriculture on a large holding in return for a suitable premium. In his view, this led to the farmer's family acquiring expensive tastes and idle habits from the young man, while 'his agricultural tutor, who received an ample fee with him, made it a point of honour to keep what was called "a liberal table," and to indulge in luxuries which, if left to himself, he would have thought beyond his station'.[200] Advertisements in the farming press, offering potential pupils 'hunting and fishing', as well as instruction, would surely have confirmed Kebbel's worst fears. Labourers, too, complained of 'too much pride' in their employers. In Cornwall, a county not renowned for its large holdings, one man claimed that 'a farmer now-a-days will not give a man a lift in his cart along the road; he would be ashamed to be seen with him'. Another grumbled that the men could hardly approach the farmer's house: 'You can scarcely get to the back door. They are all for hunting and going to meets.'[80]

But by the end of the century these criticisms were wide of the mark for most farmers. At that stage few could have afforded to conduct their affairs in such an extravagant fashion. Those who had once sought to do so had gone to the wall, or had reformed their ways. As early as January 1881 the *Banbury Guardian*, when commenting on the Banbury Horse Show, had quoted the Earl of Jersey as regretting that circumstances did not allow so many farmers to go hunting 'as used to be the case a few years ago'.

As for the farmers' wives, although by the 1890s they may still have avoided the dirtiest jobs, most had to help with the milking and dairying, or with feeding the chickens. As a Staffordshire man wrote in 1900: 'On almost all the farms in my immediate neighbourhood it was, forty years ago, the habit for the household to be served by two female servants. On most of the same farms now, there is no service of females other than that of the farmer's own family.'[115] For 'the amenities of domestic life in the farmhouse of a generation ago [were] no longer within reach of the farmer's purse'.

Life for the small to medium agriculturist was, of course, very different from that of his larger counterparts. Such men had always worked in the fields alongside their labourers, taking to heart the Spanish proverb that 'the best manure is the master's foot'. The families, too, were expected to lend a hand, while the spending of every penny was watched with care. 'Devon farmers live close and never spend a bob', was how one of their number put it.[252] They were inherently conservative, distrusting new ideas unless they could observe them in successful operation in the fields of a more advanced neighbour, and keeping machinery and equipment to a minimum. On small farms in the North Riding of Yorkshire, even up to the First World War, a cart, a waggon, a plough, a set of harrows and a grass cutter were deemed sufficient, supplemented by the occasional hire of a reaper. Some men, like Gabriel Oak in Thomas Hardy's *Far From the Madding Crowd*, lacked the capital to purchase their stock outright and had to rely instead on credit. In Oak's case, this meant that when his sheep were lost in an accident, he had no alternative but to sell all he possessed in order to settle the debt, and then to seek employment as a shepherd.

By the 1870s, on most farms in the grain growing areas, the annual visit of the travelling steam thresher had become as much a part of the farming year as the harvest itself. During the depression years the practice of hiring machinery grew more popular, with the number of agricultural machine proprietors and attendants almost trebling between 1871 and 1901 (numbers jumping from 2,152 at the former date to 6,480 at the latter). Steam engines, too, were more widely applied to farming purposes. By 1890 at least two-thirds of all the corn produced in England was being threshed by steam.

Augustus Jessopp, rector of Scarning in Norfolk, described the narrow routine of the smaller farmers, occupying perhaps 60 or 100 acres. Each lived by

> his hen-house, his ducks, and his pigsty; his garden is not often an ornamental *parterre*, but at any rate it brings in a trifle. He eats no eggs – it would be eating money. He shambles to the next brewery with any beast of burden that can jiggle along and fetches his load of grains. . . . His wife or daughter takes her basket of butter to the next market, or gets rid of the apples or the cabbages, or turns an honest penny by the flowers. The big man tells you that geese and turkeys don't pay. Of course they don't, if for weeks you have to pay a lad a shilling a day to look after the one, and the others have to take their chance against the rats.[198]

But the small farmer, with the help of his family, could raise them at a profit.

In fact, despite Jessopp's contemptuous tone, it was often these humbler men, whose outgoings were minimal and who were prepared, along with their children, to work long hours for little return, who weathered the depression years best of all. In so doing, however, they drove their families and themselves desperately hard. In Cumbria, children as young as nine were expected to rise by 6 a.m. to tend the sheep, or bring in the cows from pasture and help with the milking. On their return from school in the evening at 4 p.m. they would resume their duties, assisting with the animals and delivering milk and eggs. Similarly, in Lancashire during the 1890s it was claimed that farmers, their wives and their children 'worked from early dawn to late at night, with an industry that can [not] but excite the admiration of those who witness it . . . at the present time in some districts it is the farmer's sons and daughters who have suffered rather than the land for they have been and are giving their best energies toward its cultivation, receiving no reward in the present, and with but little prospect of any in the future'.[54]

Where there were too many daughters to be found full-time work at home, the 'surplus' girls would often be sent out as maids to neighbouring farms, like Elizabeth Jackson of High Ickenthwaite Farm in High Furness, Cumbria. In 1914, at the age of thirteen, she went into service on a nearby holding. Her contract was for six months, as was customary in that part of the country, and she had to rise at 6 a.m. to light the kitchen stove, wash and whiten the farm steps, and help prepare breakfast. Later there were rooms to clean and lunch to serve at 12.30 p.m. Tea was at 4 p.m., and in between she had to scrub floors. Supper was at 8 p.m., and when that had been cleared away, her working day was over. She does not seem to have had any dairy work to carry out, although many farm servants had to lend a hand there, too. Elizabeth was provided with free board and when she left at the end of six months she was paid £4 10s. She returned home to help her father with the haymaking.

Often the smaller occupiers also took up profitable sidelines to help make ends meet. In Lancashire market gardening increased very considerably, especially in the vicinity of the larger towns, while 'those farming in such localities have the great advantage of an unlimited supply of manure without incurring railway charges for its carriage'.[54] Poultry rearing and fruit growing also became more popular. Likewise in Wales it was estimated that a farmer needed at least 40 acres of land to make a living; those with holdings below that level required a supplementary income. Hence the arrangement in Carnarvonshire and Merioneth, where holdings of between three and twenty acres were cultivated by occupiers who depended primarily for a livelihood upon work in the slate quarries.[191] Colliers and coal-carriers in the anthracite district of south Pembrokeshire similarly cultivated tiny farms, while on the Acland estate in Devon, of 208½ acres let out as small holdings to thirty-five different tenants in the early 1880s, twelve combined farming with market gardening; eleven worked as tradesmen; four acted as journeymen; three were agricultural labourers; and one was a higgler, or dealer.[55] And in the neighbourhood of Penzance in Cornwall, it was common practice during the early 1880s for local miners to hire four or five cows from a farmer. From this some managed to raise themselves to become substantial farmers in their own right. However, it was stressed that the relative success of agriculturists in this county was due to the fact that they were engaged in breeding and rearing cattle, which, unlike corn growing, had remained comparatively profitable. In addition, the practice of laying down land to grass for three or more years had kept down the labour bill, the increase in which, following the advent of agricultural trade unionism in the early 1870s, had contributed to farmers' anxieties in the arable eastern counties.[55]

These small men were normally prepared to assist their larger neighbours when the opportunity offered, and in return would perhaps be allowed to borrow horses or machinery to cultivate their own holdings. In parts of south-west Wales it was customary for farmers to let holdings of three or five acres to their workers, as well as to send along their horse teams and machinery to help with ploughing and harvest, on the understanding that each small tenant's wife and family would make their services available to the farmer at turnip hoeing and harvest. And at Austrey in Warwickshire, early in the present century, my own great-grandfather relied upon his brother's mowing machine to cut the hay on his fifty-acre dairy farm. As recompense, he would give his labour free when that brother's own haymaking commenced. The farm diary of a smallish tenant farmer on the Earl of Harrowby's Sandon estate in Staffordshire shows how this network of aid, often reinforced by family ties, worked out:[9]

1878

6 August: Helped Mr Hulme shift the Machine . . . Sent for Cousin John Shaws Horses

5 October: Mr Shemilt sent His Horses to help us finish sowing . . .

7 October: Sent the colt to be weaned to Mr Shemilts.

29 November: Took Mr Schemilt's sheep back & fetched the Lamb.

30 November: Fetched the colt back from Mr Shemilts.

1879

22 January: Fetched the Machine across from Mr Hulmes.

23 January: Thrashed two Ricks of Wheat . . .

10 February: . . . Lent Bro. Joe the old Mare.

11 February: Helped Mr Hulme shift the Machine . . .

31 March: Mr Moreton sent his horses to help us two days, finished ploughing . . .

15 August: Mr Moor brought His 2 Horses to help us burst the fallow up again.

16 August: Thos. Shaw lent me His Mare for two days.

In the sheep-raising areas of the country, similar co-operation occurred between neighbours for the washing and shearing of the flocks. At Sheldon in Derbyshire, for example, the farmers highest up the village would start with their sheep to the communal washing at about 8 a.m., 'having first taken the lambs away, and amid a tremendous amount of bleating gradually all the sheep in the village would be collected'. Later, when the shearing had been completed, all the wool from the village would be sold to one firm, and as soon as it was ready to be weighed and packed, the boys would rush from school to the packing room 'to help tread [it] tight' in the sheets in which it was sent away. There was great excitement to discover whose wool would weigh heaviest.[187]

These, then, were some of the variations to be found on the farming scene in mid and late-Victorian England. It is now time to look more closely at the course of agricultural change during those years and to consider to what extent it influenced the differing groups of farmers.

The difficulties of arable men began in 1875, with bad weather in every growing season from then until 1879, itself the worst farming year on record. Not only was the harvest abysmal but there was an outbreak of pleuro-pneumonia and foot-and-mouth disease among cattle, and a disastrous attack of liver rot among sheep, which inflicted great losses on their owners. After 1884 weather conditions improved temporarily, to give six reasonable harvests, only to be followed by drought in the early 1890s and another disastrous summer in 1895. During these years many farmers were driven to financial ruin. Only milk producers and those selling poultry, vegetables, fruit and fodder crops to nearby urban markets faced the difficulties with a degree of equanimity. Sometimes, as in parts of Kent and Worcestershire, larger farms were subdivided to provide profitable outlets for market gardening in areas where the soil, climate and marketing arrangements were suitable. In Kent the acreage of small fruit increased by around 80 per cent between 1887 and 1897. By the early years of the present century it held foremost place amongst the counties of England for the growing of fruit. In the Evesham district of Worcestershire, too, market garden cultivation expanded until by the turn of the century it covered 10,000 acres and was the basis of the area's prosperity. Each day special trains, loaded with market garden produce, travelled to all parts of the country, particularly Birmingham, the North of England, South Wales and Scotland.

But for the less efficient arable producers or those paying high rents, even before 1879, the cold wet summers, poor harvests, shortages of hay and growing imports had caused difficulties. One sufferer, a tenant farmer from Lew in Oxfordshire, failed in the early winter of 1878 owing rent arrears of about £1,000 to his landlords, the Dean and Chapter of Christ Church, Oxford, as well as sundry other debts, amounting to around £1,200. The college responded by distraining on his property and then agreeing with the other creditors to allow him to remain on the holding as a manager until the following Michaelmas, at a weekly wage of £2. In the disaster he himself lost everything – including his furniture.[4]

Elsewhere, as we saw in Chapter 2, farms became more difficult to let. Sir George Brooke-Pechell, writing from Alton in Hampshire in August 1876, reported that within eight miles of his property 'there were eighty farms left on the landlords' hands'. On his own estate in Essex, he was experiencing some of these difficulties at first hand.

But the problems in the mid-1870s were of minor significance when compared to the 'black year' of 1879. Snow fell at rye-seeding time; the summer was continously wet, and wheat was still being carted in Suffolk on 4th October. The young Wiltshire farmer S. G. Kendall commented on the 'damp, dank, cold atmosphere which struck a chill almost into one's bones', and which resulted in blackened, unsaleable wheat, and oats which when carried into stacks, 'began to sweat and heat like a dung mixen'. The diary of another man from Charlton near Wantage in Berkshire similarly recorded, on 1 October: 'About 50 Acres Wheat not carted, only 10 acres Barley carried and only about half cut'. In this case the harvest was not finished until 31 October.[9] Yet, as a result of imports (chiefly from the United States), the price of cereals, following this worst harvest of the century, actually declined. In 1879 wheat sold at 10s. 3d. a hundredweight and barley at 9s. 6d., compared to 13s. 8d. and 11s. 4d., respectively, only six years before. Nor did the problem end there, for the slide continued in the adverse seasons which followed. Even when, as in 1887, there were abundant crops, the farmer was unable to rejoice. For as Kendall recalled bitterly, only 'ten years before as a boy, in charge of my father's big Somerset farms . . . we had sold wheat at £3 per quarter – now it was down from 80% to 90% below that level.'[20] In the event, the lowest price of the century was not reached for wheat until 1894 (when it stood at 5s. 4d. a hundredweight) and for barley until 1895 (when it was 6s. 2d.).

Nor did the livestock men escape unscathed, for, apart from the severe outbreak of disease among cattle and sheep in 1879–80, imports began to take a toll. Wool prices started to fall early in the 1870s, as a consequence of growing supplies from Australasia. By the mid-1890s they were only at about half the level of twenty years earlier. During the 1880s the development of marine refrigeration led to price falls for meat and dairy produce, too, while Welsh farmers complained of the 'diminished demand for store cattle to go to the Midland pastures', to be fattened. A Staffordshire dairy farmer noted gloomily that on 5 July 1879 he had taken some cheese to market but 'did not get A bid' for it; not until 2 October in that year was he at last able to make a sale.

Admittedly, British produce normally commanded a higher price than most of its foreign competitors, while cheaper imported fodder helped to keep down the costs of the livestock men. Nevertheless, despite an expanding urban market and a shift in consumers' taste in favour of meat, cheese, butter and bacon, the prices of these home-produced commodities fell by perhaps 10 per cent in the final quarter of the century, at a time when those of their foreign counterparts dropped by around 20 per cent. By the early twentieth century, British farmers were still providing almost half of the meat consumed in this country, though less than a quarter of the wheat and cheese and only an eighth of the butter. Faced with the efficient competition of farmers' co-operatives overseas and in Ireland, with their high standards of grading and packing, British cheese and butter producers found themselves in difficulties. Rider Haggard, for instance, found in 1901–02 that even village shops sold French and Danish butter, American bacon and tinned meat, and Canadian cheese.

Many occupiers, confronted by the disasters and uncertainties of 1879 and beyond, simply threw up their holdings, in order to avoid bankruptcy; others delayed too long, with receiving orders against farmers reaching a peak in 1886 and again in 1895.[229] By the early 1880s in parts of Huntingdonshire, the worst affected county at that date, perhaps one farmer in every twenty or thirty was failing; and in East Anglia as a whole (excluding Norfolk) bankruptcies were running at around one for every 250 farmers each year. Advertisements in the press confirm the sorry tale, with announcements of farm sales 'under distress for rent' or 'In Liquidation – By order of the Trustee'. A few men followed the example of an

Essex farmer who, facing heavy losses in January 1886, offered his landlord £500 if he could be released from the remaining term of his lease.[223] Those with annual agreements left as soon as their notice had expired. A number subsequently emigrated to North America and Australasia, while others sought more attractive holdings with lower rents in England itself, or merely decided to live upon their capital. A sprinkling, like the man quoted by Richard Jefferies, found themselves driven to accept posts as bailiffs, agents or farm managers. Significantly, as the number of farms taken in hand by landowners increased, the demand for bailiffs grew. In 1871 there had been 16,476 of them employed; by 1901 there were 22,623, an increase of more than a third.

Within the worst affected villages, the constant changes seriously threatened the stability of community life. At Barford St Michael in Oxfordshire, the incumbent complained in 1884 that bankruptcy had 'prevailed among the Parish' during the last three years. 'All the farms are changed in occupation. . . . The labourers have grown disorganized & out of condition.'[21] And at Ingatestone in Essex, of twelve farming families in the parish in 1870, only four remained in 1886. Even in more fortunate areas, perhaps where grain growing was less important or the soil more fertile, the turnover was considerable. Thus, in the mixed farming village of Hambleden in Buckinghamshire, only six of the fifteen farming families resident in 1869 were still there in 1887. And at Harefield, Middlesex, despite the benefits derived from its close proximity to the London market, just seven of the sixteen farming families listed in 1870 were there sixteen years later. Many similar cases could be quoted.

In some cases the changes were due to emigration, and as early as 1879 the *Annual Register* recorded the departure of the steamship 'Helvetia' from Liverpool with eighty farmers aboard who were setting out for Texas:

So large an exodus of farmers had never been chronicled before. Most of the farmers who sailed by the 'Helvetia' were what is called 'small men', but some of them had 400 l. or 500 l. of capital, and the less well-off had clubbed together so that all were more or less capitalists. An emigration agent, a sort of tout from the directors of a new railway in Texas, was the moving spirit in the matter. Throughout the summer and autumn many letters and advertisements appeared calling the attention of farmers to the great openings for men with a little capital in the United States and in the Colonies.

During the 1880s this outflow was to intensify for both farmers and labourers, with peak emigration to the United States taking place in the later years of that decade. Beguiling advertisements appeared in the farming newspapers. The Roseland Co-operative Colony in Louisiana, for example, boasted in 1891 that a mere £50 would purchase twenty acres of land: 'If you want to own a home and farm of your own with NO RENT TO PAY, In a beautiful country and a delightful climate, where it costs but little to live and money can be made easily, write for particulars. . . . From £100 to £200 per acre yearly can be made in small fruit and vegetable growing. Large profits can also be made in stock, dairy, or poultry farming. Land in this colony is sold only to temperate and industrious men of good moral habits.'[45] Similarly, the government of Ontario, Canada, proudly proclaimed the province to be 'a HOME for the BRITISH TENANT-FARMER who desires to become his own Landlord'. There were many other offers in this optimistic vein.

More usually, as a first stage, tenants appealed to their existing landlords for rent remissions and reductions to help them out of their difficulties. And there were complaints that owners were too slow to make the necessary concessions, with a good tenant often driven out of business before the reduction was secured. Then his successor came in at a much reduced rent and with other benefits. These complaints about rent levels were, to some extent, confirmed by the Royal Commission on Agricultural Depression in the mid-1890s.

For most farmers, retrenchment became the order of the day. They reduced their labour forces to a minimum, hired or purchased machinery from the growing number of contractors to help them through the busy haymaking and harvest seasons, or for threshing, and generally farmed 'low', neglecting the hedging, ditching, and weeding which had once been their pride. Clare Sewell Read, an influential spokesman for tenant farmers and a former MP, writing from Norfolk in January 1891, underlined the new attitude:

The days of trim, neat farming are ended. . . . It was a . . . delight, but it never did pay, and is an expensive luxury, in which only rich farmers can now indulge. . . . Fences are much rougher. . . . Farm roads and the homestead are not scraped so often as formerly, the rickyard is terribly untidy, stacks are ragged and ugly, thatching is uneven and shabby, weeds which spring up in the turnips after harvest too late to mature any seed are left to be cut down by the frost, and thistles in the meadows, instead of being constantly mown, are only cut once in the summer. Gates won't open, hurdles are broken, and the old dilapidated implements remain unpainted. And most of the work upon the farm, ploughing, drilling, mowing, hoeing, etc., is not executed with the skill and precision of former days.[45]

A son of Cornelius Stovin recalled the economy measures introduced on his father's holding during the 1880s and 1890s, with all the children of the family called upon to help on the farm before and after school. In this way they were able to keep going and to make a bare living. Yet in earlier, more prosperous days, Stovin had been an enthusiastic supporter of new ideas.

On the positive side, the search for economies encouraged farmers to maintain better accounts, something in which they were sadly deficient. Even a man like Henry Overman, a large tenant farmer on the Holkham estate, had to admit in the early 1880s that he could not calculate how much profit he made on each cow, while Clare Sewell Read declared that farmers found it impossible to ascertain their true financial condition: 'They just keep going from year to year.'[208] Even the Royal Commission on Agricultural Depression concluded that accurate 'detailed accounts' were seldom kept: 'It is noteworthy that most of the farmers who keep good accounts have had, either directly or indirectly, some experience of, or connexion with, mercantile business.' By the end of the Victorian era these weaknesses were being tackled, although on the smaller farms, especially in Wales, the situation still left much to be desire. As late as 1919 it was noted that the farmers in Cardiganshire transacted nearly all their business 'by word of mouth, and it is but rarely that [they make] any engagements of any kind in writing'.[60] In this county, as in other predominantly Welsh-speaking parts of the principality, the language barrier doubtless reinforced their commitment to the old ways, since farming journals were normally printed in English only. It was consequently more difficult for such men to learn of modern procedures.

Marketing, too, began to receive attention. Men like my great-grandfather no longer blindly sent their butter and eggs to market by carrier's cart, to realize the best price they could, as had formerly been their custom. Instead they sought direct outlets with the larger shops, or with the newly established private creameries, dairy processors and manufacturers of condensed milk and baby foods, thereby obtaining a better and more secure rate of return. In the case of my great-grandfather an agreement was reached with Tamworth co-operative society, and not only were eggs and dairy produce sold on improved terms, but purchases of animal feed were obtained at a discount, thanks to the co-operative 'dividend'. In this way he was able to reduce the cost of his inputs.

Elsewhere a minority of farmers in dairying and horticultural districts formed their own marketing co-operatives to dispose of their produce on a communal basis, though these never proved very popular. The same was true of the co-operative cheese and butter factories established in the midlands during the 1870s. English and Welsh farmers were too individualistic. They preferred to deal with the middle-men on a personal basis, even though by so doing they were weakening their own bargaining powers. One exception to this was a scheme for the joint marketing of eggs established in the Framlingham district of Suffolk by a local clergyman. Instead of selling their eggs to travelling 'higglers' or taking them once a week to the nearest grocer, the farmers despatched them every day to a collecting station, and from the many separate depots they passed to a central collecting station at Ipswich. The scheme got under way in the 1880s and within a few years the number of eggs sold was immense, 'and huge vats had to be made where they could be stored in summer when the prices fell below a certain level'.[140]

The majority of men, though, responded to the changed conditions by slowly adjusting their output. Many produced milk and hay for the town markets, with liquid milk sales growing rapidly. Large numbers of farmers in Dorset, north Wiltshire and Berkshire now delivered their milk to the railway stations for onward despatch to London, and the capital's supplies came from as far afield as Leicestershire and Derbyshire. During these years it was common for advertisements of farms for sale or to let to mention the distance of the holding from the nearest railway station, and Richard Jefferies commented on the processions of carts visiting the stations twice a day, with as many as twenty or thirty of them travelling to one station.[197] The industrial centres also acted as outlets for the dairymen, with Leicestershire milk going to Leeds and Newcastle, and at local level, production in the north-east being encouraged by sales in the expanding colliery villages of Northumberland and County Durham. In the valleys of the Chilterns, too, the outflow increased, not merely to London but to a condensed milk factory at Aylesbury and to Huntley and Palmer's biscuit factory at Reading, as well as to growing towns in the area, like Watford. Farmers gained from the fact that the cash return on these liquid milk sales was almost immediate, whereas cheese, for example, had to be stored for several months before it could be sold.

Eggs and poultry provided ready money for other farming families: 'Plenty of young farmers' wives on 200 acres', it was said, made 'over 100 1. a year' from poultry farming, and in this way helped their husbands to survive.[54]

Market gardening provided a third source of income. In Holland, Lincolnshire, men turned to the growing of vegetables and fruit, while mustard, turnips and mangolds were grown from seed, and there was a start to the bulb business. In 1885 there had been only one bulb grower recorded in the whole of Lincolnshire. By 1892 the trade directory was reporting twenty-two, more than half of them living in Spalding.[265] Around Histon in Cambridgeshire it was the Chivers jam factory which provided a major marker for nearby smallholders, who brought their fruit in carts for direct sale to the factory. Similarly, at Wisbech, Rider Haggard commented on the great and profitable increase in fruit and flower growing which had taken place between 1885 and 1900, with strawberries, raspberries, gooseberries, plums, apples, pears, onions, cauliflowers, asparagus, rhubarb, narcissi, pansies, and other flowers all despatched in quantity to the major population centres. In Herefordshire, a county long famous for its fruit, there was a switch to the large-scale production of strawberries, one large farmer claiming that from 6½ acres of the fruit he had made £200 clear profit during 1900.[177]

Unfortunately, not all farmers had the Herefordshire men's easy access to a large urban market. They gained by their proximity to the industrial midlands, which also provided a large temporary labour force to help with picking. In this county much of the fruit was gathered by women and children brought in from the big cities. They were lodged in huts or tents for the season, rather like the hop pickers in Kent. But a major hurdle remained the conservativeness of the farmers. As Rider Haggard remarked caustically: 'How many English farmers can grow a strawberry, or, being ignorant, will take the trouble to learn the craft?'

It was here that the growing numbers of agricultural societies and farmers' clubs which had appeared since the middle of the century could play a part. By the early 1870s there were about 600 of them, and through the shows, journals, reports and implement trials they organized, agriculturists were made aware of the need to improve the quality of their stock, or the standard of their husbandry. Lip-service began to be paid to the need for a more scientific approach to farming, a view which the problems of the depression years intensified. In 1890 the Central Chamber of Agriculture called for 'scientific and practical agricultural education' to be provided so as to enable 'the farmers of the United Kingdom to meet the pressure of the present active competition with the markets of the world. Old methods may have to be abandoned, new methods may have to be introduced'.[209] As early as 1888, the Bath and West and Southern Counties Agricultural Society had begun to tackle the variable quality of English butter and cheese by holding special migratory butter and cheese schools. These efforts were expanded when in 1890, under the Local Taxation Act, county councils had government funds placed at their disposal for the promotion of technical education. Several of them appealed to the Bath and West to conduct dairy schools on their behalf, and within a short time the Society had set up nearly 170 butter-making classes and fifteen for cheese-making, the former operating on a migratory basis, with sessions held in different districts, and the latter remaining fixed in one place for the whole of a cheese-making season, and then moving on the next year.[186] In Wales, the county councils took the lead in providing dairying instruction, while both Aberystwyth and Bangor Colleges taught dairying at their mobile dairy schools. A few farmers benefited from the work of the Rothamsted Experimental Station near Harpenden in Hertfordshire, though it is significant that when a new director took over in 1902 he confessed that his heart sank when he came to take possession of the laboratory. It was like a museum. Progress thus remained slow and piecemeal. In the case of butter and cheese, the greater part consumed in this country continued to be imported up to the time of the First World War.

But, as the secretary to the Bath and West Society, Thomas Plowman, observed in 1885, without the exertions of the various farming clubs and associations, English agriculture would have been still farther behind. Such bodies helped to counterbalance governmental deficiencies in encouraging agricultural improvement, while men who followed their advice were anxious not to be behind their neighbours in the neatness, style and success of their husbandry or in the quality and condition of their livestock.

The benefits of artificial fertilizers were also more widely canvassed in these years, with the fertilizer consumption of the United Kingdom approximately doubling between the late 1880s and the eve of the First World War.[222] Manufacturers, for their part, sought to exploit the anxieties of farmers by their sales campaigns. One advertisement which appeared in the *Mark Lane Express* during May 1890 firmly declared: 'The only way for Farmers to compete successfully with foreign grain growers is by obtaining the largest possible yield for their land. To ensure heavy crops of wheat, barley, grass, roots, potatoes, &c., they should use SULPHATE OF AMMONIA which is now only half the price it was a few years ago.' During this period there was a growth of farmers' purchasing co-operatives to arrange the bulk buying of seeds, fertilizers and feeding stuffs for members. By 1914 two hundred such organizations had been formed, with a membership of about 24,000.

Efforts were likewise made to raise the quality and reliability of livestock. Flock books began for Shropshire sheep in 1883, for Oxfords in 1889, and for Hampshires in 1890, while among cattle the Guernsey Society dated from 1885 and the Welsh Black Cattle Society from 1904. There were many others. Even horse-breeding shared in the new movement, with the first of the heavy horse societies, the Suffolk Stud-Book Association, commencing in 1877 under the sponsorship of the Suffolk Agricultural Association.

Sometimes migrants coming from a distant part of the country, where a different pattern of husbandry prevailed, would be the vehicle of change and adaptation. In East Sussex the milk-producing industry, which was later to become the most important branch of agriculture in the area, was introduced by farmers moving into the county from Cornwall, Dorset and Devon. In Essex there was an influx of agriculturalists from Lancashire, Scotland and the south-west of England. For, in contrast to the position in the eastern counties, demand for land in the livestock districts of England and Scotland continued relatively buoyant, and rents were well maintained. Consequently, ambitious farmers, who were unable to obtain a holding in their home area or who wanted a larger property, seized the opportunity of getting a low-rented farm somewhere else. Accessibility to major urban markets, particularly London, attracted some, while a few were influenced by social considerations. Welsh farmers who moved to Herefordshire praised the greater amenities available as compared to life on lonely upland farms in the principality.[252]

Among the many Scottish migrants was Walter Lyon, who moved from Balquaharrage near Glasgow to take a 376-acre farm on the Luton Hoo estate in Bedfordshire in 1884. Earlier in the year he had asked for a reduction in rent from his Scottish landlord and, when this had been refused, had decided to move.[9] Another farmer who travelled south was Mr Primrose McConnell, who wrote of his experiences in the *Journal of the Royal Agricultural Society* in 1891. By that time the Ongar, Brentwood and Chelmsford areas of Essex had become so attractive to Scotsmen that the district was often dubbed the 'Scotch Colony'. McConnell, and men like him, were attracted by the advertisements of vacant farms which appeared in the press, notably in the *North British Agriculturist*. 'First one or two came, and finding the taste good, sent back a satisfactory report to their friends behind.' They followed in their turn.

These new men cut back on labour requirements, relying instead on their own families, as they had been accustomed to do in Scotland. The wives and daughters superintended the dairy department, while the sons drove the horses and fed the cattle. In Suffolk, it was said that the Scottish women would 'undertake work which no Suffolk woman would dream of doing', such as 'mucking out byres and pig pens which not even the female labourers would stoop to do'.

But one of the greatest changes in the system of farming brought about by these incomers was the development of dairying in the eastern counties. Although the dry climate of eastern England was not ideal for grass growing, and the migrants had to endure some hostility from the native farmers, who referred to them contemptuously as 'cow-keepers', by dint of hard work most of them made a profit. Some, on moving south, 'simply transported the whole of their live and dead stock' with them, 'hiring a special train for the purpose, and starting a fully-equipped herd of cows at the very first'. Many also continued to purchase their stock north of the border, where prices were lower. 'Dealers, or friends left in the North', wrote McConnell, 'can send up a few truck-loads of sheep or cattle on the shortest notice', adding, 'there is no doubt this choice of markets gives a better chance of profit very often.' For the sale of their produce, most relied on the growing milk trade with London.

In the early days the Scottish farmers in Essex were extremely clannish, clinging together for purposes of marriage and friendship, and nurturing their ties with their native land. Commercial travellers even came down from Scotland to sell their wares to the Essex families. They were known as Scottish 'Cuddies' and would stay on a farm, while they visited their compatriots in the neighbourhood in a hired horse and cart. Drapers brought samples of stockings, blankets, woollens, underwear and tweeds. When they had filled their order books they returned home and sent down the requisite goods. Even tea arrived in crates, as well as oatmeal and cheese. A number of Scottish social customs also survived, such as 'shows of presents' prior to a wedding. These were social gatherings, with shortbread and scones served with the afternoon cup of tea.[29] In this way, the Scots remained for a long time a community within a community, looked upon with some suspicion and occasional resentment by the native farmers. Overall, between 1880 and the mid-1890s, approximately 120 to 130 Scotsmen moved into Essex, and the movement continued at a high level until 1914.[54]

Elsewhere, for example in Oxfordshire, farmers migrated from Devon, where 'certain land agents recognizing their aptitude' for introducing and working the new livestock system, continued 'to go . . . for tenants as often as farms have been vacant'.[252] In Hertfordshire, it was Scottish and Cornish agriculturists who came to the attention of Rider Haggard. Both were heavily engaged in dairying and potato growing, though Haggard stressed that to be successful a man must have easy access to the railways. 'Where means of communication are lacking, as a Scotch gentleman said to me, there is "agricultural death."' Although some of the old farmers remained in Hertfordshire, in general 'the whole victory [was] to the Scotch and Cornish'. Hard work and a sensitiveness to the needs of the market were the secret of their success.

Naturally these changes in personnel and in husbandry patterns led to an alteration in cropping arrangements within the counties. Given that in some 'predominantly arable farming localities, the farming population . . . underwent a hundred per cent change in its personnel' during the last two decades of the nineteenth century, this was scarcely surprising.[252] In counties like Essex, Bedfordshire and Suffolk in 1870, 23.1, 20.7 and 19.8 per cent, respectively, of the cultivated area had been devoted to wheat production. By 1890 the comparable figures were 17.4 per cent, 17.3 per cent and 16.2 per cent, while the area under permanent pasture had increased.[57] But, significantly, those counties which in 1870 had produced little wheat (such as Westmorland, Lancashire and the North Riding of Yorkshire), grew even less twenty years later. In the case of the two first-named counties the 1.1 per cent and 5.1 per cent of cultivated acreage so devoted in 1870 had become a mere 0.2 per cent and 2.8 per cent by 1890. Access to profitable markets for the livestock· and livestock products on which they concentrated provided the explanation.

In summary, then, farmers responded to the depression by abandoning cereals where they could and concentrating upon more remunerative lines, especially the sale of liquid milk and fruit and vegetables. They paid more attention to costs and to the maintenance of accurate accounts, and they sought economies where possible. In some areas rent reductions, coupled with the inflow of migrants with new ideas, provided the principal solution to the problem.

It would be a mistake to assume that farmers endured these vagaries of fortune without complaint. Although a majority recognized that the days of agricultural protection had gone, given the anxiety of politicians to please a large urban electorate dependent on cheap food, that did not prevent some from secretly hankering after import restriction. Clare Sewell Read claimed that in Norfolk, even in the mid-1890s, 'nine out of ten . . . farmers wanted Protection', although 'they would never get it'.[162] At around that time another farmer, from Northumberland, proposed that there should be a protective duty on imports of barley. These were not used for food but mainly for making beer and spirits and, in his view, there was no fear of the prices of these drinks being affected by an increase in barley prices resulting from the tax. For, he sourly observed, 'when barley was double the present price, beer was no dearer to buy. . . . My suggestion may be regarded by some as savouring too much of protection, but surely we have not rendered ourselves so hoarse or weak by shouting for free trade that we have no voice left to advocate, or independence of mind to adopt, a change which might be for the good of the country.'[54]

But most men recognized that it was impossible to expect reforms which raised the cost of living for the community at large, merely to help the farming interest. They turned their attention to more easily remedied grievances, such as the lowering of railway freight charges for farm produce, a reduction in game depredations to crops on estates where the landlord was an enthusiastic preserver and, most importantly, the payment of compensation to tenants for improvements previously carried out, should they be required to leave their holding. Other concerns included the more equal distribution of rates between landlord and tenant and the inequities of the tithe system, whereby payments had to be made to tithe owners even when the farmer himself was making no profit. It was to espouse these various causes that a new body, the Farmers' Alliance, came into existence in 1879.

The primary objective of the Alliance was to secure for tenant farmers a *compulsory* payment of compensation for unexhausted improvements (such as the application of fertilizers or drainage works) they had carried out prior to leaving their holding. For most landlords had ensured that their tenants opted out of the permissive 1875 Agricultural Holdings Act, which had been designed to achieve this end. The Alliance was also anxious to obtain greater representation of farmers in Parliament. Significantly, its first chairman was James Howard, an agricultural implements manufacturer and farmer from Bedfordshire, who had been Liberal MP for Bedford from 1868 to 1874.[102] Its secretary and treasurer was William Bear, the editor of the influential farming newspaper the *Mark Lane Express*, which took as its watchword: 'Tenant-Right. Live and Let Live'.

During the 1880 election campaign the Alliance pressed for

reform on the various issues with which it was concerned, and when the Liberals were returned to power in that year, it renewed its demands. Howard, now MP for Bedfordshire, proved a particularly effective spokesman in Parliament. At the same time its local organization was extended, with new branches formed among farmers in the north-east, Cornwall, Hampshire, Lancashire and Berkshire during 1880/81. Other bodies joined in, with especially rapid progress apparent in Kent. Although the Alliance was praised for its publicizing of the 'excessive' charges levied by some railway companies, its main interest remained the securing of effective legislation on the tenant rights issue. This was finally achieved in 1883, when a new Act made the payment of compensation compulsory, and limited to one year the time during which a landlord could distrain upon his tenant's property for rent arrears. The previous maximum had been six years. But a major weakness in the legislation from the tenant's point of view was that the landlord could counter-claim for alleged infringements of cropping provisions, etc., by the occupier. According to the *Mark Lane Express*, the strictness with which valuers interpreted these 'infringements' soon deterred farmers from making use of the Act, since the landlord's counter-claim could amount to more than the compensation to which the occupier was entitled. In May 1892 it quoted a case in Cumberland, where the tenant had claimed £260 for compensation for improvements. The landlord had counter-claimed for £235 for dilapidation and mismanagement. 'Result: the tenant receives £34 and the landlord £144, each party to pay their own costs'.

The *Express* cannot be considered an impartial witness, but its complaints were largely upheld by the Royal Commission on Agricultural Depression. Of the Garstang area of Lancashire, the Assistant Commissioner observed:

It is a common expression to hear used that 'if tenants claim for unexhausted improvements the landlords counterclaim for dilapidations' and, though no one suggests that the landlords have not a just right to do so, still the tenants say they think it cheaper to avoid a contest. . . . In the Garstang and Fylde Unions, where yearly tenancies without any agreements in writing are so prevalent, landlords and tenants seem to leave the Act entirely alone.[54]

Other witnesses described the measure as a 'lamentable failure', or as 'too expensive and cumbrous in its working'. By this time the Farmers' Alliance itself had largely faded away, having split over the issue of protectionism. But the battle for reform continued. In Lancashire it was spearheaded by two pressure groups established in 1892 – the Lancashire Federation of Farmers' Associations, claiming a membership of 600, and the more radical Lancashire Tenant Farmers' Association. This later became part of the National Federation of Tenant Farmers' Clubs, based on Lancashire, Cheshire, North Wales and Cumberland. Whilst the Lancashire Federation concentrated on securing a reform of the Agricultural Holdings legislation, its National rival demanded much wider changes, including absolute fixity of tenure, to be backed up by a Land Court, fair rents, and a free sale of improvements carried out by the tenant.[112] Needless to say, this proposal for the securing of rights guaranteed by law was greeted with hostility by landowners. They saw it as fostering class organization by unifying farmers across estate boundaries and as undermining the organic system of society which they sought to promote, in which all groups were bound together by mutual obligations. Despite an attempt by the National Federation's president, a Lancashire corn miller and merchant who was also a Liberal MP, to present a Land Tenure (England) Bill in 1892 incorporating the demands of the more radical tenant farmers, nothing was achieved.[295]

Not until the Agricultural Holdings Act of 1906 was there an ending of prescribed courses of cropping by landlords or of prohibitions on the sale of specified crops. After that date a tenant could farm as he chose, provided that the fertility of the soil was maintained. The only exception was that landlords had the right to prescribe the rotations in which a farm was to be left in the last year of the tenancy. The Act also allowed compensation not merely for the tenant's investment in the land but for excessive damage caused to crops by game which the tenant was not permitted to kill. In practice, few occupiers were bold enough to take advantage of these latter powers, especially where their landlord was a keen preserver. But by the early twentieth century the tenant right issue at least had been largely settled and the State had so far altered the balance of economic advantage between landowners and tenants that occupiers could farm in any way they pleased; and they could claim compensation at the end of their tenancy for the unexhausted value of any improvement made, and for the costs of disturbance. Landowners still had the right to choose their tenants, to agree with them the rent properly payable and . . . to terminate any tenancy on a year's notice or at the end of a dated lease, subject only to the payment of such costs.[222]

Another grievance, that of rates, was also tackled in these years through the 1896 Agricultural Rates Act, which halved rates on farm land, thereby easing the local tax burden of agriculturists.

Finally, there was the question of tithes. The giving of a tenth of one's income towards the maintenance of the Church was an ancient custom founded upon biblical texts. But over the years the system had been much amended, notably by the 1836 Tithe Commutation Act. This had established that the amount of tithe rent-charge payable was to be based upon the average of corn prices over the preceding seven years. It also placed responsibility for the payment of the impost upon the landlord, though in practice, under most tenancy agreements, the occupier continued to pay. In this way he acted as the landlord's agent. But to most farmers the whole thing appeared an unfair levy upon their income for which they received no benefit. Their resentment grew during the depression years, as cash became tighter and as tithe-owners refused to grant remissions or rebates in the way that landlords were prepared to do for rent. Typical of most was the attitude taken by the Dean and Chapter of Christ Church, Oxford, who firmly informed some reluctant tithe payers from Benson in Oxfordshire:

> Tithe Rent-Charge is . . . a first charge on the produce of the land and takes precedence of any claim for rent. The right to such Tithe Rent-Charge cannot . . . be affected by any arrangement made between Owners & Occupiers of land for the payment of tithes by the latter who are in this respect merely agents of the owners for the discharge of their obligations. . . . The Governing Body of Christ Church have always been ready to consider individual cases of real distress, but they are unable

to acknowledge themselves under obligation to make a general reduction in the payments due to them on account of Tithe Rent-Charge.[4]

The college treasurer, for his part, confidently asserted that 'the recovery of Tithes is always possible by extreme measures'.

But despite this dissatisfaction in England, it was in Wales that hostility to the tithe system reached a peak, partly because the poverty of many small farmers in the principality made any additional financial burden hard to bear, and partly because Nonconformist tenants resented having to pay to support an alien Church. Instead they demanded that if tithes were to be levied they should be applied to some lay purpose for the benefit of the whole nation. The serious unrest which developed is examined in detail in Chapter 6, where the relationship between Church and Chapel is analysed. Suffice it here to point out that after several abortive attempts at legislation, the 1891 Tithe Rent-Charge Act at last placed responsibility for the payment of tithes unequivocally upon the landlord. With the implementation of this measure the unrest died away, aided by the fact that after 1900 farming conditions began to improve as the price of agricultural produce increased.

But whatever the situation after 1900, for most farmers the final quarter of the nineteenth century proved a time of great uncertainty, as they struggled to adjust output and methods to meet the challenge of the new conditions.

4

Agricultural Labourers and their Families

Landowners and farmers provided the capital and the managerial abilities necessary for the running of British farming, but it was the skill of the agricultural labourers which ensured that the wheels of that industry were kept turning smoothly. This remained true despite the effects of mechanization in the final quarter of the nineteenth century. Equally, it was they and their families who dominated, in numerical terms, the Victorian village community. Only in areas like Cumbria and parts of Wales, where small farmers abounded, or in sheep-rearing districts like the Glendale area of Northumberland, was this not the case. There the Cheviot hill farms might cover many thousands of acres, and the only inhabitants were shepherds, who worked on a semi-independent basis, keeping some sheep of their own alongside those of their employer. These were later sold for profit, and in that way they became almost small farmers in their own right.[80]

But if the labourers' role in the nation's agriculture was of major importance, they shared to only a limited degree in the prosperity of that industry in the later 1860s and early 1870s. While landowners benefited from rising rentals and farmers gained from increases in food prices, particularly during the boom years from 1870 to 1873, the prospect for their workers was far bleaker. Admittedly, as we saw in Chapter 1, there were considerable regional differences, with men in the north and midlands able to secure higher wages and better conditions than their counterparts in the rural south-west and East Anglia, where there was little alternative employment. Often, too, such alternatives as did exist were associated with the land and were relatively poorly paid. Thus, around Langport in Somerset during the early 1890s, the winter jobs available included cutting osiers in the withy beds, or working in the woodlands, cutting timber. And in the Bromyard district of Herefordshire, it was felling and sharpening hop poles and bark stripping which helped to eke out the winter work.[80] In both of these areas, it was also common for some labourers to seek piecework contracts in neighbouring counties, especially during haymaking and harvest, while others moved between local quarries and agriculture.

Unfortunately, even with these various job opportunities, earnings remained low. Between 1867 and 1873 the average agricultural wage rate, adjusted for differences in retail prices, was only about 52 per cent of the average industrial rate; without these adjustments, it was a mere 47 per cent of the industrial rate.[215] Even at the end of the century, despite some improvements, the average agricultural wage rate, adjusted to take account of prices, was over the period 1884–96 only 55 per cent of its industrial counterpart. Stockmen fared slightly better, usually securing a shilling or two a week above the general labourer's basic rate in recognition of their specialist skills and of the fact that they had to work on Sundays. They also often received a rent-free cottage. Piecework earnings supplemented the income of other workers, though as Table 3 indicates, by no means all men shared equally in these, and the loss of time through illness or bad weather could easily cancel out any benefits thus gained.

Table 3   Wages and Piecework Earnings on the Harcourt Estate at Nuneham Courtenay, Oxon., in 1872[13]

Name	Position	Basic Wage Rate*	Annual Earnings	Piecework	Average weekly earnings
W. Attewell	Carter	13s. & 14s.	£43 18s. 3½d.	£8 10s. 2½d.	16s. 10½d.
W. Brockland	Cowman**	13s. & 14s.	£42 6s.7¾d.	£4 14s. 11¾d.	16s. 3½d.
T. Brockland	Under Shepherd	12s. & 13s.	£37 3s. 5d.	£2 13s. 11d.	14s. 3½d.
R. Palmer	Labourer**	11s. & 12s.	£37 11s. 5¾d.***	£9 6s. 5¾d.	14s. 5d.
G. Phipps	Labourer	11s. & 12s.	£39 6s. 10d.***	£9 13s. 5d.	15s. 1½d.
G. Kent	Labourer	11s. & 12s.	£39 17s. 10d.***	£11 17s. 6d.	15s 4d.
T. Baker	Labourer	11s. & 12s.	£35 10s. 5¼d.	£4 8s. 6¼d.	13s 7¼d.

* The basic wage rate was increased to the higher figure in April 1872.
** These workers also obtained a rent-free house and garden and free wood.
*** These workers secured 8d. per day for beer during the harvest season.

Piecework earnings clearly influenced average wages very considerably. The under shepherd, whose basic rate was above that of the general day men, in fact earned less in the year than some of them because of reduced piecework opportunities.

Nor was this all. Working hours in agriculture were longer than in most urban industries, the usual arrangement being from daybreak to nightfall during the winter months and from around 6 a.m. to 6 p.m. in the summer. For stockmen, who had to come early to feed their animals and return in the evening to settle them down for the night, the working day could be still longer. Furthermore, during haytime and harvest, it was the custom for men to spend many extra hours in the fields, labouring amidst dust and dirt under a hot summer sun. As compensation they received higher wages, and a number of them entered into special piece-work contracts to 'take' the harvest. These detailed not only the crops to be carried. but the methods to be used in harvesting and, frequently, the allowances applicable in the form of beer and food to the workers. Significantly, even in 1871 three-quarters of the corn was still cut by hand. A typical harvest contract at Blaxhall in Suffolk also noted: 'Should any man lose time through sickness he is to throw back 2s. per day to the Company [of workers] and receive account at harvest. Should any man lose any time through drunkenness he is to forfeit 5s. to the Company.'[158]

Women and children, too, played a part in gathering the grain, with the former helping to bind the corn into sheaves and the latter assisting them, or leading the horses, or carrying food and drink to the harvesters. In *Tess of the D'Urbervilles,* Thomas Hardy described the scene at sunrise in one Dorset village as the reaping-machine started work:

Presently there arose from within a ticking like the lovemaking of a grasshopper. The machine had begun, and a moving concatenation of three horses and the . . . long rickety machine was visible over the gate, a driver sitting upon one of the hauling horses, and an attendant on the seat of the implement. Along one side of the field the whole wain went, the arms of the mechanical reaper revolving slowly. . . .

The reaping-machine left the fallen corn behind it in little heaps, each heap being of the quantity of a sheaf; and upon these the active binders in the rear laid their hands – mainly women, but some of them men. . . . The women – or rather girls, for they were mostly young – wore drawn cotton bonnets with great flapping curtains to keep off the sun, and gloves to prevent their hands being wounded by the stubble. There was one wearing a pale pink jacket, another in a cream-coloured tight-sleeved gown, another in a petticoat as red as the arms of the reaping-machine; and others, older, in the brown-rough 'wropper' or over-all – the old-established and most appropriate dress of the field-woman, which the young ones were abandoning. . . . This morning the eye returns involuntarily to the girl in the pink cotton jacket. . . . Her binding proceeds with clock-like monotony. . . . A bit of her naked arm is visible between the buff leather of the gauntlet and the sleeve of her gown; and as the day wears on its feminine smoothness becomes scarified by the stubble, and bleeds.

The disadvantages experienced by agricultural workers in the matter of wages and employment conditions, compared to the situation of their urban counterparts, were also reinforced by housing problems. Although rural areas escaped the worst health hazards of the town slums many country cottages were poorly maintained and insanitary, despite the passage of public health and housing legislation in 1875 and 1890, which had been designed to correct such abuses. The high fertility rates of the labourers contributed to the difficulty, for the large size of their families aggravated the difficulties of overcrowding.[92] Illegitimacy levels, too, were highest in the rural counties. In 1869 the Annual Report of the Registrar-General of Births, Deaths and Marriages estimated that around one in ten babies born in Cumberland, Norfolk, Shropshire and Westmorland was illegitimate. It is true that birth and illegitimacy rates did fall a little in the last years of the century, but they remained well above the average for the nation as a whole, and country households continued to contain large numbers of children. Even over the years 1888–97, 7.4 in every one hundred births in Shropshire were illegitimate; in Cumberland and Herefordshire the figure was 7.2, and in Norfolk 6.7, at a time when the national average was only 4.3. The prevalence of residential farm service, which precluded early marriage, was probably a factor in the high levels recorded in the first three counties listed, together with ignorance of contraceptive methods, and perhaps a tacit acceptance by the community at large that such 'slips' did occur from time to time, regrettable though this might be, and need not be regarded as disasters.

Another difficulty was the 'tied' cottage system, whereby workers who lost their job inevitably lost their home as well. As one Yorkshire labourer put it: 'There is a feeling about tied-houses that it is not your home. You do not seem able to plant fruit trees, nor work any little paying hobby, because you know if the least little screw goes wrong, out you go at a month's notice or less.'[204] As late as 1913 the Liberal Party's Land Enquiry Committee discovered that in 23 per cent of the parishes they investigated, the ordinary labourer received a free cottage as part of his earnings, while for stockmen, the figure rose to 36 per cent.

Inadequate and polluted water supplies added to the catalogue of grievances in many villages. At Goosey in Berkshire, even in the early 1890s, the people depended upon a dirty stream for their water, whilst the farmers brought in supplies in milk churns from springs some distance away. Of nearby Denchworth and Grove it was grimly stated that strangers were 'apt to be poisoned by the water', though the local inhabitants had apparently grown immune to it.[80] The heavy toil involved in fetching and carrying water over considerable distances is also easy to envisage. And so the labourer who sweated in the heat of the harvest field, or endured the dust of threshing operations and the mud of winter ploughing, often existed without that first essential of civilized life, a plentiful water supply. Only in estate villages was the position likely to be more satisfactory. But, as we saw in Chapter 1, accommodation in such places tended to be strictly limited – sometimes not even sufficient to house those who worked there.

It was in these circumstances, too, that the public gang system evolved in the sparsely inhabited districts of the eastern counties, with groups of men, women and children recruited from more heavily populated 'open' parishes in the area. Although the passage of the Agricultural Gangs Act of 1867 removed some of the worst elements of the system, gangs continued to operate in East Anglia until the end of the nineteenth century. In the Swaffham area of Norfolk during the early 1890s widows, young girls and boys were particularly prominent in them, driven on by poverty and the need to find work of some kind. Around North Witchford, Cambridgeshire, the system was also common, with gangs starting work in March or April of each year and continuing until December. The girls here had evolved their own practical style of dress, consisting of a short skirt, usually made of cotton and designed to keep out of the mud, a rough woollen apron, heavy boots, and a large cotton bonnet on their head, 'with a curtain for neck and front'.[80]

In Northumberland, women workers likewise remained relatively numerous, with annually hired male labourers still required to provide females as part of their contract of employment. In the Glendale district during the early 1890s it was, indeed, reported that as many women were employed as men, and in the county was a whole in 1911 more than one in five of all agricultural labourers were female. The following agreement signed between Thomas Loftus, labourer, and Mr Foster, a farmer of Budle, near Glendale, gives an idea of the arrangements in operation at the end of the century;[80]

> We agree to serve on Lowick farm for one year, commencing on May 12, 1892, for the following wages:- Thomas and Martin 17s. per week each, and 1,000 yards of potatoes each. Four sisters, Margaret, Mary, Bridget, and Catherine to have 1s. 6d. per day, and 3s. per day for 20 days in harvest. Julia, wage according to work done.
>
> (Signed) Thomas Loftus.

The family was provided, in addition, with a rent-free house, and their coals were carted free of charge.

In view of the difficulties and uncertainties of their daily life, it is not surprising that the discontent of country people grew during these years. Many decided to move away to take advantage of expanding employment opportunities in mining, manufacturing industry and transport or, for the girls, in domestic service. Recruitment to the police also proved attractive to a minority, while others, like the future trade union leader Ernest Bevin, were able to turn farming skills to account by taking a job working with town horses. Others again moved to farm jobs on the higher-paid fringes of the industrial belt as a first step. In the Vale of Glamorgan, it was claimed in the early 1890s that locally born farm workers were almost unknown. Instead their places had been taken by men from Wiltshire, Somerset, Herefordshire, Devon and the Cirencester district of Gloucestershire: 'But even the new comers do not, as a rule, remain very long on the land, for higher wages and shorter hours almost invariably succeed in attracting them to the mineral districts, so that other labourers have to be continually drafted from the same English counties to replace them.'[80] For the most adventurous, emigration to the colonies or the United States of America was another possibility.

During the 1860s the number of male agricultural labourers, farm servants and shepherds in England and Wales had fallen by 16 per cent. This decline continued thereafter to the end of the century, speeding up in the late 1890s under the influence of the Boer War, as men entered the armed services or other war work. Among the female farm servants and labourers the drop was even more dramatic, by 35.8 per cent in the 1860s and by approximately comparable percentages in the succeeding decades. For as the men became slightly better off, they grew anxious to prevent their wives and daughters from going to the fields, save for casual employment during the busy summer season. Land work was considered degrading for females, while the lower wages they received helped to undermine the bargaining strength of the menfolk. Often the girls, too, had little relish for farm work. They preferred the relative gentility of domestic service. Not until the early years of the twentieth century was this downward trend to be temporarily halted (see Table 4).

Improvements in education also affected the attitude of younger people, and reinforced their determination to seek a better life elsewhere. Contemporaries commented disapprovingly on the way youngsters were beginning to read and to think for themselves. As

Table 4 (a) Total of Agricultural Labourers, Farm Servants and Shepherds recorded in the Census Reports

	1861	1871	1881	1891	1901	1911
Male Workers						
Agricultural labourers	914,301	764,574	807,608	734,984	583,751	622,279
Farm servants	158,401	134,157				
Shepherds	25,559	23,323	22,844	21,573	25,354	20,838
Female Workers						
Agricultural labourers	43,964	33,513	40,346	24,150	11,951	13,214
Farm servants	46,561	24,599				

N.B. the totals of agricultural labourers and farm servants were not recorded separately after 1871. These figures include only *permanently* employed workers.

(b) Percentage Changes in the Numbers of Agricultural Labourers, Farm Servants and Shepherds

− = *decrease*
+ = *increase*

	Period	Percentage Change
Male Workers	1861–71	− 16·0
	1871–81	− 9·9
	1881–91	− 8·9
	1891–1901	− 19·5
	1901–11	+ 5·5
Female Workers	1861–71	− 35·8
	1871–81	− 30·5
	1881–91	− 40·1
	1891–1901	− 50·5
	1901–11	+ 10·6

Calculated from the *Census Reports*: for 1861, P.P.1863, Vol. LIII, Pt. 1; for 1871, P.P. 1873, Vol. LXXI, Pt. 1; for 1881, P.P.1883, Vol. LXXX; for 1891, P.P.1893–94, Vol. CVI; for 1901, P.P.1903, Vol. LXXXIV. For 1911, *General Report of the Board of Agriculture and Fisheries: Wages and Conditions of Employment of Agricultural Labourers*, P.P.1919, Vol. IX, P.36.

---

one critic sourly observed: 'You will see teammen sitting on their corn bins reading their penny newspapers, when at the same time they should have been grooming and feeding their master's horses.'[255] Cheap railway excursions and, during the 1890s, ownership of bicycles similarly helped to widen their knowledge of the outside world and to encourage their dissatisfaction with their lowly status in village society. Migration seemed the obvious answer to their problems.

For farm servants, a further factor in these declining numbers was the growing reluctance of farmers and their wives to accommodate workers in their own households because of the catering and supervisory problems involved. Equally, among the men themselves there was an increasing dislike of the controls and limitations which living in an employer's house normally entailed. Few indeed would have relished the conditions imposed on resident workers by the Reffell brothers on their one-thousand-acre holding on the Buckinghamshire/Middlesex border in the 1890s. Under their contract one farm servant, William Burtchell, had to give the blanket undertaking to hire myself to Alfred William and Joseph Reffell for one year as carter at 7s. per week for the first half, 8s. per week for the second half-year, and £3 at Michaelmas, October 11, 1890, to make myself generally useful at all kinds of work, and to do anything I am asked at any time. In case of any illness or accident I agree to support myself; to be in the stable at 4 o'clock every morning in order to get my horses ready for work at 6 o'clock; to rack up my horses every night at 8 o'clock; to find my own whip, masters to keep it in repair; to get up in the morning when called by the carter; to be in every night by 9 o'clock, except when required to be later by my masters; to clean boots and shoes on Sunday morning.[9]

Out of his 7s. a week Burtchell had to feed himself, and for warmth to rely upon visiting a public house, since no fire was permitted in the loft where he slept. After about two months Burtchell left the job, only to be charged by his employers with a breach of his contract of employment. When the case came before the Slough bench, however, the magistrates condemned the agreement in no uncertain manner, and although they agreed that Burtchell had technically broken the conditions of his contract, they fined him only 6d. At the same time they rescinded the contract and remitted the costs.

Needless to say, most contracts for farm service by the 1870s and 1880s were more advantageous to the worker than this. For as the men congregated at the annual hiring fairs, which were still held in the north of England and Wales, where the system of residential service was most widespread, they exchanged notes on previous employers. All of them sought what was called in Yorkshire a 'good meat house', and for that a lot depended on the generosity of the farmer's wife.

It was on the smaller, livestock enterprises and in sparsely populated districts that farm servants were most numerous, and the close proximity to their employer in which they lived and worked often led to warm ties being forged between master and men. In Wales, this good feeling was reinforced by the fact that many of the servants were themselves the sons of small farmers, who would hope later to be able to set up on their own account. Frequently, too, as with the shepherds and hinds of Northumbria, they were allowed to run a few animals with their employer's stock. At the end of a year, these would be sold and gradually a little capital would be amassed.[60] In some parts of the principality it was also the custom for male servants who had remained with an employer for seven years to receive a heifer as a gift at the end of that time, while maids with a similar record of service would receive a pair of blankets. In this fashion, despite the poverty of farming families, links were created between master and men which differed considerably from the harsher, more authoritarian relationships favoured on many English farms.

In Wales, too, men who failed to get hired at one of the annual fairs or by means of personal contacts would migrate 'in North Wales to the quarries, or in South Wales to the "works"'. In Glamorgan, it was not unusual for a labourer to leave his employment on the land 'and go to the "works" for a period, and then return to work on the same farm'.[80]

Of course, rural migration was not solely attributable to the changing attitudes of *workers*. As the agricultural depression deepened in the 1880s and early 1890s, farmers sought to economize in their use of labour by neglecting tasks like hedging, ditching and weeding which were not absolutely essential for the cultivation of the holding. In other cases changes in husbandry methods, with the phasing out of arable farming in favour of pastoral, or alterations in the tenancy of farmsteads, could have a similar effect. There were numerous claims that Scottish farmers in East Anglia preferred to rely only on the help of family members, as we saw in the last chapter. In many instances, too, the greater use of machinery limited the demand for casual workers at harvest time. Already by the mid-1860s the new reaping machines could save the labour of ten to thirty human mowers, using instead two men with two or three horses, plus a complement of pitchers, stookers and other helpers. Twenty years later the self-binders were even more effective: 'the grain-growing farmers could cut, bind, stook and cart their corn crops with probably no addition to their regular staff but the boys on holiday from school, and only a slight addition to the strain on their horses'.[222] By the late 1880s there was a noticeable reduction in the number of migrant Irish harvesters employed on English farms, though some farmers still reserved their most difficult stands of wheat for the Irish to cut by hand. After 1870 it was often only Irish workers who could be relied upon to carry out a cheap and efficient job using hand tools, and they continued to be employed in the East Anglian fens, when the corn was too laid and twisted for a machine to be used, up to the time of the First World War. In the north of England they were also welcomed to compensate for the fall in the local rural population, which was a particular problem at hay and corn harvest time.

At the same time agriculturists complained that younger English workers were unable to carry out the skilled jobs of thatching and hedgecutting in the way earlier generations had done. This led to exaggerated and largely untrue statements about the composition of the labour force. Even in the late 1860s one critic claimed that 'farm work [was] now practically left to boys and old men', while another declared that because younger men were being attracted to the towns, 'only the old or the ignorant' were left behind.[103] Thirty years later Rider Haggard, on his tour of rural England, heard much the same story. 'Young men', declared one Wiltshire farmer, 'are now seldom to be seen upon the land, while hedgers, ditchers, and thatchers are all over fifty years of age. The race is dying out.'[176] Yet the age structure of the agricultural work force, as revealed by the census reports, contradicts these assertions – certainly as regards the age of workers. The quality and skill of the men cannot be so easily assessed. The censuses show that within the overall decline in the size of the labour force it was among the *older* men, those aged 65 and above, that the greatest fall occurred between 1871 and 1891. By contrast, the proportion of those under twenty increased, and of those between twenty and sixty-five remained fairly static. Seemingly farmers responded to the harsher economic climate by divesting themselves of those they deemed too old to pull their weight. They turned instead to younger and cheaper workers to help fill the gap, though these were inevitably also inexperienced and unskilled. Only around 1900, partly under the pressures of the Boer War, did the position temporarily change and the percentage of older men increase. Even among shepherds, where experience and skill were at a premium, the proportion of workers aged 65 and above fell from 9.2 per cent of the labour froce in 1871 to 8.2 per cent in 1891, and then rose a little to 8.5 per cent in 1901 (see also Table 5). Admittedly, agriculture had a higher proportion of older workers than any other industry at the end of the nineteenth century, but it must be emphasized that this was no *new* phenomenon.

Table 5   Percentage of Agriculture Labourers, Farm Servants and Shepherds in Different Age Groups

	1871	1881	1891	1901
Under 20	26.8	27.0	27.9	24.8
20 to 54	54.0	n.a.*	53.8	56.1
55 and above	19.2	n.a.*	18.3	19.1
(65 and above)	(9.1)	(8.6)	(8.0)	(8.6)

N.B. For most of the period the percentage of the labour force aged 20 to 64 inclusive remained fairly constant, at 64.1 in 1871; 64.4 in 1881; 64.1 in 1891; and 66.6 in 1901. The 1871 census figures included retired agricultural workers as well, where they gave their former occupation to the census enumerator.
* At the 1881 census the percentage aged 20 to 64 was 64.4 per cent. Changes in the arrangement of the census report prevents calculations for the age group 20 to 54.
Calculated from the *Census Reports*

At the same time, the proportion of older people living in most rural counties increased. Even in 1881, as Charles Booth pointed out, there were 43 people in every 1,000 who were aged over 65 in rural districts, compared to only 28 per 1,000 in that age group in the urban areas.[92] During the succeeding years, that trend continued. Inevitably, in the face of reduced employment opportunities for old people, this raised the likelihood of more of them having to depend on the Poor Law for support in their declining years. On 1 January 1899 the five most pauperized counties in the country were Dorset, Hereford, Norfolk, Wiltshire and Devon, respectively. All were predominantly rural. And in the first three, more than four persons out of every hundred were paupers.[81]

Other, less significant, factors contributing to the rural outflow included resentment at the existing power structure of village society, and dislike of the administration of the poor relief system and the game laws. As regards the first point it was often the petty restrictions that rankled, like the prohibition exercised by some farmers on their men keeping a pig or chickens, in case they were tempted to steal grain and meal to feed to them.

Equally, throughout the period, detestation of the Poor Law and the workhouse remained overwhelming in country districts. As George Dew, a relieving officer in the Bicester Poor Law union, Oxfordshire, recorded in his diary during December 1870, the very name 'workhouse' was to many villagers 'as the depths of fathomless degradation'.[7] A year later he noted how an elderly woman who was offered the 'house' as the only means of relief refused it, even though she was destitute, because she, like 'every poor person in the land', hated its name.

In practice only about 5 per cent of all old people in rural areas ever received their relief in the form of indoor assistance, and among younger people the proportion was lower still, being confined principally to vagrants, the sick, or women (and their children) whose husband had died or deserted them. But it was indoor aid which most of them fiercely struggled to avoid. This remained the case even in the 1890s, when a more enlightened approach applied, with guardians allowed to provide newspapers and books for the aged (from 1891), and to issue tobacco or snuff to all non-able-bodied paupers (from 1892). Prior to this latter concession being granted, some of the more desperate old people had apparently been smoking hawthorn leaves! Three years later the Local Government Board, as the national supervisory agency, recommended that older inmates should be allowed to wear individual clothing instead of pauper uniforms. It was a policy adopted reluctantly by some Poor Law unions, a guardian at Braintree in Essex observing sourly that he did not think men over the age of sixty who were able to work should be 'dressed up in fine clothes; they made a convenience of the Workhouse in the winter and went out in the spring'.[143]

In Wales, hostility to the workhouse as an alien English institution was early established. Even in 1873, a number of Poor Law unions in the principality were without this first essential of the 'deterrent' relief system. And where they did exist, they were often little used. Thus, in England as a whole, the ratio of outdoor to indoor paupers in 1872–73 was five to one, but in Aberayron and Newcastle Emlyn unions in west Wales the respective figures were eighty to one and seventy to one.[81] Small wonder that one of the Poor Law Inspectors in Wales wrote gloomily to his masters in Whitehall of the 'practice of giving too freely small weekly doles . . . in some of the Welsh and other agricultural Unions', though he added realistically that 'the objection to the workhouse in country districts is very great'. Despite pressure from London, as late as 1 January 1899 South Wales had, on average, only 3.9 indoor paupers per 1,000 of the population, as compared to 25.9 per 1,000 in receipt of out relief; in North Wales, the respective figures were 4 per 1,000 and 33.4 per 1,000. Wales still had a lower indoor pauper rate than any English county. By contrast, in those parts of England where, at that date, a sterner attitude prevailed, indoor rates might reach 8.2 per 1,000 of the population, as they did in Berkshire and Gloucestershire, or eight per 1,000, as they did in Shropshire and Sussex.[81]

Fear of the workhouse was especially strong among the aged, who dreaded ending their lives within its unsympathetic walls. For this reason they struggled on as long as they could on out relief, supplementing the paltry payments of one or two shillings per week and a loaf, which was the weekly allowance in many rural areas, by charity or the help of children, who might perhaps provide vegetables from the garden, or an occasional meal. Unfortunately, strains were often placed on family relationships by the requirement of the Poor Law authorities that children should also pay towards the support of aged parents in receipt of relief, even when their own earnings were low. Those who failed to do so could be brought before the courts, with an effect on family ties only too easy to imagine. As Thomas Pitkin, a labourer from Swanbourne in Buckinghamshire, declared in evidence to the Royal Commission on the Aged Poor in 1894, there would not be 'so much objection' if the sum contributed were added to the old person's weekly allowance. Instead it was deducted from the parent's relief, so that the recipient was no better off: 'That is what they grieve about'.[53] In his district, the basic weekly payment to old people on out relief was 3s., with 6d. extra to 'help buy them a bit of firing' during the winter.

The following entries, taken from the Minute Book of the Winslow Board of Guardians in Buckinghamshire in 1897, underline the essentially cheeseparing nature of the relief system:

12 March: Mr W. Hedges moved and Mr O. S. King seconded that the cost of the coffin for Emma Perridge who died at Winslow and the Burial fees be recovered from the person who received her Insurance money.

9 April: Mr J. Mead proposed and Mr G. Clarke seconded that a 1/- per week for 19 weeks be stopped from the relief of Rachel Tofield of Stewkley to repay the cost of the Coffin and Burial Fees of her late husband.

7 May: The Clerk was . . . directed to communicate with Mr D.

T. Willis of Leighton Buzzard in whose hands are the affairs of a deceased person through whom Sarah Webb of Stewkley benefits, giving him notice of the Guardians' claim in respect of her maintenance.

Apparently no stone was left unturned to ensure that the ratepayers were protected against all needless expenditure. Even pauper burials were not exempt from this approach.

In 1891, it was estimated that around 30 per cent of all country men and women over the age of sixty-five received some form of poor relief.[187] In these circumstances it is not surprising that the granting of old age pensions in 1908 by the Liberal government should cause so much rejoicing. For receipt of a pension did not carry with it the stigma (including disfranchisement) which poor relief brought. The pensions were tiny, the full sum of 5s. per week being payable only to those who were aged seventy or more, were of good character, and whose income from other sources (such as a pension from a previous employer) did not exceed 8s. per week. But these restrictions did not worry most retired labourers and their wives, for few of them had any additional income at all. So it was that when the old people of Swaffham, one of the most pauperized areas of the country, went to collect their first payments on 1 January 1909, the local newspaper described the 'predominating note' as 'one of nervous anxiety . . . there being, perhaps, a lurking fear that, after all, there might be some mistake; but after the coveted amount had been safely handed over the old people left with smiles and with an absolute disappearance of doubt'.[46] More dramatically, at White Horse Hill, near Westbury in Wiltshire, a huge bonfire was lit on 'pension' day in celebration, while at Rippingale in South Lincolnshire one of the new pensioners, a retired baker, dressed up in his Sunday best and 'with tears of joy' went to the post office to draw his first five shillings.

Desire to escape the indignities of the rural Poor Law was, then, one factor contributing to the migration from country districts in the later Victorian years. Resentment at the game law system was another. Many country people would doubtless have agreed with George Dew when in December 1871 he wrote bitterly in his diary:

All *wild game* in my opinion belongs as much to one person as another. . . . It is the common stock of the land, & is not under any ordinary circumstances confined to one person's Estate. . . .

The aristocracy have taken all they can & are still striving to get more. They pursue every poacher with almost bloodthirsty vengeance, they reserve every particle of game for themselves & their cliques, & they never stay to enquire of the hundreds of thousands of acres of common lands which they have wrongfully taken away from the poor. . . . The Aristocracy hold game almost as tightly as gold, & every infringement of the game laws is proceeded against with the utmost vigour.[7]

Particularly disliked was the 1862 Poaching Prevention Act, which authorized the police to search any person on the road or in a public place whom they suspected of poaching or of having in their possession a gun, nets, or snares for the purpose of killing or taking game. Magistrates could order that a convicted poacher's nets, snares and gun be confiscated, but what most villagers objected to was the greater right of search which the Act gave to the police. As the agricultural trade union leader Joseph Arch declared angrily: 'Before this Act passed a working man might trudge home at night in peace, carrying his little basket or his bundle of perquisites; but after it became law the insulting hand of the policeman was hard and heavy upon him.'

The way the Act was interpreted is indicated by an entry in the diary of a police constable from West Sussex. In April 1876 he was travelling by train in pursuit of another case when he observed 'J.J. a noted poacher' joining the train. When 'J.J.' alighted a little farther along, the policeman followed him and, as he left the station premises, stopped him and demanded to see 'the contents of a basket he was carrying. This I found contained 156 pheasant eggs and not giving a satisfactory explanation how he obtained them I took possession of the eggs and returned by next train to Horsham and handed the basket and contents to Supt. Henderson'. Two days later he attended the petty sessions and gave evidence against 'J.J.', who was subsequently fined 5s. for each egg – a total of £39 – plus costs. In default, he was to serve three months' imprisonment with hard labour. Although there is little doubt that the man was guilty, the mode of his arrest was such as to cause concern to many law-abiding citizens.[11]

Night poaching was still more severely punished with those found guilty required to serve three months' imprisonment with hard labour and 'at the expiration to find two sureties in £5 with themselves each in £10 that they will not so offend again for a year and in default of finding such sureties to be further imprisoned' for six calendar months. Yet, despite the penalties, for the most determined the risk seems to have been worth taking, for around 5 per cent of all game offences, even in the 1890s, fell into the 'night poaching' category (see Table 6). And of course, whilst some men were driven by hunger and poverty to engage in their illicit activities, others were concerned with the profits they could earn by selling their ill-gotten gains to hawkers or to nearby town traders. Some were also motivated by a desire to 'cock a snook' at those in authority, like salmon poachers on the River Wye, who fixed a stale salmon to the Market Hall in Rhayader with a note attached:

Where were the river watchers when I was killed?
Where were the police when I was hung here?

Although, by the final quarter of the nineteenth century, poaching was far less violent than it had been in earlier years,

Table 6   Number of Game Law Convictions: Annual Averages of Non-Indictable Offences

Years	Total	Trespassing in Day-time Pursuit of Game	Night Poach-ing	Unlawful Possession of Game, &c.	Illegal Buying and Sell-ing of Game
1870	10,600*	9,089	522	914**	75
1878–82	11,144	9,458	548	1,109	29
1883–87	10,955	9,123	525	1,278	29
1888–92	8,923	7,351	430	1,113	29
1893–97	8,720	7,077	465	1,152	26
1895–99	7,838	6,348	386	1,085	19

* In addition there were 59 indictable cases reported of men being 'Armed taking Game and Assaulting Gamekeepers'

** In 1870, this total appeared under the heading '1862 Poaching Prevention Act' From *Return of the Number of Convictions under the Game Laws in England and Wales in 1870*, P.P.1871, Vol. LVIII, and *Judicial Statistics*, for 1897, P.P.1899, Vol. CVIII, Pt. 1, and for 1899, P.P.1901, Vol. LXXXIX.

D. J. V. Jones, 'The Poachers: A Study in Victorian Crime and Protest' in *Historical Journal*, Vol. 22, No. 4 (Dec. 1979), p.83, suggests that poaching incidents reached temporary peaks in 1869–70; 1874–77; 1881; 1885; and 1894. He notes, too, that increases in poaching figures had a regional character, with the south-west particularly prominent in the late 1860s and East Anglia in the 1880s.

battles between gamekeepers and poachers still took place, with men on both sides killed or injured. Over the period November 1880 to July 1896 there were at least thirty serious affrays involving poachers and keepers in various parts of the country. In seventeen, either poachers or keepers were killed.[187] Similarly, on the river Wye, between 1875 and 1881, skirmishes involving salmon poachers became so serious that in 1881 the Inspectors of Fisheries were required to investigate the situation. The gangs, often numbering as many as one hundred people, went out with blackened faces and wearing white under-garments or night-shirts over their everyday clothes, and armed with bludgeons and guns.[108] They called themselves followers of 'Rebecca', that legendary focus of unrest in the principality during the 1840s against the high level of tolls charged on turnpike roads and the introduction of changes in the system of poor relief. In the 1870s and 1880s the grievances were different, but many of the methods used to express them were the same. One of the gravest incidents in their campaign occurred on 6 December 1880, at Llanbadarn-fynydd, when around a hundred armed men congregated and a constable's arm was broken; shots were also fired at the local police station. Already by January 1878 the chairman of Quarter Sessions had complained of 'a system of terrorism and positive danger' in the area, and in the months that followed conditions deteriorated.[237]

The immediate cause of unrest was local resentment at the introduction of new restrictions on fishing by the board of conservators of the Wye, reinforced by the support of a group of 'better class . . . people in Radnorshire and Breconshire who . . . conceive that they have been unjustly deprived by the inclosure of commons of ancient rights of fishing which they had previously enjoyed'. In the end, the police force in Radnorshire had to be temporarily increased from seventeen to thirty-seven men to cope with the disturbances, while the conservators were persuaded to modify their restrictive policy.[74] In these conditions, the unrest subsided.

It was, therefore, only in the last years of the nineteenth century that the number of game law offences dwindled noticeably, as living standards improved and respect for law and order increased (see Table 6), though to the end of the 1890s the number of cases remained substantial. Rabbits and hares comprised perhaps two-thirds of the total catch of the poachers, and to most country people the daytime pursuit of these animals was no crime. It was merely taking a share in the beneficence of the countryside, to which all were entitled.

So, although the greater part of rural crime in the last decades of the nineteenth century involved relatively minor offences like drunkenness, infringements of the highway regulations, assaults and petty theft, as late as 1897 in Bedfordshire 18 per cent of all non-indictable offences still involved the game laws; in West Suffolk the figure was 13.3 per cent, and in Norfolk and Nor-thamptonshire around 9.5 per cent.[78] The attitude of the police and of magistrates and the seriousness with which game preserva-tion was viewed in a given county clearly had a role to play in the scale of convictions. For where the question was taken lightly, the number of convictions was likely to be relatively small. In Radnor, it is clear that a number of the magistrates had some sympathy with the poachers, one JP declaring plaintively that the performance of his duty as a magistrate 'with regard to the salmon laws was the most irksome duty he had to perform in public life'. Another man objected to the police being used as supplementary water-bailiffs: 'I do not like to have police const-ables mixed up with the watchers in these affairs', he commen-ted.[108] In this county, despite the substantial unrest of the late 1870s and early 1880s, relatively few people were actually convic-ted of offences against either the Fisheries or the Salmon Fisheries Acts. They were far less numerous than in neighbouring Brecon, where a firmer attitude towards policing seemingly applied.

But even where offences against the game laws were not rigorously pursued, there remained a residual unease among many villagers – an awareness that that approach could easily be changed at the behest of those in authority. As George Sturt observed, it led to 'an unreasoned but convinced distrust of propertied folk, and a sense of being unprotected and helpless against their privileges and power'. It manifested itself, too, in their attitude towards the village policeman. 'There is probably no lonelier man in the parish than the constable', wrote Sturt. 'Of course he meets with civility, but his company is avoided. One hears him mentioned in those same accents of grudging caution which the villagers use in speaking of unfriendly property-owners, as though he belonged to that alien caste. The cottagers feel that they themselves are the people whom he is stationed . . . to watch.'[261]

It was, therefore, to escape the social controls associated with village life that a number of labourers moved away. Although in their new environment real wages 'might not be higher, housing was very often worse, . . . in the towns the hours of work were usually fewer, the opportunities for economic improvement were present in some measure, and the social and political pressures of Bladesover and the Vicarage were absent. The towns had their own forms of oppression for the working people, but there was nothing quite equal to the deadweight of custom and tradition in the countryside'.[249]

Meanwhile on the national scene the scale of the rural outflow began to arouse concern. For to many it seemed that the agricultural population formed the real backbone of the nation. 'At the last, it is to the countryman, to the ploughman, and "the farmer's boy" that a land in difficulty looks for help', wrote Richard Jefferies in 1887. During the 1880s and 1890s, efforts were made to tackle the problem by promoting legislation designed to give the labourer a 'stake in the soil' by increasing the number of allotments and smallholdings available. The process began with the Allotments Extension Act of 1882, which required the trustees of charity land in a parish to set apart a suitable portion for allotments. If they failed to act, the Charity Commissioners could enforce the legislation. Further measures came in 1887, 1890 and 1894, with the aim of requiring rural sanitary, district, or parish councils to make provision.[122] Thus, under the Local Government Act of 1894, parish councils were empowered to hire allotment land, and if they were unable to secure suitable property by agreement, they could apply to the County Council for it to be hired compulsorily. The introduction of compulsory powers was an interesting departure from traditional attitudes towards property rights, but in practice it had little effect. By June 1897, a mere 75 acres had been acquired compulsorily in the whole of the country.[81] A similar lack of enthusiasm informed the efforts of County Councils to provide smallholdings under legislation passed in 1892 and 1907. It arose partly on ideological grounds – councillors regarding this as an unwelcome move towards public ownership of land – as well as on grounds of cost, while a relatively small number of would-be smallholders could afford to pay the rents needed if the venture were to be a financial success. Yet, if the measures had little direct impact, indirectly they encouraged the *voluntary* provision of allotments by landowners and clergy; and by June 1897 almost 13,000 acres of land had been secured by parish councils through private negotiations.

The seriousness with which many labourers regarded the allotments issue is illustrated by a letter which disgruntled cottagers at Hoggeston, Buckinghamshire, sent to the agent of their landlord, Lord Rosebery. The latter had promised that a suitable plot would be provided to meet the men's needs, but they felt that the agent was responding tardily to that undertaking. Eventually they plucked up courage to write and tell him so: 'In our humble way we uphold the integrity of his *Lordship's pledged word* at least equally with yourself; we claim at your hands the redemption of his Lordship's kind & unmistakable promise, nor shall we abandon our suit until the latter has been made good.' Nor did they, for they even wrote to Lord Rosebery himself on the subject. In the end their persistence had its reward with the granting of the necessary plots more than a year later. But most villagers lacked the stubborn determination they showed in approaching their social superiors.[16]

In cultivating their allotments the men often displayed a friendly rivalry, vying with one another to see who could grow the best vegetables or the heaviest crop of corn. At Haddenham in Buckinghamshire, by the 1880s, the allotment had become the most significant part of a cottager's life, according to the village carpenter, Walter Rose:

> A stock of potatoes could now be grown and stored against each winter; it became possible to grow and fat a pig and to hang its flitches on the cottage walls. To these ends every available hour – except Sunday – throughout the spring, summer, and autumn was given to their cultivation; and often, when the work was in arrears, the husband would rise early and put in an hour or two before beginning labour on the farm at seven.[243]

Most families consumed the produce themselves, but sometimes surpluses were sold in nearby towns or disposed of to occupiers of neighbouring smallholdings. The latter would then retail these with their own vegetables. This happened in the Woburn area of Bedfordshire, for example, while at Corsley in Wiltshire, Maude Davies found one woman who had earned more than eight pounds in a year by selling soft fruit, apples, poultry and vegetables, all produced on fifty poles of ground. Most of the produce from Corsley was sold in nearby Frome.[146] In this way extra cash could be earned to supplement a husband's wage on the farm.

At Haddenham, as in other parts of the Vale of Aylesbury, and at Fencott and Murcott in Oxfordshire, cottagers also followed a more unusual money-making sideline by rearing and fattening ducklings for the London market. The trade dated back to at least the eighteenth century, though it reached its peak in the 1890s, when the prosperous middle classes had joined the ranks of its customers. It owed its success to the close proximity of the producers to their principal outlet in the capital. The birds were despatched, carefully packed in hampers, by carrier's cart, although by the later nineteenth century the railways, too, were organizing both the collection and the sale of the ducks for a small commission. The number of birds reared and sold each year by an individual producer might range from a few hundreds to several thousands. At Weston Turville, one major centre, there were in the 1890s eleven men who each fattened about one thousand ducks annually, a total of between 16,000 and 17,000 birds being sent from that village each year.[54] Cottage gardens were divided by planks into makeshift pens, and shedding was erected to protect the birds from the weather. The stench exuded, especially after a warm June shower, and the noise at feeding time were extremely unpleasant, but the profits earned helped to compensate for this. During the season, which lasted from February or early March – after the end of the game season – until late August, a man selling a thousand ducks a year could expect a gross return of over £160. Even when payments for rent, food, brood hens to hatch the duck eggs, and other expenses had been met, a reasonable profit remained – better than anything a man could earn as an ordinary agricultural labourer. At Haddenham, though, according to Walter Rose, the business was in the hands of the wives, while their husbands continued to work on a farm. The women's only assistance was provided by fellow-villagers, who plucked the birds for 1½d. a duck.[243] With the cash thus secured, some thrifty families were able to purchase their own cottages, while a few moved up into the ranks of smallholders and even farmers. Where a garden was given over to 'ducking', an allotment was essential for the growing of vegetables and its availability reinforced the attractions of the duck trade.

Only in the north of England and in Wales was interest in allotments minimal. There, even at the end of the century, payments in kind were still common, at a time when perquisites had been phased out for the ordinary labourer in much of central and southern England save, perhaps, for the provision of beer or cider as part of wages. This was a practice which lingered on, for example in Somerset and Worcestershire, even after being made illegal by the 1887 Truck Act. Men who had potato ground in an employer's field naturally had little interest in cultivating that vegetable in an allotment. Perhaps, too, the availability of large gardens and the fact that cash earnings in the north were higher acted as further deterrents. Workers preferred to buy additional vegetables they needed rather than engage in the laborious business of digging, setting and harvesting their own. In these areas it was the acquisition of cow pastures which proved the prime attraction, and in those parishes where land for the purpose was in short supply, it was common for cow-keepers to tether their animals at the side of the road. Around Driffield, in the East Riding of Yorkshire, cow owners often banded together to engage a child or an old person as a 'tenter'. He or she would collect the cows from the different owners in the morning, would look after them during the day, and then drive them home again in the evening, often blowing a horn as they passed through the streets, as a signal to the respective owners to collect their animal. At Kilham in the East Riding thirty-two cows were grazed in this fashion in the lanes during the 1892 season.[80] 'Three acres and a cow' was also the ambition of labourers in Cheshire, where perhaps 40 per cent of them owned their own cows, as well as in the Garstang district of Lancashire. Both were traditional dairying areas, and in Cheshire a large number of cattle clubs existed to provide insurance against the loss of an animal. They were widely supported by farm workers.

The provision of land for allotments and the existence of these various small-scale farming enterprises were two – admittedly imperfect – answers to labouring discontent. Another more obvious manifestation of that dissatisfaction was the growth of agricultural trade unionism. Although there had been sporadic attempts to form localized societies from the days of the Tolpuddle Martyrs in 1833/34, it was not until 1872 that a national body was set up among this most numerous section of the workforce. It was led by a determined and skilled Warwickshire hedgecutter named Joseph Arch. The timing of the upsurge was significant, for it came at a period of industrial prosperity, when urban jobs were widely available, and shortly after the passage of the Trade Union Act of 1871, which had confirmed the legality of such organizations. It also followed a successful movement for a nine-hour working day among engineering and building workers, which underlined the benefits combination could bestow.

It was, therefore, in a mood of hope and of firm resolve that Arch began work organizing the labourers of his native county in February 1872. The theme of his speeches was simple – the need for higher wages, improved housing and better working conditions for the labourer and consequently greater comfort for his wife and family.

Early in March some men in the Wellesbourne area, taking this message to heart, decided to come out on strike in support of a demand for higher wages, a shortening of the working day, and the payment of overtime. The appearance of unrest among a group of workers hitherto dismissed as quiescent 'chaw-bacons' quickly aroused the attention of both press and public. The strikers were aided by sympathetic reports of their case which appeared not only in local newspapers but in national ones, like the *Daily News* and the *Daily Telegraph*. Soon much-needed funds began to flow into the union's coffers. According to Arch, when the men first struck there had not been 'a pound's worth of silver among the lot'; 'they had to get credit from the shop for the barest necessaries. Kettle broth and tea made from crusts burnt black and scraped into the pot to give a little colour to the "water bewitched," was no new food and drink to the half-starved labourers; it was what they and their children had been fed upon year in and year out; but the bit of bacon could be no longer counted on'.[120]

As the dispute dragged on, a number of the strikers migrated to alternative employment in the north of England, while a few emigrated, mainly to New Zealand. But most stayed firm, and were eventually rewarded by the granting of an increase in pay when the strike was wound up in the middle of April.

Meanwhile, Arch's fame had spread far beyond the borders of his own county. Labourers elsewhere came together informally and decided to follow his example and form a union. At Old Buckenham in Norfolk two hundred men met at the White Hart Inn 'to consider agricultural wages'. There was no chairman. Instead they all sat round on benches and each, as he rose to speak, asked for silence. A committee was chosen to apply to the farmers for an advance in wages, and to raise funds for the continuation of the agitation.[255] In Kent, the initiative was taken by a group of labourers meeting at Shoreham in the middle of April. They invited a member of the Maidstone Trades Council and Alfred Simmons, editor of the radical local newspaper, the *Kent Messenger and Maidstone Telegraph*, to address them.[91] For some years the paper had been pleading the rural labourers' cause, and as early as 6 April 1872 had expressed support for the Warwickshire movement. A singular example of the self-generating character of these meetings is provided by Hoarwithy in Herefordshire, for in this case not only did the convenor of the gathering remain unknown but its eventual chairman proved to be a man who had merely been attracted by rumour as a spectator![100]

Soon labourers in most of the low-wage counties in southern and central England were joining in, though in the north, where annual hirings were common and conditions fairly satisfactory, the movement made little impact. In Northumberland the men used the hiring fairs to extract the best conditions from future employers, and to this end often held meetings to co-ordinate action before the hirings took place. Once they had committed themselves, it was difficult for them to strike, since by so doing annually hired workers risked action by employers for breach of contract and the subsequent imposition of cash penalties.

It was against this background of rising agitation that Arch's supporters called a conference in Leamington at the end of May to consider bringing all the differing organizations into one national body. The conference was attended by about sixty delegates, many of them Methodist local preachers, like Arch himself, and on 29 May the National Agricultural Labourers Union (NALU) came into existence, with Arch as its president.

In their struggles the labourers were able to secure the help of a number of outsiders, including some leading Liberal politicians and several non-agricultural trade unionists, who were anxious to undermine the Conservative party's traditional power base in the countryside. But at district and branch level the administration remained largely in the hands of the farm workers themselves, despite their educational limitations and lack of experience in maintaining records and accounts. But the NALU's general secretary was Henry Taylor, treasurer of the Leamington branch of the Amalgamated Society of Carpenters and Joiners. Upon appointment to this new post, he gave up all other employment. The treasurer was the sympathetic newspaper owner and journalist J. E. Matthew Vincent, also from Leamington, whose newspaper the *Royal Leamington Chronicle*, had already given detailed coverage of the labourers' affairs. The following month Vincent helped to found the NALU's newspaper, the *Labourers' Union Chronicle*, which by 1873 claimed a circulation of 35,000. It continued in existence, despite difficulties and some changes of name, until 1894. Through its columns members could learn of the actions of fellow-unionists elsewhere, and could doubtless derive encouragement from them. Information on emigration opportunities was also provided. For example, in its issue of 4 October 1873 the *Chronicle* included a report that one of the union's district secretaries, James Crick of West Suffolk, had emigrated 'thirty- three souls to Canada last week'. It then added: 'The application for emigration is enormous. We wait anxiously a liberal scheme for Canada. Numbers are enquiring for Queensland.' Several union officials acted as emigration agents, and in all, during the 1870s and early 1880s, perhaps forty to forty-five thousand unionists and their families went abroad under NALU-sponsored emigration schemes.[106]

Meanwhile, in the months following the formation of this new organization, the workers continued to press for higher wages, with some success. Over the period 1872–74 it has been estimated that basic wage rates were increased by 20 to 30 per cent.[100] Often, progress was made only in the face of severe opposition, and there were charges of victimization as men were threatened with the loss of their jobs or of their allotments if they joined. At Lower Heyford in Oxfordshire George Dew indignantly noted that two men who had merely attended an open-air meeting in the village on 8 May 1872 had been discharged by their employer 'on account of having participated in the movement, but I cannot hear that they entered their names as being desirous of joining . . . such a course is subversive of civil & individual liberty'.[7] Agriculturists were particularly opposed to the intervention of 'outsiders' in their dealings with their men. As a Suffolk farmer bluntly declared in 1874: 'This is not a struggle for a paltry rise of 1s. in wages. It is not a question of wages at all. The question is, "Are these delegates to rule over us?"'

In the Cirencester district, farmers gave their men notice to quit their cottages and resolved in the future to rent only by the week, so that unionists could be more easily evicted. In the Brampton district, an innkeeper was threatened with the loss of his licence if he allowed meetings to be held on his premises. Elsewhere there were claims of unionists being summoned before the courts for trivial offences. In one case, at Compton Abbas in Dorset, two men were kept in prison for nine days before they were tried on what proved to be a trumped-up charge. An employer was heard to remark: 'They are union men, give it to them.'[150] So common did these cases become that in June 1873 Auberon Herbert, a Liberal MP, moved in the House of Commons that a Royal Commission should be appointed 'to inquire into and report upon the state of the Law giving powers of summary jurisdiction to magistrates in criminal cases', and into the general methods of appointment of magistrates.[90] He was counted out, and no action was taken.

The bitterness engendered by these methods led one Bedfordshire clergyman to complain of the '*rank communism and covetousness*' of his parishioners: 'A squire rides through his Parish. "Why should he be on horseback? . . . Why shouldn't he walk as we do? We ought to be all alike." . . . "Why shouldn't Master's horses and cattle be mine as much as his?"'[100] It found expression, too, in publications like *The Farm Labourers' Catechism*, which in 1884 listed the ten 'landowners' and farmers' commandments', among them the fourth commandment:

Remember that thou, and those that thou hast begotten, are mine, to fetch and carry, to dig and plough, sow and reap, and that my will is law. For six days from five o'clock in the morning till late in the evening, shalt thou toil and do my service, and on the seventh day thou shalt work if I require thee, if not, thou shalt attend Church, sit on the benches set apart for thee, and do honour to the parson, having thy hand to thy head, and thy knees bended in readiness to do homage when I condescend to sit in the same Church with thee.

Nevertheless, despite the opposition faced by the movement and the establishment in some areas of anti-union farmers' associations, membership continued to grow, rising from around 71,000 in 1873 to over 86,000 in 1874. Independent unions also existed in Kent and Sussex, in Herefordshire and the West of England, and in Lincolnshire and the neighbouring districts of East Anglia. In 1873 the Kent Agricultural and General Labourers' Union had a membership of 8,000, and the Lincolnshire Amalgamated Labour League, of around 18,000. Overall, the various unions claimed a total membership of about 150,000 by the beginning of 1874, not all of them agricultural labourers. Yet despite this formidable progress, it must be remembered that that figure represented less than one in six of the nation's male and female agricultural work force (see Table 4 p. 95). Even in the most heavily unionized counties, members were never overwhelmingly dominant. Thus in Norfolk, where the NALU and the Lincolnshire League had between them over 18,000 members, this represented only about 43 per cent of the male agricultural labourers, farm servants, and shepherds in the county. And not all of the members fell into these employment categories; nor were all of them males, even though the vast majority were. Similarly in Herefordshire, where the NALU and a local body, the West of England Union, claimed a combined membership of over 7,800, the proportion of members among the county's farm workers was still only about 65 per cent. Inevitably, when the difficult times came, the existence of large bodies of non-unionists made strike-breaking by employers easier and ultimately undermined the whole structure.

During their early days, the unions exercised a powerful influence on village life in the areas most heavily affected. The labourers could no longer be treated contemptuously as mere 'Johnny Raws', but had to be recognized as men determined to secure their just rights. Naturally there were complaints that the upsurge of militancy had disturbed formerly 'good relations' between employer and worker, though an impartial witness might wonder just how 'good' those relationships had been in pre-union days, given the low wages and poor living conditions of many workers. Even in the early twentieth century farmers in Oxfordshire still retained memories of Joseph Arch, and attributed everything 'in the way of agitation, complaints or anything to disturb the grooved ways of the agricultural labourers' conditions . . . to the disturbing influence of Joe Arch'.[60] Similarly, in the Swaffham area of Norfolk during the early 1890s it was claimed that the union had done 'a great deal of harm between employers and employed. It made the farmers give up giving beer, harvest suppers, and carting coals, also they gave up giving prizes at garden shows'; while according to Lord Walsingham, it had deluded the workers 'with numberless absurd promises, and putting forward grievances which are for the most part wholly imaginary'.[80]

For the men, however, the movement achieved a great many short-term benefits, with earnings raised, overtime rates conceded, and the payment of wages arranged on a more regular basis than hitherto. In pre-union days it had not been uncommon for the men to be paid only once a month – a fact which, given their low earnings, made family budgeting extremely difficult and contributed to the debt problem. There was, too, a growing trend to pay wages wholly in cash instead of partly in cash and partly in kind.

But trade unionism involved more than just economic matters. There was an important social side as well, with tea parties and other junketings arranged in many villages. Members would parade the streets headed by brass bands, and with flags and banners waving. Such a meeting was held at Horndean in Hampshire at the end of September 1873 when, according to the *Labourers' Union Chronicle*, 'About 150 sat down to tea, previous to which dancing and other amusements were resorted to, accompanied by the very efficient brass band from Compton.' At seven a public meeting began, with speeches from local union leaders and, between the addresses, 'the band played some very appropriate pieces'. At such gatherings special songs were sung, like 'We'll all be Union Men', or 'We Demand the Vote'. In many, tribute was paid to the union president, Joseph Arch, as in 'We Demand the Vote', one verse of which ran:

With Arch our commander
The strife is begun,
We have fought sharp engagements
And Victories have won.[185]

Unfortunately for its supporters, however, the movement was unable to sustain this early momentum. The onset of agricultural depression in the mid-and later 1870s in the arable districts where its main strength lay, and the increasingly determined opposition of the farmers, led to a gradual decline in its fortunes. Inevitably, given the nature of the industry, many of its struggles were localized affairs, centred on one or two villages here, or a single farm or several farms there. They were 'a series of local engagements fought separately'.[175] By 1874, however, the farmers had decided to respond to these tactics by generalizing the conflict and locking out men over a wide area. It was in that year that the movement had its greatest battle, centred mainly in the eastern counties but eventually affecting at least twelve counties to some degree. In all, nearly 4,000 NALU members were locked out, along with around 1,500 to 2,000 workers associated with the Labour League and other independent unions in the area.[138] The dispute began in a virtually unplanned fashion with labourers in the small Suffolk village of Exning demanding a 1s. rise in their basic weekly pay of 13s. The employers, who belonged to the Newmarket Farmers' Defence Association, not only rejected the demand but resolved that 'all Union men be locked out, . . . and that such lock-out continue so long as the men continue on strike'.

Soon the conflict had spread beyond the confines of the New-market area. By 23 March, three weeks after it had begun, at least 2,500 members were locked out in Suffolk, Cambridgeshire, Norfolk, Essex, Bedfordshire, Lincolnshire and Hampshire, and a union lock-out fund had been established. Ultimately perhaps one-half of the unionists in Suffolk were to be sucked into the struggle.

The pressures on both sides were immense, but for the men, seeking to bring up families on the union dispute pay of 9s. per week, the hardship was especially severe. There was also a considerable drain on resources. In all, the NALU was to spend £24,432 10s. 7d. from its central funds, excluding cash raised and disbursed locally, and excluding, of course, the outgoings of other

1 'Leaving Home'

2   Agricultural trade unionism

unions in the area.[138] Special fund-raising meetings were organized in the industrial districts, and union members in the unaffected regions also contributed. Yet, in the end, the unionists had to
admit defeat. With the greater use of machinery, and the recruitment of family labour and non-union workers, farmers were able
to carry on. When the dispute was finally called off towards the
end of July, it was amidst bitter recriminations. Yet, given the
financial plight of all the unions involved, it is difficult to see what
alternative strategy could have been adopted. Significantly, the
Times correspondent, Frederick Clifford, blamed the farmers
more than the men for the ill-feeling engendered: 'They would not
treat; they chose rather to fight, and to fight upon an issue which,
though nominally resting upon an extra shilling of wages, really
involved the rights of the men to combine.' Certainly the Lincolnshire farmer Cornelius Stovin showed little spirit of compromise.
As late as 16 March 1875 he noted in his journal that the strike had
encouraged him 'to invent some method of sowing with less
labour'. As a result he had purchased a new drilling machine and
now 'one man performs the work of three'.[256]

Against this unhappy background, conflicts developed between
the union leaders themselves. In the summer of 1875 J. E.
Matthew Vincent, the NALU treasurer, led a breakaway organization called the National Farm Labourers' Union. It had as its
principal aims the provision of allotments and smallholdings and
the avoidance of strikes. In the months that followed, the leaders
of this organization and the NALU proceeded to cast doubts upon
one another's probity, with the leaders of some of the independent
unions also joining in. In these circumstances, support for all the
organizations dropped. Membership of the NALU fell from 86,214
in 1874 to 40,000 in 1875, though it recovered a little to 55,000 in
1876, before again slumping to 20,000 in 1879 and 4,254 a decade
later.[185] Most of the other unions shared the National's fate, the
Labour League's membership declining from around 18,000 in
1873 to 5,500 in 1876 and 1,020 by 1881. Only the Kent and Sussex
Union, which had remained outside the Eastern Counties dispute,
managed to hold membership at around 10,000.

One of the principal causes of discontent among NALU members
was the practice of sending the greater part of their weekly
subscriptions of 2¼d. each to headquarters in Leamington. As
one of the Oxford district leaders later complained: 'We raised

funds by paying our twopences; three parts of it was sent to Leamington and spent in high salaries for officers and strikes in the Eastern counties, and we, who were plodding on had neither funds to fall back on and no prospect of getting allotments.'[149] Exaggerated though the charges were, they were an indication of rank-and-file disillusionment with the union.

To add to the problems, the effects of agricultural depression led employers to cut wages from the high level reached when the movement began in 1872/73. Doubtless, the farmers were emboldened to take this action by the declining effectiveness of the unions, and the fact that these could offer so little protection on the vital matter of wages weakened support for them still further. The only consolations were that in most cases, weekly rates remained above pre-1872 levels, and that thanks to the fall in prices in the last quarter of the century, *real* wages were moving upwards.

During the 1880s, a number of unionists turned their attention to political matters – a subject dealt with in Chapter 7 – and to ineffectual attempts to secure a reform of the land laws so as to give the labourers their much desired 'stake in the soil'.

Then, in 1889, came a general revival of economic activity within the country, and with it a successful strike for improved wages and conditions by London dockers. The victory of the unskilled dockers gave new confidence to poorly paid workers everywhere. In the early 1890s the Dockers' Union itself recruited farm worker members in Oxfordshire and Lincolnshire, no doubt with the ulterior motive of discouraging them from migrating to the towns and thereby weakening further the bargaining position of unskilled men already there. In addition, a number of new unions were formed at around the same time among labourers in Suffolk, Norfolk, Wiltshire, Berkshire, Hertfordshire and Warwickshire.[216] Most were associated with a Radical body called the English Land Restoration League, which aimed at land reform and the abolition of landlordism. The first tour organized by this new body was in Suffolk in 1891, when 'missionaries' came out to the villages to work alongside the recently established Eastern Counties Labour Federation. Others followed, but these new societies failed to capture the support of the labourers in the way that the NALU and the Labour League had done two decades earlier. Most lacked a firm financial base and were consequently

120

anxious to avoid all disputes. The Norfolk Federal Union, based on Harleston, stressed the need for boards of arbitration to be set up in wages disputes 'to prevent disputes and disagreements from taking the shape of Strikes or Lock-outs'. This union also had the novel notion of lending small sums of money to bona fide members to enable them 'to improve their position by hiring land and securing their own houses and homesteads'.[20] With its cash tied up in this fashion, it is difficult to see how it could ever have supported members involved in industrial action. Not surprisingly, within a few years all these organizations had faded away.

The National Union, too, shared briefly in the upturn of the early 1890s, especially in Norfolk, where by the end of 1891 over 12,000 men had been recruited. Overall, NALU membership rose to around 15,000 once more. Then came further economic recession, exacerbated by the effects of serious drought in many rural areas. Farmers' resistance to union demands increased and in 1896 the NALU was itself wound up. Not for another decade was there to be any effective trade union organization among the farm workers.

Nevertheless, during the revival of the early 1890s, wage rates were increased, and these gains were largely retained in the years that followed. Thanks to the effects of migration, there was also some harmonization in the general pattern of wage differentials, with the emergence of labour shortages even in some predominantly rural areas. Although by 1907 regional differences still applied, the *maximum* wage now earned in agricultural labouring exceeded the *minimum* only by some 28 per cent. In 1867–70, it had exceeded the minimum by 44 per cent.[92]

During the 1870s the trade union movement gave a much-needed boost to the position of the agricultural worker, and although in the final two decades of the nineteenth century his progress was little influenced by unionism (save, perhaps, in the political field), other factors now conspired to raise living standards. By the early 1890s, there were widespread comments on the improvements secured as a result of relatively steady wage rates at a time of falling prices. In areas, too, where cottage industries were being undermined by industrialization, the loss of this source of income for a wife and family was to some degree compensated by the advance in the real wages of the menfolk. Elsewhere, as we have seen, women could afford to stay at home rather than go out to work in the fields as they had once done. They were also becoming more fashion-conscious. A Northamptonshire landowner, Sir Herewald Wake, commented on the way in which once upon a time 'the whole female village population used to turn out and collect stuffs for winter fuel . . . at other times, the women and girls were always available to do such work on the farm as they could do'. But, 'Nowadays, with their high heels and pretty hats and hobble skirts, they are not at all anxious to do any manual labour in the fields, or their own allotment gardens, for that matter.'[32]

And in 1892 an assistant commissioner in connection with the Royal Commission on Labour reported of the Dorchester area in Dorset: 'The circumstances of the agricultural labourer in this district have considerably improved during the last 20 years. . . . I very much doubt if the labourer in the Dorchester Poor Law Union was ever better off than he is at the present time. . . . I was told by one retired labourer that he remembered the time when barley cakes were the usual food of the labourer as he could not afford wheaten bread. Now all eat wheaten bread.'

Another man commented that the cheapness of the necessaries of life and the 'greater spending power of the wage' had brought about the main advance.

This is particularly the case with regard to bread and tea, and manufactured articles like clothes, hats, and boots; . . .
The old wage in North Witchford was reckoned to be a bushel and a half of wheat at 8s. a bushel; the present wage, if put at 14s., is equal to 4 bushels at 3s. 6d. a bushel. . . . Boots are from 2s. 6d. to 3s. 6d. cheaper than they used to be, and clothes of all kinds show even a greater reduction.

The result of all this is seen in a variety of ways. The old smock-frock is very nearly extinct, and there is no real difference in the style of dress adopted by the labourers and their wives and that of the class above them. On the clothes lines, instead of rags, good linen is to be seen; in the cottage there is more furniture, and lights are burning late into the night; at the school, children appear neatly dressed, with their boots blacked; and at the farm, every young man of 16 years of age carries a watch. Butchers' carts go round the villages once at least every week on a Saturday. . . . At the village shops there is an increased demand for tinned meats of all kinds; and it is surprising to find what distance tradesmen's carts from the market town will travel for the sake of the labourers' custom. Men are often extremely particular in the joint of meat which they buy, they will not buy fat bacon, and they will only take the whitest of flour. Tea, which used to be looked upon as a luxury, is now considered a necessary, and a good supply of vegetables is seldom wanting.[80]

In the light of this evidence, some of the more extreme allegations of poverty and deprivation in the rural areas appear wide of the mark, at least in the 1890s, although it must be stressed that regional differences still persisted. The assistant commissioner for the Royal Commission on Labour quoted above noted, for example, that basic rates for ordinary labourers could range from the average of 10s. to 11s. per week secured in the Wantage Poor Law union, or the 11s. to 12s. per week in winter and 12s. to 13s. per week in summer obtained in the Thame district of Oxfordshire/Buckinghamshire, to 13s. to 15s. per week paid in the Atcham district of Shropshire and the neighbourhood of Truro in Cornwall. Significantly, both of the latter were in areas where opportunities for employment outside of agriculture, especially in mining, were to hand.

In Cornwall there were also complaints that proximity to the mines and the constant 'going to and fro between Cornwall and America' by many of the miners had contributed to a growing 'independence' among the labourers. Strikes, especially among threshing gangs, were not uncommon in the early 1890s, even though there was no formal agricultural trade union in the area.

Nor were the charges of 'independence' confined to Cornish labourers. In other areas which had had no recent experience of unionism, similar complaints were made. As a large farmer from Upper Winchendon in Buckinghamshire declared in 1895: 'I find . . . that now those young fellows get so pert that you cannot speak to them, and if you see anything going wrong, and say anything to them, they say, "Give me my money; I will go." They do not trouble about getting work about home, many of them, they go right away.'[54] But to twentieth-century eyes, it seems that what employers resented was a belated move towards greater equality between master and man, and the advent of a system whereby contract would replace status in employer/worker relationships.

If variations in cash incomes and the changing level of prices were two major factors in deciding the level of prosperity of labouring families, a third was the size of the families themselves. Where these were large and the children were too young to earn, then even in the 1890s household diets were likely to be very heavily dependent upon bread and potatoes. The plight of old people living along has already been touched upon, especially where they relied on poor relief. Poverty had certainly not been eliminated from the late Victorian village – merely reduced. As Sir John Gorst, former Vice-President of the Education Department, pointed out in evidence to the 1904 Inter-Departmental Committee on Physical Deterioration: 'In every country district there are an immense number of widows with seven or eight children, and it is almost impossible for a woman to provide necessary food for her children.' Another witness complained of the shortage of milk to feed to youngsters in areas where commercial dairying was followed and there were no smallholders or labourers with a few cows to meet the need: 'It pays the farmer better to send it to big centres of population or the neighbouring towns and the children do not get it at all.' In her view, there was less milk used in rural areas in 1904 than there had been thirty or forty years earlier.[83] A third witness claimed that hard-pressed mothers gave their babies brandy and gin to keep them quiet, while the use of opiates, such as Godfrey's cordial, was common.

On the plus side, both infant mortality and adult death rates throughout the period were lower in the rural areas than they were in the industrial districts. Poor earnings could not entirely cancel out the benefits to health of fresh air and a country environment. The Registrar General of Births, Deaths and Marriages in England and Wales pointed out that mortality rates amongst farm workers during the period 1880–92 were only 66 per cent of standard mortality among all occupied males.[187] Similarly, among babies the 1898 infant mortality rate in Wiltshire, Dorset and Westmorland was only 99 per 1,000 birth registered, and Oxfordshire 101, compared to rates of 181 in Lancashire and 185 in Durham at that date. Although the fact that even in the best counties almost one baby in ten died before it reached its first birthday could hardly be regarded as a cause for complacency.

Leisure interests, too, were widening, as some of the younger man and women purchased bicycles upon which to visit the nearest town, or took advantage of cheap railway excursions. In parts of Wales, instead of visiting local fairs, people saved up to go on railway trips to Cardiff, Birmingham and even London. The Cambrian railway timetable in the early 1900s included four pages of 'market ticket arrangements', giving details of the departure times and fares from over 150 local stations to the twenty-two market towns which the company served. Special market returns were sold, in many cases at less than 1s. and in some at only 3d.[216] Other companies made similar arrangements.

The there were the villagers' own celebrations, such as the feast day, when friends visited from miles around and there were bands and processions, stalls selling sweetmeats, swings and roundabouts, and usually a dance. On a rather different level a number of traditional festivities likewise survived, including morris dancing, which was found in several Oxfordshire parishes. When men from these villages travelled to London and the south for seasonal work in the hayfields, they would often give exhibitions of dancing and singing on their journey.[217]

Harvest homes were still held by some farmers for their own workers, to celebrate the successful gathering in of the corn. Hams were boiled, sirloins of beef roasted, pies baked, stacks of plum puddings prepared, and casks of ale made ready. It was a recognized custom for guests to fast, and to make their children fast, for a meal in advance so that they could do justice to the plentiful fare provided. After the meal there would be toasts, followed by games, singing and dancing, perhaps to the music of a fiddler. But in many areas during the later Victorian years harvest homes lapsed in popularity, partly, it was said, on account of the ill-feeling engendered between master and man by the union movement, but also because of growing disapproval of the drunkenness which they often encouraged amongst the attenders. In certain parishes more sedate harvest festivals, held in association with the church, became the order of the day.[189]

In the North of England, hiring fairs continued to have their 'merry bucolic side', with the young newly recruited farm servants able to spend the 'fastening penny' they had received from their future employer at boxing booths, coconut shies and roundabouts, or in flirtations with the servant girls. 'Many a match was made at the Hiring Fair', it was said.[14]

In these circumstances, an assistant commissioner with the Royal Commission on Labour could comment perceptively that despite the apparent limitations of country life, the daily round was not dull

> to those brought up to it. . . . Strange as it may appear to those who have not experienced it, there is an intense delight to the cultivator of luxuriant crops in a garden or allotment, or to the feeder of a prospering pig, in the contemplation of the results of his efforts and in the exhibition thereof to appreciative neighbours. Then, the village gossip, vacuous as it seems to an outsider, is interesting above all other things to the villagers. There is no lack of merriment in the gatherings of men and lads to be found in village streets on summer evenings and on Sunday, or in the meetings of familiar acquaintances in the public-houses.

Over their evening half-pints, the men would exchange anecdotes, or discuss the affairs of the day, or perhaps merely engage in a communal sing-song. By now, many of the traditional country tales and folk songs were fast being forgotten in favour of more modern entertainments, but a few lingered on, like the old ballad 'Lord Lovell stood', favoured by the stalwarts at the public house in Juniper Hill.[268]

In parts of Wales another, more controversial, survivor of the old ways also continued, namely 'night courting'. Up to the time of the First World War, farm servants in Pembrokeshire would abandon the badly lit and uncomfortable lofts which their employers provided for their bedrooms to spend the night with their sweetheart on a neighbouring farm. The girls secretly admitted them to the house, and there they remained until '2 and even 5 o'clock in the morning. "Though the parties are generally careful not to disturb the household, still this kind of courting is done with the connivance of the employer, who excuses himself on the alleged ground that it would be too difficult for him to keep any servants if he restricted them in these respects" '. In 1919, an official report on agricultural employment sourly observed: 'Many young men "sit up" three nights or even four nights a week, each night with a different girl, and they can scarcely be expected to be such efficient workmen on the days that follow these customary vigils.'[60] One reporter claimed to have met a young man in

Pembrokeshire who asserted that 'he had not been to bed at all on eleven nights during the preceding fortnight'.

But outside the borders of the principality these exotic forms of 'courting' did not apply, and workers had to be content with more circumspect pursuits. Those who were not prepared to accept that unsophisticated way of life, and wanted to experience the excitement of the wider world, simply moved away. Significantly, in the early 1890s it was noted that the migration of the girls from the villages to positions as maids in the towns was encouraging the men to move. They acted as 'magnets to the lads they [left] behind them'.[80]

5
Crafts, Trades and Professions

If agriculture, despite its difficulties, remained the economic power-house of the late Victorian and Edwardian countryside, a wide range of crafts and trades were needed to keep that machine running effectively, and to promote the smooth flow of community life. Some men concentrated on building and repairing houses; others produced the clothing and boots that people wore. Others again satisfied the needs of the farmers or of their fellow-tradesmen, with the wheelwright dependent on the skills of the blacksmith to fit the metal tyres needed to complete the wheels of carts and waggons, and the baker reliant upon the miller for his supplies of flour and upon the brickmaker for the tiles required for lining his oven. Many of these men also had their favourite fellow-tradesmen. At Great Horwood, Buckinghamshire, early in the present century, the wheelwright would invariably choose one particular blacksmith, saying that his competitor 'always made a pair of odd 'uns', if he were asked to supply a couple of wheel tyres for a cart.

Local gazetteers confirm that some workers also followed several lines of business on their own account in order to make a living. Among them were George Bonham of Bierton, Buckinghamshire, who took on the joint tasks of grocer, baker, brickmaker and postmaster during the 1880s and 1890s, and George Price of Newport Pagnell, in the same county, who advertised himself as a corn, cake, coal and lime merchant, and a brickmaker. Elsewhere, as in parts of Yorkshire, blacksmiths would act as agents for commercial lime-burners, while small farmers in the vicinity of Pickering took up besom-making. The besoms were made by the thousand to send to the foundries or shipyards in the north of England and Scotland, where they were used to take off the scum from molten metal as it came out of the furnaces.

Among these craftsmen it was the blacksmith who was the key figure in the village economy, at a time when horses reigned supreme as working animals on the farm. Not only was he employed in shoeing them, but he was expected to make and repair the implements they hauled. One smith, who followed his trade in East Anglia both before and after the First World War, recalled that in his shop there were nine workers, each of whom had his special tasks to perform:

> two were on the shoeing – two more were brought in if there was a rush; the guv'nor would be making mill-bills – a tool for trimming a millstone; two were on farm-work, sharpening the tines of harrows, mending ploughs and so on; the last four were normally on outside jobs, on pumps for wells – outside work of all kinds.[159]

In their capacity as farriers the smiths were also required to treat animals which fell ill, while through their skills in shoeing they could correct faults in a horse's feet. Good feet were considered the first essential for a working horse, and it was not uncommon for farmers to ask for a smith's professional opinion before making a purchase.

Surviving account books confirm the close links between farmer and smith, whilst some of the major cultivators in the eastern counties, with large arable holdings and numerous horse-teams, would employ a full-time worker of their own.[208] The following extracts show the varied jobs carried out for a Gloucestershire farmer late in 1904 by George Amos, a blacksmith from Weston-sub-Edge in that county:[1]

November 25	1 lb. Tar	4d.
	Repair manure drag	6d.
26	4 Removes (i.e. the shoes had been taken off, the hooves trimmed, and the shoes replaced]	1s. 4d.
	Work to Sawbench	6d.
	Mending saucepan	3d.
28	4 Removes	1s. 4d.
	Rep. Ploughwheel & scraper	6d.
30	Frostnailing 6 shoes [carried out in icy weather to prevent the horse from slipping]	1s. 0d.
	2 shoes	1s. 4d.
	Rep. Plough	1s. 0d.
December 6	Work to cake crusher	6d.

Alongside these tasks, the blacksmith also satisfied the needs of fellow-villagers by making and repairing hoes, scythes and fagging hooks for the labourers, and inserting rings in the noses of cottagers' pigs to prevent them digging up the floors of the sties. Leaking kettles and pots and pans would be repaired for the housewives, while children would purchase iron hoops. Some men specialized in the production of edge tools, like scythes and billhooks, and would achieve a more than local reputation. And almost everywhere the smithy became a general meeting place for men to gossip about the affairs of the day as they waited for their horses to be attended to, or merely stood around watching with fascination as the blacksmith worked at his forge.[160]

Wheelwrights were equally involved in the agricultural scene, and in East Anglia it was common for blacksmiths and wheel-wrights to have their shops next door to one another, as a sign of the co-operation between the two trades. Neither horses nor waggons could be kept in good order without the help of the smith and the wheelwright. George Sturt, who took over the family wheelwright's business at Farnham in Surrey in 1884, stressed the local nature of most of the work carried out:

> Farmers rarely more than five miles away; millers, brewers, a local grocer or builder or timber-merchant or hop-grower – for such and no other did the ancient shop still cater, as it had done for nearly two centuries. And so we got curiously intimate with the peculiar needs of the neighbourhood. In farm-waggon or dung-cart, barley-roller, plough, water-barrel, or what not, the dimensions we chose, the curves we followed . . . were imposed upon us by the nature of the soil in this or that farm, the gradient of this or that hill, the temper of this or that customer or his choice perhaps in horseflesh. . . . To satisfy the carter, we gave another half-inch of curve to the waggon-bottom, altered the hooks for harness on the shafts, hung the water-barrel an inch nearer to the horse or an inch farther away, according to requirements. . . . The field, the farm-yard, the road and hills, the stress of weather, the strength and shape of horses, the lifting power of men, all were factors which had determined in the old villages how the farm tackle must be made, of what timber and shape and of what dimensions, often to the sixteenth of an inch.[262]

He emphasized, too, the importance which the men attached to doing their job in a proper manner, using appropriate materials. They knew the circumstances of each customer, understood his carters and his horses and the character of his land, and took pride in satisfying his specific needs.

The saddler, the hurdle-maker and the carpenter were other craftsmen who were closely linked to the farming round. The saddler produced collars and harness for the horses, as well as headstalls, halters, horse-covers, and the plough-reins or cords which were made from hemp. Later, when the self-binder harvesting machines came into use, some saddlers repaired the canvas conveyor-belts which delivered the sheaf of corn after it had been tied. Carpenters had much domestic work to carry out, repairing and constructing window frames, doors and cupboards, or mending furniture, but they, too, were likely to gain the greater part of their livelihood from the farms. There were always gates to make, outbuildings to repair and cow-cribs, sheep troughs and ladders to produce. Often the men had to work out in the fields, mending gates and the like, and they would go to their task carrying a large basket, lined with canvas, in which were stored their tools, a pot of grease for the saw, and a file to sharpen it. During the winter months, as the Buckinghamshire carpenter Walter Rose recalled, the making of field gates provided a 'fall-back job' in the workshop, at a time when other assignments were in short supply. In those days the making of a gate 'was considered a day's work for a qualified carpenter, and was expected to be done in the ten hours which . . . constituted a day of labour'. And he added significantly: 'No one ever suggested that it was possible to make one in less time!'[242]

Traditional attitudes to work were, indeed, characteristic of most village tradesmen in the Victorian era, and often son would succeed father at the same forge or workbench. It was an approach which the apprenticeship system did much to reinforce. In trades like those of blacksmith, wheelwright and carpenter this normally meant a learning period of at least five years, at the end of which a practical test had to be passed. Then, as George Sturt noted of his own trade, the newcomers were expected 'to live up to the local wisdom of our kind; to follow the customs, and work to the measurements, which had been tested and corrected long before our time in every village shop all across the country'.[262] Experimentation was discouraged and 'reasoned science' firmly ignored. There was also a strong pride in the craft and a spirit of friendly rivalry towards those with competing occupations. Wheelwrights, for example, held the view that while anyone who could make a wheel knew enough to be a carpenter, a carpenter could not do a wheelwright's work, for want of training.

Alongside the craftsmen whose primary concern was with the agricultural needs of the community were those whose main interest lay in meeting the personal wants of the villagers themselves. They included bakers, butchers, tailors, and boot and shoemakers. The butchers, who normally bought and sold their meat locally, also made large quantities of lard and dripping for sale to their poorer customers. These would arrive at the counter bringing their bowls and basins to be filled, for hot dripping toast was considered a great treat in many labouring households. As for the bakers, although a number of country people made at least some of their own bread, scarcity of fuel and the lack of suitable ovens in many cottages ensured that they enjoyed a profitable business in most parishes. The bread was usually sold in 2 lb or 4 lb loaves, made from stone-ground flour, and the baking itself was carried out in a brick-built, domed oven, whose tiled floor was heated either by a furnace or by faggots of wood burnt on the floor of the oven. When the correct temperature had been reached, the baker would carefully remove the glowing embers and wipe down the floor with a damp cloth, before slipping in the loaves. Afterwards, when the bread was ready, the baker often allowed housewives to take their pies, cakes and stews to be cooked in the residual heat. Or perhaps, as at Akeley in Buckinghamshire, the ovens would be lit specially on Sunday mornings so that Sunday dinners could be cooked, for the modest charge of 1½d.

The village boot-maker was another familiar figure. Already cheap mass-produced footwear was appearing in the shops, but many local men managed to hold their own, at least to the end of the century (see Table 7, p. 139). Orders for boots were usually arranged to coincide with the additional harvest earnings of labouring families, and the more astute shoemakers adjusted their work pattern accordingly. Often they would make a number of pairs in advance, on the understanding that the bill would be settled after harvest. At Haddenham there was even a special celebratory supper arranged for those making the harvest payments, when they would feast together 'to the honour of the boots' that the shoemaker had produced.[243] Whilst they were new their leather was very stiff and extremely uncomfortable to wear, until softened by liberal applications of oil.

Tailors, sitting cross-legged on their benches, made anything from the breeches, jackets and overcoats worn by farmers to the heavy cord trousers and sleeved waistcoats favoured by their labourers. Orders for these would also be placed at harvest time, and one Suffolk tailor recalled travelling out from his workshop to the outlying districts to arrange special harvest sales. He took a large quantity of merchandise with him and would hire a club-room in a country pub in which to conduct sales. Business began in leisurely fashion with a drink in the tap-room. Then the men strolled in and ordered what they wanted – cord trousers, shirts, waistcoats, and probably 'a little bit of best wear: black jacket and waistcoat and a muffler. . . . We used to have these mufflers in all colours of the rainbow'.[160] Tailors rarely made clothing for the women, for if a wife could not make her own, and perhaps those of her children, she would turn to one of the dressmakers who were to be found in all but the tiniest of villages.

The kind of clothes worn was regarded as an indicator of social status. Most labouring men wore corduroys but, according to Walter Rose, at Haddenham painters were regarded as the 'aristocrats of the crafts' because their work was lighter, and 'they wore cloth trousers'.[243] Likewise all 'respectable' persons would wear a head covering of some kind, however battered it might be.

A third category of tradespeople were the dealers. They ranged from rabbit-skin men, purchasing skins at cottage doors for twopence apiece, to the horse and cattle dealers and the drovers, who still plied their trade over short distances, despite the effect of the railways in taking away most of the long-distance traffic. Often, like some of the craftsmen mentioned earlier, they would have their fingers in a number of different pies, perhaps working part-time as labourers, or running a smallholding, or keeping a public house. One Kent horse dealer combined this with cultivating a thirty-acre farm, collecting poultry from neighbouring farmers for sale in Canterbury and London, purchasing pigs and bullocks to fatten for market, supplying ferrets for shipment to France, selling milk in the village, and dispensing 'Whitstable whelks at local fairs. He even found time to run a small hire service taking local residents to and from the station . . . and provided transport for weddings and funerals'.[283] Then there were the pedlars and hawkers, who brought to cottage and farmhouse doors anything from a reel of cotton or a length of tape, to pots and pans and oil for the lamps. In remote upland areas, where there were few shops, their arrival was warmly welcomed. Alison Uttley, who spent her childhood on an isolated farm in Derbyshire, recalled that every two months an elderly pedlar would visit the family 'bearing a basket of tinware on his head, bright nutmeg graters, kettles and dishes, scissors and colanders. Besides this he had a pack on his back containing coloured ribbons and cottons, combs, tapes, and all the odds and end of the truckster.'[291] When Alison's mother and her maid had completed their purchases, her mother would brew some tea and prepare slices of cold bacon on home-made bread for him to eat. After he had finished the simple meal he would examine any rabbit-skins they had, perhaps exchanging them for a sieve or a strainer. Sometimes he would also take an order for a length of material for a dress, or for a sunbonnet, which he would deliver the next time he called.

Similarly at Wood Norton, Norfolk, as late as 1910, people were regularly visited by an old man driving a donkey cart, in which he brought clean silver sea sand to sell to housewives for scouring pots and doorsteps and for spreading on the brick floors.

Carriers, too, played an important role in the retail chain. Not only did they collect poultry, eggs, fruit and dairy produce to sell in the nearest market town on behalf of the farmers, but they would also take shopping orders and passengers as well. At Austrey in Warwickshire it was the carrier's wife, Mrs Orton, who drove the covered cart each week the seven miles to Tamworth market. Her passengers, seated on benches placed across the cart, had to share their journey with ducks and hens, tied by the legs and placed in the front of the van, and with baskets of butter and eggs, packed in straw, which were stowed at the rear. In season, baskets of plums were also taken – all this produce being collected from local farmers. On their return in the afternoon these carriers, for a small payment, would deliver any merchandise ordered, and would also remit the cash obtained from sales of produce.[236] Usually carrier services would be arranged to coincide with market day in the principal town with which they communicated. During the 1880s country carriers entering Leicester made half of their weekly calls on Saturday, the town's main market day, and another 39 per cent on Wednesday, its second market day.[216] Sometimes, too, higgler-farmers who carried produce to market for themselves and their neighbours would bring coal as a cheap back-carriage; this would subsequently be sold in the parish.

Village shops also provided a valuable service at a time when, despite the railways and the advent of cheap bicycles, visits to a town were often difficult for labouring people to arrange. Their shelves were stocked with cheese, bacon, tea, butter, hogsheads of moist sugar, jars of treacle and canned goods, as well as a miscellany of drapery, matting, linoleum, ironmongery and candles. Surviving account books reveal the dire poverty of many of their customers, with some having the greatest difficulty in paying off even small debts. Joseph Arch complained in the 1870s that farm workers were 'nearly always in debt to the shop a week a-head', but there were some who allowed their debts to run on far longer than that. The accounts of a shopkeeper from Bletchley, Buckinghamshire, show that one customer bought an overcoat for £1 7s. 6d. in November 1880, for which he made a down payment of 2s. 6d. By early December he had paid a further 5s., leaving £1 owing. Then on the 18th of that month he added to the debt by purchasing a blue serge jacket for 4s. 6d. and two pairs of hose for 3s. 1d. Not until April 1881 were these debts settled. However, within a week he again owed the shopkeeper 9s. 6d. for a pair of 'Cord Trowsers' purchased on credit. His first payment towards the cost of these (2s. 6d.) came six months later, and it took a full year, until April 1882, for this item to be finally cleared. More pathetic were cases like that of 'old Robert Jones', who spent 3s. 7½d. in July 1881 on pigs' feet, a length of shirting, and some other small items. He was able to put down only 3s. in cash and the remaining 7½d. was not cleared until the following September. In other instances, where farmers and fellow-tradespeople dealt with the shop, a barter system prevailed. Butter and eggs were purchased from the farmers, and in return they were provided with groceries and drapery. But this Bletchley shopkeeper appears to have been more fortunate than a Devon colleague, who had to accept fowls, ducks, turkeys, bushels of oats, bundles of straw, and even potatoes from his smallholder customers in order to cover their debts. In the case of one client, who owed £7 11s. 2d. in 1901, the man's wife altered suits, and made trousers, shirts and frocks for members of the shopkeeper's family in order to reduce the debt. By the end of 1904 her efforts had brought down the sum owing to £5 7s.; nine years later, it had been reduced still further to £1 5s. 4d. At that stage the shopkeeper seems to have tired of the whole business, since the smallholder's name disappeared from the list of debtors, even though there is no evidence that any further payment was made.[207]

Alongside these more general trades and crafts, there were those which were associated with a particular locality, perhaps on account of its soil and climate or because of the crops which were grown. Quarrying and stone-dressing provide obvious examples of the first type, as does brickmaking, which in country areas was frequently combined with agriculture. For farmers were well placed to exploit the clay found on their own land, and of forty-six master brickmakers working in Buckinghamshire in 1903, at least eight were also farmers.

Among the crafts associated with produce grown in a particular area were the chair-making trade of the Chilterns and basket-making and hurdle-making in parts of Oxfordshire and Berkshire. All were concentrated in woodland districts. In Berkshire, it was quite common for a hurdle-maker-cum-thatcher, once he had amassed sufficient funds, to rent a copse, for which he would pay 5s. in the £ at the time of hiring and the remaining 15s. at the end of the year, when his wares had been sold. The winter months were spent in cutting and sorting the wood, disposing of the waste as firewood and pea sticks, while the larger poles were sold to turners or made into hurdles and similar products. Often he would also work at the busy seasons on the land until his business had expanded sufficiently to permit him to devote himself to it full-time.[284] In the Lake District, where similar arrangements applied, the principal goods made were clogs and oak-spelk baskets, known locally as swills, which were manufactured from shaven strips of wood and were used for household, farm and garden purposes. The stripping of oak-bark for use in tanneries was a further industry associated with the swill trade.[163]

Yet another variation on this theme is described in Thomas Hardy's novel *The Woodlanders*, whereby George Melbury, a timber, bark, and copse-ware merchant, entered into an informal partnership with a young man who specialized in the apple and cider trade. The bulk of the work in the timber trade came in the spring, while the main requirements of the apple and cider trade, as regards cartage and other activities, came in the autumn. So horses, waggons, and even workers were lent to the younger man when the apples began to fall, while he, in return, helped Melbury at the busiest wood-cutting season.

In the hop-growing districts of Kent, Herefordshire and Worcestershire there was scope for other specialities. No crop needed so much attention throughout the year as the hop, in digging, poling, wiring, training, shimming, manuring, weeding, washing and picking, this latter continuing as a hand task until after the Second World War.[283] The pickers themselves normally came from the large towns, although they were supplemented by local people, especially women and children. The regular workers on a farm usually did no picking, but took over specialist tasks on a contract basis, such as those of binmen, or pole pullers, who hoisted the hop bines down so that the pickers could work on them. Each group of pickers would be assigned a bin, and four or sometimes five times a day the measurer would come round to record their pickings. These would then be carried away to the oast house for drying. That process was particularly skilled, and the men concerned with it would live in the oast house for six days a week, snatching their sleep when they could, cooking their food outside to avoid contaminating the hops with smoke, and drinking copious quantities of beer provided by their employer. Special equipment was required, including bine knives for cutting down the hops for the pickers, drying forks, hop shovels, and the 'pokes' used to carry the hops from the bins to the kilns, the manufacture of these forming another minor local industry. On a more general level 'hopping' also stimulated other trades. In Kent, it was customary for village stores to stock up with extra food in readiness for the arrival of the 'foreign' pickers, and extra assistants were engaged to serve the additional customers and to keep an eye on them to make sure that they did not steal anything. Bakers gained, too, not only by their extra bread sales but by roasting the pickers' Sunday joints in their ovens for a small charge. During the season normally peaceful village streets were thronged with people, after work at night and at the weekends. According to one local farmer it was almost impossible to get up Goudhurst high street on a Saturday night![292]

* * *

So far, the country trades and crafts have been considered in static terms, as if their role and importance remained unchanged during the late nineteenth century. But, of course, that was far from the case. As Table 7 shows, there were sharp falls in the totals of those engaged in many of the occupations. In Cumberland the number of wheelwrights, for example, fell by two-thirds between 1871 and 1901, while that of shoemakers more than halved. In Hereford-shire and Devon, similarly dramatic declines in those groups are recorded. In some counties (e.g. Cumberland) the figures may be distorted by the requirements of local manufacturing or mining industries. This applied to Cumbrian blacksmiths, who were needed by the iron industry as well as by agriculture. Similarly, predominantly arable counties such as Essex were likely to have more millers than Herefordshire and Cumberland, where the grain harvest was of minor significance. And Westmorland farmers, with their sheep farming preoccupations and rugged terrain, were likely to have relatively little need for the waggons and carts and other equipment which were the stock-in-trade of the wheelwright. Nevertheless, important though these regional differences were, they could not disguise the overall process of change and decline which was under way in many crafts. It is to that process that we must now turn.

One of the prime factors behind the new situation was the influence of urban technology and the way in which, as a result of an improved transport network, the output of town factories could be sent quickly and cheaply to country districts. In some cases old-established products were replaced by new ones, like the metal buckets which took over from wooden pails, or the oil lamps which were substituted for candles in room lighting. From Wiltshire there were reports in the 1890s of the work of hurdle-makers being made obsolete by a wider use of barbed wire, and that of coopers by the greater sales of galvanized utensils of all kinds. The farming press began to include advertisements like that of a Wol-verhampton firm which offered iron sheep hurdles 'from 30s. per dozen; Cattle Hurdles five bars, from 39s. 6d. per dozen, delivered free. . . . Specially low prices quoted on application for all kinds of Fencing, Hurdles, Palisading, Gates, Tree Guards, Poultry Houses, Tanks, Troughs, &c.' Not surprisingly, the number of men engaged in making wooden fences and hurdles fell nationally from 3,014 in 1871 to 2,232 thirty years later. Similarly, as the slate

*Table 7   Employment in Crafts and Trades in Selected Counties –
1871 and 1901*

N.B. The 1871 total relates to all ages; that for 1901 is concerned
with those aged ten and above

Male occupations	Year	Essex	Berk-shire	Westmor-land	Devon	Hereford	Cumber-land
Wheelwrights	1871	911	407	26	921	351	64
	1901	1,058	242	34	790	269	21
Saddlers, &c.	1871	416	261	60	503	92	174
	1901	725	254	56	482	88	160
Blacksmiths*	1871	2,066	1,092	358	3,485	764	1,385
	1901	3,524	1,105	286	2,834	575	1,433
Millers	1871	1,045	410	111	1,151	287	419
	1901	760	242	54	681	181	268
Tailors	1871	1,120	922	425	3,302	599	1,403
	1901	693	943	288	2,842	362	1,107
Shoemakers	1871	2,863	1,647	724	5,782	989	1,665
	1901	3,478	683	572	2,621	373	717

Female occupations	Year	Bucks	Berk-shire	Westmor-land	Devon	Hereford	Cumber-land
Straw plaiters	1871	3,412	44	11	84	14	26
	1901	173	–	–	–	–	–
Lacemakers	1871	8,077	38	–	4,342	–	1
	1901	789	9	1	1,524	1	–
Dressmaking & tailoring**	1871	1,837	2,886	822	12,730	1,562	3,163
	1901	1,969	3,630	762	11,887	1,185	3,738
Gloving	1871	3	16	–	2,428	379	2
	1901	–	3	–	447	14	–

* The increase in blacksmiths in some counties is probably attributable to their greater employment in urban foundries and engineering workshops.
** Includes milliners in 1871.

The number of women employed in cottage industries is likely to be an under-estimate since many part-time workers did not declare their occupation.
From 1871 and 1901 *Census Reports.*

---

industry grew and tile manufacture developed, so the need for
skilled thatchers diminished, while galvanized sheeting was used
on the roofs of farm buildings. Midlands manufacturers offered
'Iron Thatch Substitute, Great Straw & Labour Saver' for ricks,
and there was a growing demand for Dutch barns. Nationally, the
number of thatchers dropped from about 4,140 in 1871 to 3,210 in
1891. Thatching had been a craft traditionally concentrated in the
southern and western counties of England and in East Anglia, and

as Chartres and Turnbull point out, these were all 'maritime areas and thus vulnerable to the penetration of rival and simpler roofing materials'.[216]

Even George Sturt, in his old-fashioned wheelwright's shop at Farnham, felt the pressures of competition by the late 1880s:

> Now, discontented customers would buy 'steam wheels' from London. Lighter wheels than any that could be made in my shop – wheels imported ready-made from America – had to be kept in stock along with the ancient sort of naves and felloes.[262]

Eventually, in 1889, Sturt decided to install modern machinery, purchasing power-driven saws, lathe, drill and grindstone, while wooden axles were replaced by case-hardened iron arms. The firm also changed over to the manufacture of trade-vans and carts, as the agricultural side of the business dwindled; 'from the first day the machines began running', wrote Sturt, 'the use of axes and adzes disappeared . . . the saws and saw-pit became obsolete. We forgot what chips were like'.

Other men, such as George Ford, son of a wheelwright from Newborough in Staffordshire, transferred their business to a nearby town in order to operate on a larger scale. In Ford's case this meant moving to Burton-upon-Trent, where by the 1880s he was running a flourishing concern, providing fencing for nearby landed estates, as well as a wide range of waggons, carts and brewery drays. He also established a substantial timber merchant's business. But men who were unable or unwilling to respond to the altered circumstances in this fashion simply left the trade or were driven out.

Millers were hit especially hard by the decline in wheat-growing in England, as well as by the erection of large steam-powered mills at the ports to grind the increasing quantities of imported grain, and by the introduction, between 1875 and 1885, of a new system of grinding by steel rollers, instead of mill-stones. Nearly all the millers who remained at the end of the century survived primarily by turning out meal and feeding stuffs for farm livestock rather than flour for human consumption, though some English flour was still used in the biscuit trade. Manufacturers tried to ease their problems by offering 'improved machinery', with one firm in 1890 boldly advising 'any miller who finds the competition from the roller mills becoming too keen,' to contact 'users of our Combination Plants, who are now able to hold their own. Small Miller's Plant, £120'.[45] But such initiatives clearly had little success, and the number of millers in rural counties like Berkshire, Devon, Norfolk and Cumberland fell by about one-third between 1871 and 1901, and in Westmorland by more than that amount (see Table 7).

Elsewhere, blacksmiths found their position as makers of farm implements eroded by the competition of specialist manufacturers, such as the Taskers of Andover, Hampshire and the Ransomes of Ipswich, or by smaller firms like the Cameron-Rumsbys of Bungay, Suffolk. Already by the late 1860s Taskers were turning out drills, winnowing machines, cake crushers, turnip cutters, portable mills for grinding corn, straw elevators, threshing machines, mowing machines, reapers and self-rakers, and even waggons. They produced a wide range of metal ploughs, and thousands of ploughshares of different types were always kept in stock. 'On one day of the week at least, the foundry concentrated on the moulding and casting of shares and as many as 116 dozen were cast in one day by a gang of ten men, who were paid at the rate of 4½d. per dozen for their day's work.'[240] Depots were established in the larger towns of the locality, with the firm having stores in both Salisbury and Winchester, which they serviced with waggon-loads of replacements each week.

At Bungay, a member of the Cameron-Rumsby firm recalled how on market days his father would take some of the stock – smaller items like ploughshares and coulters – and lay them out in front of the King's Head inn for customers' inspection. It was the son's job to deliver any items ordered to the various public houses where the farmers had put up their horse and trap whilst they attended the market.[161]

Faced with competition of this kind, a number of blacksmiths decided to take up agencies for the bigger firms, but many others preferred to concentrate on the more mundane activities of shoeing horses and carrying out repairs. In the early twentieth century a few, greatly daring, began to paint above their shop doors a sign proclaiming 'Motor Repairs a Speciality'.

Apart from the effects of technological change, a second problem faced by country tradesmen was the decline in the size of the rural population itself. Villages which had once been large enough to support three or four shoemakers, half a dozen carpenters and two blacksmiths now found business for one or two men only. And with the decrease in their numbers came important social changes as well. For tradesmen were more likely to have moved *into* a village, thereby introducing new ideas and customs, than were the agricultural labourers. At Elmdon in Essex only about one-third of the tradesmen in mid-Victorian times had been born in the village, compared to nearly 90 per cent of the male agricultural labourers. Similarly, of seventeen tradesmen (wheel-wrights, carpenters, blacksmiths, harness-makers and millers) working in Great Horwood, Buckinghamshire, in 1871, less than a third had been born within the parish, whereas three-quarters of the labourers had. The census returns of other villages confirm that this pattern was normal.

Craftsmen were important, too, for the social leadership they provided. The radicalness of village shoemakers was notorious, while the blacksmith's shop, as we have seen, often acted as an informal discussion centre as well as a place of work. Richard Lloyd of Llanystumdwy in North Wales, the shoemaker uncle of David Lloyd George, provides a case in point. He presided over the village debating society which used to meet in the blacksmith's shop, and was much respected in the neighbourhood for his wisdom and integrity.[173] He was a master craftsman, employing at least two hands in his workshop, and men such as he, running their own small businesses, had an independence of outlook which was absent among most of their labouring counterparts. With the decline in their numbers and influence there was a danger, as one writer has put it, that the rural population would be 'composed entirely of farmers and farm labourers', and that 'the affairs of the village [would] be governed entirely according to the farmers' interests'.

But one of the main blows to the prosperity of the country craftsmen was the agricultural depression itself. Farmers were reluctant to place orders for new goods, and slow to pay for them when they did. In Spetember 1881 the *Banbury Guardian* high-lighted this problem when it commented on the bad state of trade among retail drapers in the town:

> Banbury is the centre of an agricultural district . . . and, as several hundred carriers' carts come in every week from the surrounding neighbourhood, very few towns can equal it in this

respect. Trade, however, has sadly declined during the long continuance of the agricultural depression, and property has greatly fallen in value.

Even the larger firms, especially those concerned with the agricultural implements trade, were not immune. At Dorchester, Francis Eddison saved his newly established steam plough works from collapse only by turning over to road-rollers, while at Andover the Taskers decided to form a limited liability company in 1896 in an effort to save themselves. They also began to hire out their machines to users, as a number of other agricultural engineering firms were doing, but in their case it proved a disaster. Sales fell still further, and the firm went into liquidation in 1903.[240] It was subsequently revived in 1907 under new management, though its financial problems remained up to the First World War – perhaps because it persisted in hiring out machinery. Likewise at Banbury, Bernhard Samuelson's once flourishing Britannia Works was forced to lay off a large part of its workforce in 1879/80. In 1885, Samuelson confessed to a local audience that 'if he had not laid something by for "a rainy day" he might have been in the Bankruptcy Court now'. Not until the late 1880s did the firm's position ease, as certain of the more optimistic farmers at last began to buy 'the self-binders and improved drills they had so often contemplated'.[263]

Elsewhere large firms like the Ransomes (with a labour force of 2,500 in 1911) turned increasingly to export markets. By 1913 more than 70 per cent of British agricultural machinery production was exported, mostly to Eastern Europe and the Empire. The Ransomes, for example, spent a great deal of energy in perfecting threshing machines for the Russian market, and in sending ploughs to the less agriculturally developed parts of British Africa.[168] Between 1900 and 1914 the export trade of this firm grew by 130 per cent, by which time in some classes of machinery about 98 per cent of total production was being sent abroad. Clearly, small firms concentrating on the home market were not equipped to take advantage of these foreign outlets, and they were particular victims of the agricultural depression.

A final difficulty for the small producer and village craftsman was that all too often their financial management and costing systems were as primitive as were those of the farmers. George

Sturt recalled that when he started up in the mid-1880s he priced the work by reference to his father's and grandfather's charges, which had themselves been established by tradition: 'On the subject of profits other tradesmen in the district were as ignorant and simple as myself . . . I doubt if there was a tradesman in the district – I am sure there was no wheelwright – who really knew what his output cost, or what his profits were, or if he was making money or losing it on any particular job.' Bills were sent out once a year, at around Christmas time, the idea being that farmers might have money at that season. At Farnham, 'it was worth while to ask for money then – so soon after the hop-fair at Weyhill in October'.[262] In the meantime, thanks to this dilatory system of submitting accounts, the craftsman was providing free credit to farmers for months on end. All his spare capital was tied up in outstanding debts and often he could not afford to modernize his operations, or even to carry the spare parts and stores which he needed to run his business efficiently. Both factors added to his difficulties.

The change in the structure of community life which the decline in country crafts brought about was underlined by Miller Christy in 1907. His comments related to Essex, but could have been applied equally well to most other counties.

Sixty years ago, there were in all our . . . towns – even in the smaller ones – fell-mongers, tanners, curriers, tallow-chandlers, soap-boilers, dealers in British wines, breeches-makers, boot-makers, glovers, stay-makers, mantua-makers, hatters, sack-makers, patten-makers, clock-makers, tinmen, and many others, all selling goods made actually by themselves or by their own workmen on their own premises. The number of workmen employed by each master-worker was small, but collectively the employés were numerous and all received comparatively good wages, while they and their families contributed largely to the life and prosperity of the town or village in which they lived.[225]

But by the early twentieth century, many of these local and regional markets had disappeared or had been sharply reduced, and had been replaced by a national network organized on mass-production lines.

Some of those following more specialized trades, like those of millwright or cooper, which were being squeezed out by competition from the machines, sought to meet the challenge by diversifying into general crafts, like those of carpenter and joiner. But in the long run they too came under pressure from mass-production techniques. As Chartres and Turnbull point out, Victorian England 'thus saw both the peak and the transformation of the craft activities of the countryside'.[216]

Alongside this, there was a gradual deterioration in labour relations. With the greater use of machinery, the pressures of difficult economic circumstances and a growing awareness on the part of many workers of conditions in the wider world, masters and men became alienated from one another. Partly this was because the men wanted to have a greater say in the running of their working lives, and partly because the introduction of machinery in even relatively small workshops undermined many traditional craft attitudes. As early as January 1891, George Sturt recorded in his journal that the men in his shop were demanding shorter hours, to match those of a firm of coachbuilders in the town. Reluctantly he agreed, and at the same time introduced a system of time sheets for the men – though he considered the whole business of time sheets contemptible. More than thirty years later, when he came to publish *The Wheelwright's Shop*, his concern at these changing attitudes had strengthened. Despite the mixture of sentimentality and paternalism which he displays, there is more than a grain of truth in his comments on the differences in working practices:

> In what was once the wheelwright's shop, where Englishmen grew friendly with the grain of timber and with sharp tools, nowadays untrained youths wait upon machines, hardly knowing oak from ash or caring for the qualities of either . . . . In modern conditions work is nothing like so tolerable as it was say thirty years ago; partly because there is more hurry in it, but largely because machinery has separated employers from employed and has robbed the latter of the sustaining delights which materials used to afford to them. . . . Is there – it is worth asking – such laughter about labour, such fun, such gamesome good temper, as cheered the long hours in my shop in 1884?

Meanwhile, the problems faced by so many country tradesmen also applied to the majority of cottage industries. Some, like domestic lacemaking and straw-plaiting, which were largely concentrated in the south midlands, succumbed to the twin pressures of competition and fashion changes. In the case of pillow lacemaking, which was done by women and children, the problems stemmed from cheap machine-made goods, coupled with new fashions, which called for a less expensive article than real lace. For plaiting the danger lay in cheap imports from Italy, China and Japan. Here the collapse came rapidly during the 1870s and 1880s. In Essex, for example, there were 2,889 engaged in the trade in 1871; a decade later, they had dwindled to 930; and in 1901 no one at all was recorded as being so employed. As early as 1881, a visitor to the county had observed that it was followed by a few women only, who were 'seated on the cottage steps or leaning against the doors or garden gates, busily twisting the straws . . . they told me it was starving work, and the price per score [i.e. per 20 yards] was getting worse and worse. They said they only did a little at odd times because they could get nothing else to do. They are not bringing their girls up to it.'[225]

Buckinghamshire and Bedfordshire, two of the major plaiting centres, suffered a similar fate. The industry was, indeed, particularly important in the latter county, where it supplied the hat and bonnet trade of Luton and Dunstable. In 1871 it was estimated that nearly one in three of all Bedfordshire girls aged from ten to fifteen was a plaiter, while there were 20,701 female workers of all ages in the county engaged upon the trade. Thirty years later that total had dwindled to a mere 485. In Buckinghamshire the respective figures were 3,412 and 173. And whereas at the height of the trade it was possible for a wife and children engaged upon plaiting to earn more than the husband of the family, if he were an agricultural labourer earning a basic wage of 12s. a week, by the end of the century 'much labour' was needed 'to earn very few shillings'. Certainly not many were prepared to emulate the single-minded determination of a woman from Aston Clinton in Buckinghamshire, who made twenty score of plait in one week, for which she received the relatively high price of 1s. a score. To achieve this she sat up in bed at four in the morning each day, so that she could plait for an hour or two before rising.

With the decline in the cottage plait and lace trades there was also a loss of business for the specialists who had made the equipment they used, such as the bobbins, patterns, and pillows for lace making and the splitters and plait mills used for straw-plaiting.

However, whilst most observers recognized that it was mechanization and competition which had destroyed these domestic crafts, a few critics attributed at least part of their demise to the effects of new factory and education legislation enacted during the 1860s and 1870s. It was claimed that these measures, by protecting children from early employment had deprived them of the chance to acquire the dexterity needed to produce the best work in later life. This applied particularly to lacemaking, plaiting and glovemaking, where it had long been the custom to send children as young as four or five years of age to so-called 'schools', where they would be taught the rudiments of the craft under conditions of strict discipline; academic instruction was almost entirely neglected. Then in 1867 came the Workshops Regulation Act, which fixed eight as the minimum age of employment for any child engaged in a domestic industry; in 1878 this was raised to ten. Between the ages of eight (or ten) and thirteen a boy or girl could be employed only in accordance with the half-time system already used in the factories. In other words, each child must attend an approved elementary school for at least ten hours per week, between 8 a.m. and 6 p.m., and must obtain a certificate from the teacher stating that this had been done.

Initially the legislation proved difficult to enforce, especially as responsibility for its implementation was put into the hands of the local police and sanitary authorities. Not until 1871/72, when the Factory Inspectorate took over, did conditions slowly improve. However, as late as 1875 a critic from Crewkerne in Somerset wrote bitterly of conditions in local gloving 'schools':

Children begin to learn gloving at a *very* early age, not unfrequently at six years of age. They generally became 'learners' at the house of a 'teacher', and serve a sort of apprenticeship, earning at first nothing, but are allowed a few pence per week as they become able to improve themselves. The house of the teacher is almost always an ordinary small cottage, and containing only one sitting-room with one window. . . . For the sake of the light children in winter have to sit as close to this window as possible, and this place of work is generally in the line between the outer door and the fire, between which there is necessarily a

147

through draught. The floor is mostly mud or stone, and their shoes not being of the best, their feet are seldom warm . . . in cold weather, notwithstanding all ventilation is prevented in order to keep out the cold air, their feet are numbed by the cold, and their hands rendered incapable of working from time to time by contact with the brasswork of the gloving machines . . . it is not surprising that young children should soon begin to suffer in health, and their feet get crippled with broken chilblains often leading to bad ulcers on the toes. Colds, coughs, consumption, and anaemic diseases are very prevalent, while from the close attention required for some kinds of work, and the strain on the eyes being kept up for so many hours, the sight frequently becomes impaired.[72]

Skin diseases were also alarmingly widespread, while the hours of work extended from 5 a.m. to 7 or 8 p.m. during the busy seasons. In country villages in south Somerset, it was said, 'there is no compulsory education, and often no sufficient inducement to voluntary education, where the earning of a few pence is an object to a family'.

Conditions in the lace and plait 'schools' were similar. In one Essex establishment, during 1874 a factory inspector discovered thirty-six children crammed into a single small cottage room, and such conditions were by no means unusual.[73] Often, too, the children would slip out through the back door when anyone in authority called at the 'schools', thereby defeating the object of the inspector's visit, while the number plaiting at home was too great to be dealt with by the Factory Inspectorate or the police.

A further unsatisfactory aspect of the domestic trades was the prevalence of the 'truck' system within them, with workers paid partly in cash and partly in kind. Although such practices were illegal cottage workers, employed in scattered communities and with no central organizing agency, were poorly placed to enforce their right to money payments. In the lace trade around Honiton in Devon, a large dealer frankly admitted to one of the factory inspectors that 'about 10 per cent of his payments were in tea or some other commodity, and that payments made entirely in money were extremely exceptional'. According to this inspector it was common to see, in the windows of village shops in South Devon, pieces of fine lace lying alongside 'packets of dips and bottles of brandy balls. . . . These the shopkeeper will have taken from the workers in exchange for his groceries, &c. I am told that where money alone passes the price given is considerably lowered, and that the worse the state of trade the greater the amount of truck'.[72] In such circumstances, it was hardly surprising that lacemakers' earnings were put at a pathetic 1d. or 2d. per hour.[163]

Only when the domestic trades themselves declined did these abuses at last disappear. Although, as regards the children, an important contributory factor in that process was the passage of fresh education legislation, notably the Act of 1880, which imposed compulsory school attendance on every child at least to the age of ten.

Not all domestic industries, however, did vanish at the end of the nineteenth century. Even in the case of lacemaking, efforts were made by middle-class sponsors to preserve craft skills through the creation of specialist associations. The first to be established was the Midlands Lace Association, formed in 1891; it was followed six years later by the North Bucks Lace Association, and then by the Bedford Lace Education Committee, which received a County Council grant from 1907. By the early twentieth century the North Bucks Association alone was employing some three hundred makers and had established classes for children and young girls in various centres. Its main objective was to ensure that high-quality work was produced which could be disposed of to the workers' best advantage, usually from depots in London.[216] But in the long run, the associations did little to arrest the decline of the trade.

A rather more successful survivor was the netmaking or 'braid-ing' industry carried on around Bridport in Dorset. Before the First World War there was no satisfactory machine able to make nets with square meshes, or those whose meshes varied in size within the same net, and here the cottage workers were able to make their contribution. Individual villages specialized in a parti-cular kind of net, and the twine was given out by the Bridport mills; it was brought to the villages by carriers, who returned the finished products to the factory. Despite complaints from adult workers that school regulations prevented the children from learning the craft at a sufficiently early age, the industry continued to prosper until 1914, and to export its nets to fishing communities all over the country.

Ready-made clothing was a third home industry which survived into the late Victorian and Edwardian period. Two areas around which it was concentrated were Ipswich in Suffolk and Colchester in Essex, with garments sent out either from London or from factories established in the respective towns. The clothing was made up by cottagers' wives, most of whom owned their own sewing machines, and the firms benefited from the cheap labour available.[225] In 1893, the Factory Inspectorate estimated that there were nearly three thousand outworkers employed in the garment trade around Colchester alone. Elsewhere, in parts of Buckinghamshire, 'beadwork' took over from plaiting and lacemaking as a domestic task, with women sewing black glass beads on to silk to ornament ladies' dresses for the London fashion trade. And at Cottenham, Cambridgeshire, labourers' wives worked during the summer months in the market gardens and spent the winter sewing swansdown on to calico, also for the dress trade.[171] In Cumberland a number of women were occupied in making rag mats and knitting quilt counterpanes on frames, while in Somerset, despite the unsatisfactory circumstances of the domestic glove trade, many women and girls continued to be employed in it until 1914. The work was brought to their homes by a 'bag woman', who was responsible for returning it to the factory when it was completed.

Yet, however important these industries may have been within their own particular communities, their *overall* significance in no way matched that of the domestic industries of earlier decades. Centralization of production in factories and the influence of technological change ensured that their contribution now was a peripheral one only.

If the years between 1870 and 1914 saw a decline in the numbers of country craftsmen and domestic workers, in almost every village there still remained a core of tradespeople who supplied the general needs of the community. For more expert services, such as those of doctors, solicitors, bankers and auctioneers, villagers normally had to turn to the country towns. With their markets and fairs, their varied shops, and their professional men these acted as service centres for a 'rural hinterland of perhaps no more than three or four miles in radius'.[216] Thame in Oxfordshire, with a population of 3,334 in 1891, provides one example of the range of

3 'A Country Cricket Match at Ashington, Sussex'

4 Members of the Women's Land Army

businesses available in even a comparatively small community. In the mid-1890s its inhabitants included four doctors, two chemists, two brewers, a veterinary surgeon, a newspaper proprietor, five insurance agents, three solicitors, four auctioneers and estate agents, an umbrella maker, a photographer, and the proprietor of a private school. Craftsmen, shopkeepers and dealers abounded – there were four corn factors and six dress- and mantle-makers alone, as well as fourteen publicans, fourteen beer retailers, and four hotel-keepers.

Although the sophisticated city visitor was likely to find the wares offered in these towns old-fashioned and dowdy, to people used only to the familiar sights and sounds of their own village they seemed places of glamour and excitement. Flora Thompson, visiting Buckingham one Sunday in the mid-1880s from her Oxfordshire hamlet of Juniper Hill, remembered it as a 'large and grand' place, with its square 'where there were many large shop windows, . . . and a doctor's house with a red lamp over the gate, and a church with a tall spire, and women and girls in light summer frocks and men in smart straw boater-shaped hats'. Subsequent visits confirmed the picture, with Flora marvelling at 'the wax lady dressed in the height of fashion, with one of the new bustles, at the leading drapers; and the jeweller's window, sparkling with gold and silver and gems, and the toy shops and the sweet shops and, above all, the fishmonger's where a whole salmon reposed on a bed of green reeds with ice sprinkled over'.[268]

Professional services were important features of every country town, and were valued as such by those country visitors who had legal business to discuss, or an insurance policy to arrange, or perhaps the sale or valuation of property to consider. In agriculture the provisions of the 1883 Agricultural Holdings Act and its amendments increased the importance of the valuer when farms were changing hands. Whilst the problems of the depression in bringing about the bankruptcy or retirement of many farmers, whose property had then to be sold up, were other factors in the growing demand for the services of auctioneers and valuers. In October 1892 the *Mark Lane Express*, when describing the 'deplorable accounts of the number of farms that [were] being given up, in Hampshire and Berkshire, added sombrely: 'Every member of one large firm of auctioneers [was] last week engaged in valuations.' Many of the auctioneers were themselves farmers, or the sons of farmers, and were thus well equipped to acquire a broad knowledge of rural trends and to win the confidence of their agricultural clients.

Solicitors, too, had an important role to play in property dealings. Although by this time their activities as agents for landed estates had largely been taken over by specialists in that particular field, their other duties remained intact, as their growing numbers even in predominantly rural counties bore witness (see Table 8, page 154). To Richard Jefferies, indeed, the 'entire round' of rural life fell within their purview:

> The squire comes here about intricate concerns of family settlements which in their sphere are as hard to arrange as the diplomatic transactions of Governments. He comes about his tenants and his rents; he comes to get new tenants.
>
> The tenants resort to the solicitor for farms, for improvements, reductions, leases, to negotiate advances, to insure, for the various affairs of life. The clergyman comes on questions that arise out of his benefice, the churchyard, ecclesiastical privileges, the schools, and about his own private property. The labourer comes about his cottage and garden – an estate as important to him as his three thousand acres to the squire – or as a witness. The tradesman, the builder, the banker come for financial as well as legal objects. As the town develops, and plots are needed for houses and streets, the resort to the solicitor increases tenfold. Companies are formed and require his advice. Local Government needs his assistance. He may sit in an official position in the County Court, or at the bench of the Petty Sessions. . . . His widening circle of landlord clients have each their attendant circles of tenants, who feel confidence in their leader's legal adviser. Parochial officers come to him: overseer, rate-collector, churchwarden, tithing-man.
>
> The all-important work of registering voters fills up the space between one election and another. At the election his offices are like the head-quarters of an army. He may represent some ancient college or corporation with lands of vast extent. Ladies with a little capital go home content when he has invested their money in mortgage of real property.[196]

During the difficult depression years even solicitors found themselves under pressure, especially where they had become involved in making loans on landed estates. At Banbury, one firm of solicitors went bankrupt in April 1881 with liabilities of £66,500. According to the *Banbury Guardian* this had arisen on account of the 'losses and depreciation of value of assets, arising, no doubt, from the long-prevailing commercial and agricultural depression'. Two months later another solicitor in the town also failed, this time with liabilities of 'upwards of £30,000'.[263] Banbury's experience was certainly not unique. But these occasional difficulties in no way undermined the general high standing in which solicitors were held within the country town and its environs.

The same was true of the local banks, even though some smaller concerns suffered considerably during the final quarter of the nineteenth century. In the case of Gilletts' bank at Banbury, profits dropped by almost two-thirds between 1878 and 1884, and then continued at around that depressed level for the next few years. Despite this the banker, like the late Victorian solicitor, enjoyed an honoured position within the community, belonging to what Richard Jefferies called the 'carriage people' of the town. Some bankers, such as the Gilletts, also set social standards for their clients. At Banbury each customer was expected to take off his hat before he approached the counter, and anyone who forgot was likely to be gently reminded of his omission by a clerk. Smoking was not permitted and on more than one occasion, when a customer came in with cigar or pipe, the senior partner made him take it outside, saying that one did not smoke in 'a gentleman's bank'.[263]

Finally, in this list of 'professionals', there must be numbered the medical men. As a consequence of the provisions of the Medical Act of 1858 a system of registered practitioners had been established, to distinguish qualified doctors from the quacks who still clung on the fringes of the profession. In these circumstances, the number of practitioners increased, even in those rural areas like Herefordshire and Westmorland, where overall population levels were falling steadily from the 1870s to the First World War.

At the same time their growing expertise was reflected in developments like the cottage hospital movement, which was started by a general practitioner at Cranleigh in Surrey in 1859. By 1896 there were three hundred such hospitals at work in various parts of the country. Each was normally served by local doctors on

Table 8   Numbers of Barristers, Solicitors and Medical Men in Selected Counties: 1871 and 1901

Occupation	Year	Essex	Berk-shire	Westmor-land	Norfolk	Devon	Hereford	Cumber-land
Barrister &	1871	214	158	39	242	443	83	111
solicitors	1901	378	175	47	221	443	88	164
Physicians,	1871	256	180	44	235	518	70	116
surgeons &	1901	608	182	56	265	590	71	145
G Ps								

From the *Census Reports*

---

a rota system, and in this fashion contacts between the medical men of an area were promoted. Charitably supported nursing associations also provided trained care in the home in some areas, particularly for midwifery cases.

Nevertheless, despite these improvements, many country people chose to rely upon traditional herbal remedies or folk cures when they were ill. An Essex doctor remembered that among his patients bee stings were a popular cure for rheumatism, while mustard plasters and chilli paste were applied to the back for lumbago. Families would also help one another. A Wiltshire GP recalled that in his own village there was a 'splendid village midwife' who brought most of the babies into the world.[257] Only if complications were feared would the doctor himself be consulted. Other serious illnesses common in those years for which professional help would be sought included typhoid, diphtheria and whooping cough.

Where doctors were called in, strong ties were often forged between them and their patients. In Wiltshire, one GP noted that he was often invited to stay on and have a drink of home-made beer or wine, once he had examined the patient. At Juniper Hill, Flora Thompson recalled that when a woman went to pay her doctor's bill or, more frequently, a small instalment of it, she would take with her some little offering as well: 'mushrooms, a rabbit, a bottle of home-made wine or ketchup, saying, "I know 't isn't much and he's got plenty, but I feel that no money can ever pay for what he done for our so-and-so." '[267]

Despite the progress made in raising training standards, however, in rural districts the medical profession remained relatively poorly paid. As late as 1905, £600 was considered a good income for a rural doctor in East Anglia, and most men had to rely upon outside contracts, perhaps as friendly society or Poor Law doctors, in order to make a living. Though, in the case of the Poor Law contracts, remuneration was hardly generous. In 1870, the guardians of Kingsbridge in Devon appointed a medical officer for one year at a salary of £20 per annum, while at Berwick in the north of England another doctor was offered £25 per annum, and in his case also had to provide his own medicines, except for cod-liver oil, which the guardians purchased cheaply in bulk.[216] In the New Forest union in Hampshire, medical officers who asked for an increase in salary during 1874, on the grounds that the rates paid had not been increased for thirty-six years, were ignored by the guardians.[24]

The resentment to which this miserable treatment gave rise was underlined in a survey published by the *British Medical Journal* in July 1905. One doctor, writing from a village in Wales, claimed that among the members of his friendly society panel was a farmer 'worth £12,000', who paid, under the club rules, only 2s. 6d. a year for his medical treatment: 'I having to go over four miles to see him'. Another man complained of the 'want of professional honour' amongst fellow-doctors 'in applying for any club at any rate when a neighbouring medico resigns it in the hopes of obtaining more reasonable fees for his [private] work. Men in the town will go out miles into the country for 1d. a week, hoping to pick up some chance practice at the country practitioner's expense'.

Ironically, it was Lloyd George's National Insurance Act of 1911, introducing compulsory health insurance for the nation's manual workers and lower paid non-manual workers, which for the first time gave many country doctors financial security. Yet the profession had fiercely opposed this state initiative almost to the time the Act came into operation in the summer of 1912. Under its provisions, doctors were no longer forced to engage in undignified negotiations with Friendly Societies or Poor Law authorities in order to establish their contract fees; instead these were arrived at by national agreement.

Early in the twentieth century Lionel Tollemache of Helmingham, Suffolk, could look back to a time, fifty years before, when the country doctor 'used to come in at the back door, and sometimes (there being no steward's room) to take refreshment in the housekeeper's room'.[271] By 1914 such an attitude would have been unthinkable. The doctor's position as a respectable professional man was too well established. And the advance in his status was symptomatic of the general development of the professions in the half-century before the outbreak of the First World War. If division of labour and mass-production techniques had done much to undermine the status of rural craftsmen and domestic workers, the same process of specialization had boosted the position of professional men, and had increased their numbers. They found a reward for their services not merely in the cash fees they secured but in the high regard in which they were held within the communities in which they worked.

6
Organizations and Institutions

Within the intricate network of economic and social relationships which characterized village life in the years before 1914, certain institutions existed which helped to give those relationships their particular form and style. These included the school, the church and the chapel, as well as the friendly society and parish club, whose role was to offer help to the sick and the bereaved. But, like other aspects of rural life, during the uncertain years at the end of the nineteenth century many of these institutions found themselves under serious pressure. Parish clergy, for example, complained of straitened finances and diminishing congregations as agricultural depression, migration and a growing religious indifference took their toll, while dissenters saw the hostility of the Established Church and the 'induced languor' of spiritual life resulting from rural depopulation as their principal enemies. The Primitive Methodists alone lost 280 'village causes', i.e. chapels, between 1870 and 1896 – a matter of great concern for a community which had nearly three-quarters of its chapels in country districts.[279] Even the smaller friendly societies – especially those based on a single village or group of villages – found themselves in difficulty when the Liberal welfare programme was developed between 1906 and 1914. Only the village school saw its position strengthened, for it was not until the 1870s that virtually every parish had its own school. It is to an examination of this educational expansion that we shall first turn.

Prior to the passage of the 1870 Education Act, school provision had depended largely upon the charitable instincts of the well-to-do, reinforced, from the 1830s onwards, by some government assistance in the form of annual grants. In the countryside the clergy of the Established Church had been particularly active in promoting schools, at a time when religion and education were still thought to be inextricably intertwined. Many clerics also taught in the institutions which they were helping to support, combining academic and religious instruction with what they deemed an appropriate social message. At Cottisford, Flora Thompson remembered the rector stressing the importance of the social order as it then stood, but he also taught the children to memorize 'long passages from the Authorized Version, thus laying up treasure for themselves; so the lessons, in spite of much aridity, were valuable'.[268]

As a result of these initiatives, the vast majority of schools which existed in villages in 1870 were associated with the Church of England, or with the National Society, which had been set up in 1811 to promote the education of the poor in accordance with the doctrines of the Established Church. Most of the remainder were provided by the ostensibly unsectarian British and Foreign School Society which, in practice, enjoyed much support from Nonconformists.

Unfortunately, in those few villages where both a National and a British School existed side by side, this religious division could lead to bitter rivalry. At Loddiswell in Devon, the log book of the National School in the mid-1880s includes complaints that a 'Mr. C' had 'enticed four children from this school to the British . . . and ordered others to do the same – not an unusual occurrence'. The British School master retaliated by pointing out that the vicar had engaged 'in a house-to-house visitation, and is trying to persuade the parents to send their children to the National School'.[251] More seriously, at Crich in Derbyshire there were allegations of physical attacks being launched upon the National School master and his wife and pupils by children from the rival establishment. Happily, as the religious divide itself narrowed during the more tolerant Edwardian era, these examples of denominational bigotry became rarer.

Where the various pre-1870 voluntary initiatives failed to establish efficient parish schools, privately organized and usually ineffective 'dame' or 'adventure' establishments often reigned supreme, or else there was an entire absence of formal education of any kind. In Lincolnshire, the *Stamford Mercury* lamented in June 1871 that in the neighbourhood of Brigg there were parishes where the children were taught neither to read nor to write. 'Surely' it declared, 'in a Christian land where we have churches and chapels and preaching without end, and collections for foreign and other missions, our own population will not be allowed to be brought up without some education. It is shocking to find . . . numbers of young and middle-aged men with ordinary intelligence who mournfully confess they cannot read nor (*sic*) write, yet in this free country we are continually swaggering of our mission to enlighten and convert the world.'

It was against this background, and in the knowledge that matters were a good deal worse in many of the larger industrial towns, that the 1870 Education Act was passed. Under its terms a national survey of elementary schooling was undertaken and, in places where the existing voluntary agencies were either unable or unwilling to make the necessary arrangements to give every child a school place, a non-sectarian rate-aided school board was to be set up for that purpose. It was to have powers to introduce bye-laws requiring attendance up to the age of thirteen and to appoint attendance officers to ensure that those regulations were observed. The Act further laid down that in all government-aided schools, whether board or voluntary, parents were to have the right to withdraw their children from religious instruction should they so wish. Later, a number of Nonconformists claimed that if their offspring were withdrawn in the way laid down, they and their parents suffered discrimination in charity distributions and allied matters. In the event, few were prepared to risk angering those in authority within their village by exercising this 'conscience' clause.[70]

Nevertheless, the legislation ensured that for the first time a network of efficient elementary schools was established throughout the country. At the same time, its emphasis on the importance of the secular aspects of education ensured opposition from many churchmen, who saw it as undermining their influence with their flock. The Bishop of Lincoln was one of the critics, and he urged his fellow-clerics to do 'all they could to maintain the voluntary and denominational system of education', for, 'If the system of School Board teaching was spread widely he would tremble for our civil and political institutions throughout the country.'[248] Great efforts were made by the Church to meet accommodation deficiencies through a major building programme, undertaken primarily under the aegis of the National Society.

In the end, therefore, it was only in areas where Nonconformity was strong and hostility to Anglicanism well rooted, as in Cornwall and parts of Wales, that school boards came to predominate. Even in the 1890s, and despite the difficulties caused by agricultural depression, which reduced subscriptions from landowners and farmers to many village schools and undermined the incumbent's own ability to contribute, the majority of rural children attended Church schools of one kind or another, as Table 9 shows. But shortage of cash seriously weakened the standard of instruction they offered and the quality of teachers they could afford to employ. In 1902, a 'strictly confidential' memorandum issued by the Board of Education in London suggested that more than half of the voluntary schools in country districts were 'under water', with their income falling short of their expenditure. Among the more diminutive school boards, the situation was equally unsatisfactory. As one inspector of schools wrote in 1883: 'Many of the small country Boards seem to consider that their paramount duty is to keep the school rate at the lowest possible figure. The buildings . . . go from bad to worse; . . . the staff is kept at the minimum, and the inspector's requirements as regards staff, books, maps, etc. are resisted or evaded up to the last moment, and then complied with only to escape the threatened fine.'[216]

It was to meet this situation and to provide rate-aid for *all* elementary schools, not merely those under school boards, that the 1902 Education Act was passed. New local education authorities now became responsible for elementary schooling and slowly, under their broader influence, facilities were improved. Unfortunately, the fact that Church of England schools were major beneficiaries under the scheme aroused hostility among some Nonconformists, who saw it as an unwelcome bolstering of sectarian education. In parts of Wales this opposition led to a refusal by local authorities to give rate-aid to church schools, in defiance of their legal obligations. But gradually, as administrative changes were made, the hostility faded away.[186] By 1911 it had been accepted that the elementary system in Wales, as elsewhere, would follow the pattern laid down by the 1902 Act.

Once the necessary school buildings had been erected and had received the approval of Her Majesty's Inspectors, the next task was to ensure that the children took advantage of the instruction provided. This was easier said than done, for throughout the period attitudes towards education in country areas were equivocal. Farmers, in particular, attached little value to schooling, either for their own children or for those of their labourers. As a

*Table 9   Schools in Specimen Counties in Receipt of Annual
Government Grants on 31 August 1899*

| County | National or C. of E. | No. of schools on annual grant list | | | | % of total scholars in average attendance at Board Schools |
		Wesleyan	Roman Catholic	British & other	Board Schools	
ENGLAND						
Berks.	190	7	4	13	13	5
Bucks.	173	2	3	12	67	36.9
Cambs.	114	–	1	11	29	19.2
Cornwall	136	17	2	5	179	59
Devon	324	5	9	30	212	41
Gloucs.	321	5	5	26	71	23
Hereford	150	–	4	7	30	20.5
Norfolk	330	–	4	10	155	37.4
Suffolk, East	174	1	2	9	65	30
Suffolk, West	133	–	1	3	38	34
Westmorland	81	–	1	14	20	11.6
Yorkshire, N.R.	241	16	16	32	80	40.2
WALES						
Anglesey	22	–	1	2	39	63
Cardigan	27	–	–	5	75	72
Radnor	36	–	–	5	10	15

From P.P.1900, Vol. LXV, Pt. I

leading Worcestershire agriculturist declared in 1909, youngsters
needed to be trained from an early age for work on the land,
particularly if they were to deal with livestock: 'The children seem
more clumsy when they do not leave school before the ages of 13
or 14. They are not so handy with horses or cattle. My own
experience is that they never seem to show the same love for
animals or to take the same pride in them as when they begin
younger.'[84] Small wonder that an official report could conclude in
that year:

the appreciation of education as a practical factor in ameliorat-
ing the conditions of country life and work is, to say the least,
too little developed. It is not too much to say that many parents
and employers, as well as many Managers of schools and others

interested in the welfare of the rural population, frequently consider that education . . . is not a good practical introduction to agricultural pursuits. . . . They believe that village boys who stay long at school get a distaste for the country and take the first opportunity of migrating to a town.[62]

These prejudices were reinforced by the widespread decline in the rural population which occurred in the late nineteenth century. A farmer from North Petherton in Somerset expressed a common view when he informed Rider Haggard in 1901 that all the young men from his neighbourhood were going to the Welsh coalfields, where they could earn wages more than double those they obtained in agriculture.

> The initial cause of this exodus was, he thought, our system of education. Formerly if a boy went to school at the age of nine or ten years he left it to earn fivepence or sixpence a day by scaring birds or doing odd jobs upon the farm. Now he must remain at his lessons until he was twelve or thirteen, by which time he had lost all taste for country pursuits. . . . By all means . . . let a boy be taught to read and write and do the four elementary rules of arithmetic – knowledge that he could acquire by the time he was nine years of age; after which let him begin to earn his daily bread.[177]

As we saw in Chapter 4, the changing attitudes towards agricultural employment which this farmer pinpointed were due to more deep-seated economic and social influences than mere educational advance. But these broader aspects were conveniently ignored by many agriculturists, who made schooling a scapegoat instead. All save the most affluent of them also continued to send their own youngsters to the village school, their only concession to advanced learning possibly being to despatch them briefly at the end of their scholastic career to a private or grammar school in a neighbouring town. In this way they would 'break touch' with the children of the labourers. The head of one endowed school in Devon claimed that farmers' sons in his area often came for six months only, and some 'for so short a time as one term'.[86] The object of the exercise in these cases was not concern for education but a display of petty snobbery.

In these conditions, the enforcement of attendance regulations had to overcome many obstacles. On the one hand, hard-pressed farmers were anxious to take advantage of cheap juvenile labour and to discourage young workers from seeking employment elsewhere; on the other, many labouring families were concerned to maximize their children's earnings at an early age. Even when, with the improvement in farm workers' real wages at the end of the century, some of this family pressure was eased, most parents still expected their youngsters to lend a hand at the busy seasons of the year. The children, too, were anxious to make a contribution. An Essex lad, who started work at the age of eleven in 1870 at a wage of 1s. 6d. per week, later recalled the pride with which he took home his first pay – 'it was my own earnings'.[210]

Sometimes, particularly in dairying areas, employers also required their labourers to make children available for work when required. In 1909, advertisements for farm hands in Dorset included the following:

'WANTED, CARTER, with Boys, for six horses', and
'DAIRYMAN WANTED, at MICHAELMAS, with family, for 40 Cows'.[37]

In Devon, quasi-apprenticeship arrangements grew up around the turn of the century, under which boys were employed on farm work whilst they were still attending school. They lived on their employer's holding and the work they carried out before and after classes was sufficient to pay for their keep.[71] The effect of such schemes upon the health and academic progress of the youngsters concerned is easy to imagine. Similarly, in Cornwall, boys from the local workhouses were recruited as farm servants when they had reached the age of about thirteen. The farmers provided board and lodgings and a wage of 3d. per week. The boys were required to remain on these terms until they reached the age of sixteen. But, as one critic observed, it was difficult to find out whether the children were fairly dealt with and their pocket money always paid.[80] The implication was that they were exploited by their employers.

The first move to tackle directly the question of compulsory attendance came with the 1870 Education Act itself, which empowered the new school boards to draw up bye-laws requiring full-time attendance for every youngster between the ages of five and ten and thereafter, at least on a part-time basis, to thirteen, unless he or she could pass an appropriate leaving examination in the three R's (reading, writing and arithmetic). But those areas not covered by the boards – and in country districts they were the vast majority – remained unaffected; even the rural boards which did exist frequently neglected to act on the bye-laws issue. As one of HM Inspectors gloomily asserted in 1871, the tenant farmers, who were prominent members of most boards, objected 'to the removal of juvenile labour from their fields', while the parochial clergy were angered by any attempt to interfere with their 'assumed right' of sole management, denominational influence, and exclusive suprintendence of elementary education. 'Hence in those places where the managers and teachers have for so long ridiculed all attempts at real efficiency without compulsory attendance, they now refuse the very means of securing it.'

In an attempt to tackle the attendance problem on a wider scale, therefore, in 1873 a Private Member's Bill, the Agricultural Children Act, reached the statute book. Under its terms no child was to be employed on the land below the age of eight (save by its parents), while between eight and twelve a minimum number of school attendances was required. Unfortunately, the Act's failure to designate an enforcement agency quickly proved fatal. Within weeks of its coming into operation on 1 January 1875 it was a dead letter, as HM Inspectors sadly confirmed. Not until a fresh Education Act was passed in 1876 were attendance provisions effectively extended to voluntary schools as well. Under this Act, all children between the ages of five and ten had to attend school full-time, while for those aged from ten to twelve a minimum of 250 attendances a year was required and for scholars between twelve and fourteen the minimum was 150 attendances, each morning or afternoon session at school being regarded as a separate attendance. The children were then free to work for the rest of the time. Earlier full-time employment was legally possible only for those who could pass an appropriate leaving examination.

In order to enforce the regulations a new kind of local authority – the School Attendance Committee – was introduced to cover those districts which were still without boards. Parents who neglected to send their children to school could now be fined, as could the employers of such children. But even with this, a minority of education authorities failed to draw up bye-laws, and it was left to the Education Act of 1880 finally to make attendance regulations mandatory throughout the country. Later, in 1893, the *minimum* school leaving age was raised from ten to eleven, and in 1899 to twelve, though in country districts it was still possible for children to leave at eleven if local bye-laws permitted.

Slowly, therefore, the authorities were extending the legal limits of childhood. Measures like the Agricultural Gangs Act of 1867 had defined *eight* as the minimum age for employment; this had been raised by the Education Acts of 1870, 1876 and 1880 to *ten*; then during the 1890s came further advances – to *eleven*, and in 1899, to *twelve*. Unfortunately, despite such legislative provisions, the attendance difficulty was by no means solved. In defiance of the restrictions young children continued to work, especially on a seasonal basis, for years to come, while the zeal with which parents and employers who broke the law were prosecuted proved extremely variable. From Dorney in Buckinghamshire an irate inhabitant wrote to the Education Department in London during August 1880 to complain of the 'culpable neglect' of the local attendance officer: 'Since his appointment no steps have been taken either by the Board or him either to compel or induce the children to attend, and his last appearance in the district was April 5th 1880.' The writer provided a list of twenty children (out of ninety-six on the school register) who were regularly employed – including two eleven-year-old boys who were working for one of the members of the school board! As a result of this protest investigations were instituted by the Department, and a new attendance officer appointed. But as late as 1901 HMI Kenney-Herbert complained of the reluctance of magistrates to enforce the regulations within his area. In one case, at Leighton Buzzard in Bedfordshire, the chairman of the bench frankly told a defendant: 'I suppose I must administer the law, but I think the boy was much better employed by you than messing about in that stuffy school.'[71] The fact that fines rarely amounted to more than 2s. 6d. or 5s. per case was also scarcely a deterrent.

Only very slowly, therefore, did the old idea of the child as a small worker, who must begin to contribute to family income as soon as possible, begin to disappear for the offspring of labourers and small farmers, as it had already vanished for those in the higher ranks of society. An important factor reinforcing the trend was the changing character of agriculture itself. With the wider use of self-binders in the 1890s children were less necessary at harvest time than hitherto, while the expansion of livestock farming reduced the demand for youngsters to act as bird-scarers, stonepickers, weeders, and the like. Yet, when the First World War broke out, it is significant that education authorities were bombarded with appeals from farmers for a relaxation of attendance bye-laws, so that youngsters might be employed on the land to replace men who had joined the armed forces. And within weeks of the outbreak of hostilities, many authorities were acceding to those requests.[170]

Not all pupils who stayed away from school did so because they were at work. Shortage of cash was one problem, especially prior to 1891, when a new government grant brought an end to fees in most, though not all, elementary schools. Ill-health or lack of suitable clothing kept others away, as at Boughton Monchelsea in Kent, where the master noted on 26 September 1910 that several children were absent through illness or 'because their clothes [were] not ready as hop-picking only ceased on Friday'. In other cases, girls remained at home to help their mothers look after younger brothers and sisters, while bad weather was a further difficulty, since few schools had facilities for drying wet clothing. And despite increased educational provision, countless country children in the more remote areas still had to walk long distances each day to reach their classes. A Pembrokeshire doctor claimed in 1912–13 that in his area many scholars had to travel two or three miles to reach their destination, leaving home soon after 8 a.m. and not returning until about 4.30 in the afternoon. They also had to eat their midday meal at the school and often this meant the food was stored in heaps 'in different corners of the cloakroom'. 'It usually consists of bread and butter only', he declared. 'In one school with 54 children, 16 children have to walk over three miles to school, and no provision is made for warming their food.'[69]

It was to combat these problems that in 1906 the Education (Provision of Meals) Act was passed empowering local authorities to supply school meals. It was followed a year later by the authorization of a national school medical service. Both measures were to be financed primarily out of the rates, and perhaps on these grounds, and also because of local indifference, their impact in country districts before 1914 was very limited. So although all local authorities had to make *some* provision for a school medical service, most confined this to such relatively inexpensive aspects as dealing with verminous heads and weighing and measuring the children.[186]

Despite their imperfections, these schemes to enforce attendance and to improve the health and welfare of pupils were indications of a growing concern by the authorities to improve the lot of young people. A similar spirit lay behind the 1908 Children Act, which sought to protect children from cruelty and abuse not merely from strangers but from their relatives as well. It was an acceptance of the idea that a child should have rights of its own, and not merely be regarded as an adjunct of its parents.

A further area where attitudes were changing was in regard to the school curriculum itself. Under the terms of the Education Department's Revised Code of 1862, government grants to elementary education had been linked to attendance levels and, for those aged seven and above, the results of an annual examination conducted by one of Her Majesty's Inspectors in the three R's. Failure in any one of the subjects meant a deduction from the grant which that particular pupil could secure for his or her school. And because reading, writing and arithmetic alone were the grant-earning subjects, they were concentrated upon to the virtual exclusion of all else, save religious instruction and needlework, which was compulsory for the girls. Over the years some of the limitations of the system were, admittedly, eliminated, with the introduction of additional grants for 'specific' subjects, such as English grammar, history and geography from 1867. But their impact was limited, only 3.7 per cent of all pupils on the books of elementary schools in 1875 being examined for one or other of the 'specific' subjects.[186] In country districts the effect of these initiatives was particularly modest. As HMI Pickard reported of Oxfordshire in 1885–86, specific subjects were attempted in only five or six schools, 'and I am quite satisfied that it would do more harm than good if more managers were to introduce the study of these subjects.'[68] Small wonder that Chief Inspector C. H. Alderson could declare of schools in the south-western division of England at that time: 'Nothing is more deadening to children than to be kept always in the treadmill of the three elementary subjects. Such a dreary round takes the heart and spirit out of young learners.' In his area, history just flickered, 'after a moribund fashion . . . while elementary science, save for the enterprise of a single school in Devonshire, would remain a dead letter'. Textbooks, too, were criticized, with those used for history described as 'wretched little manuals which are to be had by the dozen for a few pence, all professing to be short cuts to knowledge', and 'too much a mere record of the doings of royal personages'.[216]

The monotony of the daily routine was reinforced by the teaching methods adopted, with learning by rote the normal approach. Discipline was strict and there was much use of the cane. Staff shortages added to the difficulties. In many village schools there was only one qualified teacher, aided perhaps by an unqualified assistant or by a pupil teacher (aged from thirteen to eighteen).

But it was at the time of the annual inspection that the greatest anxieties were experienced by teachers and pupils alike, for upon the results of this the financial future of the school often depended. It was not surprising that they experienced what one HMI called 'an unhealthy amount of excitement' on the great day. On that occasion the children would arrive early, wearing their best clothes and with shoes well blacked and, for the girls, pinafores freshly laundered. For teaching and examination purposes the pupils were divided into separate divisions or standards, and it was on this basis that the inspection was conducted. An HMI who worked in rural Wales recalled the customary routine:[253]

I begin with Standards I and II. They find the sums a little trying, though they count most carefully on their fingers. When you have a slate in your arms, it is hard to carry the reckoning across from one hand to the other without dropping the slate. . . . Meanwhile Standards III, IV, and V, are struggling with sums, and, at intervals, with Dictation, given out by the master in a convincing accent. Then they read with a fluency that in those early days used to amaze me, knowing, as I did, that they knew very little English; till I found by greater experience that they knew the two books by heart, and could go on equally well if the book fell on the ground. . . . All the work is done . . . the children go home with undisguised joy, and I proceed to mark the papers. [The school] has passed 92 per cent; great rejoicings follow, and I am classed above the last inspector, who drew the line at 88.

Despite the various curriculum reforms, therefore, the 'payment by results' system remained the basis of the government's grant to elementary education until the 1890s. Only with the Education

Code of 1900, which abolished piecemeal grants and offered capitation payments for all the scholars, was the way at last opened for a broader and more constructive approach to elementary schooling. In April of that year a circular was issued by the Board of Education asking managers to ensure that the teaching in their schools was 'more consonant with the environment of the scholars' than hitherto. Cookery classes, laundry work and school gardening were three subjects which were encouraged under the new regime, while small museums and nature study lessons, conducted out of doors, were other innovations. In Gloucestershire, instruction in handicraft and cookery increased notably, with the latter subject taken, after 1912, to the most remote Cotswold villages with the aid of a special van. This stayed, with its accompanying teacher, for three or four weeks' intensive tuition at each school or group of schools.[231] Elsewhere efforts were made to revive local industries. At one Radnorshire school this took the form of lessons in basket-making, which was traditional in the area. Equally typical of the more relaxed approach now encouraged was an entry for March 1909 in the school log book at Pitstone, Buckinghamshire, by HMI Kenney-Herbert: 'Some Folk-songs were rendered in a manner wholly delightful and I am pleased to hear that the introduction of Morris Dances is contemplated.'[28] In the days of the Revised Code such departures from the basic curriculum would have been impossible.

Education was now seen as having a broader role than mere instruction in a few academic subjects. It was 'to prepare the child for the life of a good citizen, to create or foster the aptitude for work and for the intelligent use of leisure, and to develop those features of character which are most readily influenced by school life, such as loyalty to comrades, loyalty to institutions, unselfishness, and an orderly and disciplined habit of mind'.[186] As HMI Henderson wrote in 1902: 'we are not merely educating future clerks, craftsmen, or labourers, but future Englishmen and Englishwomen'. About a decade later, former Chief Inspector of Elementary Schools, E. G. A. Holmes, dismissed the old preoccupation with examinations as diverting the teacher's mind 'from the proper business of education, which was the development of all the child's faculties.'

Against this background, and with a strengthening of Imperial sentiment, in 1902 the anniversary of Queen Victoria's birthday,

24 May, was officially designated Empire Day, to be celebrated throughout the British Empire as a means of training school children in good citizenship.

The changing attitudes towards elementary education were also reflected in the improved standing of the teachers. They had always performed an important role in village life as secretaries of clubs and societies at a time when few people could read and write easily. But often, especially in Church schools, these extra duties had been imposed upon them by managers as a condition of employment, which they must accept if they wished to retain their position. One man sadly reported in 1899 that in his village he had to act as choir master, organizer of the penny bank, superintendent of the Sunday school, and secretary of the temperance society. Another complained of duties in connection with 'Organ, Sunday school, stoves, lamps, candles, surplice, bell, lock gates, cleaning lamps, sweeping church', for which he was paid £1 a year. He had not had a free Sunday for more than eight years on account of the organ and choir practices, yet a refusal to perform these tasks could have brought dismissal from his teaching post.[19]

Then in 1903 came a new edition of the School Code which ended the imposition of 'extraneous duties' as a condition of employment. The greater independence this bestowed upon members of the profession advanced them in public esteem and, especially in country districts, enabled them to give greater leadership within the various social organizations and upon parish councils. Less satisfactory was the fact that on financial rather than academic grounds the profession was becoming dominated by women, as impoverished school managers sought to cut back on their expenditure. For women were cheaper to employ than their male counterparts. In Devon, where 128 of the 227 head teachers of voluntary schools in 1903 were women, *none* earned £90 per annum, although seventy-eight of the men secured £90 or more.[251] Small wonder that in 1914 about three-quarters of all elementary school teachers were women.

Yet, despite the financial difficulties of some schools and the debilitating effect upon village life of growing depopulation, the overall standard of rural elementary education was undoubtedly higher in 1914 than it had been in 1870. Under its influence, people had also become more aware of life in the wider world.

They were able to read newspapers in the parish reading rooms or to buy copies of their own, and they were better fitted to run their own societies and clubs. The old sense of helpless dependence upon the goodwill of others was no longer there. In addition, a trickle of the brightest children were able to take advantage of the scholarships to secondary education which became available, particularly after 1907.

But these positive gains on the educational front were a sad contrast to the atmosphere of depression and decline which characterized the villages' religious institutions over the same period. The Church of England found the change especially painful, as clergy saw their position threatened both by their own financial weakness and by the indifference and even hostility of certain of their parishioners. Agricultural recession was undoubtedly a major factor in both developments, but there were other deep-seated problems as well.

Among the most important of these was the growing social and political awareness of the labourers and their families, which improved education and the availability of cheap radical newspapers helped to promote. More and more came to question the traditional order, and to see the Church as something designed for the propertied and the well-to-do. In the smaller villages people might still attend Sunday services to please their employer or the squire, but as the farming population itself changed under the pressure of agricultural depression, many of these attitudes crumbled. According to 'Michael Home', in his village in the Norfolk breckland during the 1890s, the Church was scarcely regarded as a place of worship. It was merely something to which the better-off and their dependants belonged. 'Between it and us a great gulf was fixed. There was the ancient building and the fine organ; the ornate pulpit and the Reverend John in his robes and scarlet hood. Its ritual was so complex as to be incomprehensible and most of it seemed to come out of . . . the prayer-book.'[184]

In many cases the sense of alienation was reinforced by the pew system, which segregated rich and poor in what seemed a peculiarly humiliating fashion. It was something which angered 'Home's' father, while more than half a century later an Essex man bitterly recalled the way in which his mother, a devout churchgoer, had been relegated to the back pews. Local shopkeepers and tradesmen occupied the middle ground, and at the top of the church were the farmers and other well-to-do people.[269]

Some incumbents, to their credit, condemned pews and the attitudes they fostered as an affront to the Church's symbolism and its spiritual mission. Among them was the incumbent of Oundle in the Peterborough diocese, who informed the bishop that the chief hindrance in his pastoral work was 'the legalized system of selfishness in the . . . Church commonly known by the name of "Faculty Pews", which virtually shuts out the poor from the House of God – and hands them over to the Dissenting Chapels.'[187] On another level, the Revd Charles W. Stubbs, a country parson in Buckinghamshire for thirteen years, asked rhetorically how many agricultural labourers in England were churchwardens or even sidesmen: 'But I know a good many farmer and squire Churchwardens who are not even communicants. Is then "Property" or "Baptism" the test of membership in Christ's Church?'[260] Under the influence of men such as these, and of the changing spirit of the times, some of the inequalities were eliminated, but in many churches a measure of social segregation persisted up to the time of the First World War.

These attitudes contrasted strongly with those in the chapels. There the congregations were encouraged to feel that they 'belonged' and, indeed, it was frequently their hard-earned savings which had financed the buildings themselves. The Lincolnshire farmer Cornelius Stovin, for example, was so deeply committed that he continued to make loans to local chapels and to pay off circuit debts even when his own finances were depleted by the depression. The mere construction of such a place of worship was also itself an expression of independent action, almost of defiance, against the accepted order of village society. John Kent has written of these tiny bethels in their early days being seen 'as citadels from which attacks were mounted on the social and economic enemy'.[202] Certainly Cornelius Stovin regarded his own chapel as a major instrument for religious conversion: 'Scores have been born again on this little hill of Zion', he noted proudly in his journal.[256]

It was the humbler people – the small farmers, labourers, and tradesmen – who were frequently responsible for the day-to-day running of the chapels and who acted as local preachers, class leaders and stewards. In this way they learnt to take responsibility, and to speak in public without inhibition. Worship also had a greater spontaneity than was found in the Church, with congregations joining whole-heartedly in singing hymns. Many village choirs, particularly in Wales and Cornwall, started life in the local chapel as part of the process of religious worship. The lay preachers, like old Sammy Coles from Exmoor in Devon, would also frequently preach homely sermons based on their own experiences. Coles called them his 'li'l talks about the Master', and many labouring people found these simple addresses, with all their faults of syntax, preferable to the more polished performances they would doubtless have witnessed from the pulpit of the parish church.[141] They gloried, too, in the Old Testament themes, in which God intervened on the side of the oppressed, since these seemed to give support and inspiration to their own growing demands for social justice.[250]

But if Nonconformity continued to rival the Established Church in many villages up to 1914 it, too, was losing its adherents, as more and more young people left the villages and as its own missionary zeal weakened. Bitter rivalry nevertheless still poisoned church/chapel relations in some communities even in late Victorian England. At Long Crendon in Buckinghamshire, there was much feuding between the Church people and local Baptists, with the village tradespeople drawn into the dispute. 'There were Church shops and Chapel shops, and people buying groceries would go out of their way to patronise one from their own religion.' As an elderly Baptist declared, 'You can have acquaintances among the Church people, but friends, never.'[148]

Yet, despite these localized problems, over much of the country there was a gradual decline in hostility and a mellowing. That process of reconciliation was encouraged by various legislative changes, such as the ending in 1868 of the levying of compulsory Church rates – always a sore point for dissenters – and the passage of the Burial Laws Amendment Act in 1880, which for the first time authorized Nonconformist ministers to conduct funeral services in churchyards. Some incumbents, like the Revd John Conybeare, vicar of Barrington in Cambridgeshire, made it their business to get on friendly terms with the local dissenting minister. In Conybeare's case this meant attending occasional religious meetings in the chapel.[139]

Throughout the period there were also many villagers who attended both church and chapel. Some switched from one to the other as the spirit moved them, and others used the parish church for the great events of their lives, such as baptisms, marriages, and burials. Others again, as at Juniper Hill in Oxfordshire, gave their allegiance to both bodies at the same time. During the 1880s and 1890s, Flora Thompson recalled how the few Methodist families in her community attended church in the morning and afternoon, but held their own evening meeting for prayer and praise in one of the cottages, thereby earning for themselves the expressive nickname of 'devil dodgers'. A few of their neighbours who were not of their persuasion also attended, pleased to have somewhere to go on Sunday evenings, especially if it were wet or cold, for a warm fire always burned in the grate on these occasions.[268] They enjoyed, too, the feelings of comradeship and brotherly love which were displayed.

Roman Catholics, by contrast, had little role to play in village life, for they were rarely found in country districts, save where the resident squire was himself a Catholic. This was the case in parts of Northumberland, Durham and Lancashire, as well as in the North Riding of Yorkshire.[130] Pockets of support also survived in villages like Lulworth in Dorset and East Hendred, now in Oxfordshire, where even today a flourishing Roman Catholic community exists.

Among the Anglican clergy, meanwhile, growing numbers carried out their duties with a deeper sense of personal dedication than had once been the case. The mid-nineteenth century reforms, ending both non-residence of the incumbent – save in special circumstances – and the plurality of livings, had already largely eliminated two major abuses by the 1870s. The number of beneficed clergy rose from about 6,000 in the 1840s to over 13,000 by 1887. Men like Conybeare at Barrington embarked upon programmes of major church restoration, to compensate for previous years of neglect, and they set in hand a variety of societies and clubs to add interest and variety to the daily lives of their flock. When employment in the parish proved difficult, Conybeare also gave assistance. During the winter of 1893 he raised more than £100 to help relieve poverty in his parish, and when the local coprolite diggings were worked out he obtained permission from the squire to use the old workings to sink artesian wells for the village. He supervised the venture himself, employing a large number of men for the purpose, and eventually obtained three wells which gave the village a regular and reliable water supply.[139]

Another energetic cleric was Robert Hessey, vicar of Basing and Up-Nateley in Hampshire. During the 1870s he organized a night school for farm lads, an annual flower show, a musical society, a cricket club, a soup kitchen, a blanket and sheet loan society and a coal and clothing club. In running these schemes he was able to depend upon the financial support of his better-off parishioners, with the contributions of the principal landowner, Lord Bolton, at the head of all his subscription lists.

The experiences of Francis Kilvert, curate at Clyro, Radnorshire, similarly showed the deep affection which was felt for the parish clergy in many communities. Not only did he distribute wine and bedding to the sick and needy, but he also gave time and energy to assisting in other ways, as in the case of the old Peninsular War veteran, John Morgan, whom he helped with his gardening, or old Price, the gamekeeper, to whom he read.[232] When Kilvert left the parish in 1872, his departure was deeply mourned.

In displaying this whole-hearted commitment to their calling, men like Conybeare, Hessey and Kilvert were following the advice of writers on parish affairs, whose texts were appearing upon the market in growing quantities by the 1870s. Among them was *The Parish Guide*, first published in 1887. Its author stressed that to be successful a clergyman must be prepared to act as pastor, lawyer, father and even doctor to his flock.[58] Then there was the Revd Herbert James's *The Country Clergyman and His Work*, which appeared in 1890. It offered practical guidance to the would-be country cleric on such matters as preaching, parish visiting, educational work, general organization, and the handling of his parishioners. 'Avoid . . . all preference of rich to poor in the administration of Sacramental or occasional Offices', it firmly advised, 'paying no greater deference to the feelings of the one than to those of the other.'[195]

Despite this growing social awareness among the clergy, not all labouring people responded to their overtures. Some rejected the whole ethos of charitable aid which underlay many of the approaches; others, either through hostility or indifference, simply ceased to attend Church at all. Even at Juniper Hill, Flora Thompson noted that although nine out of ten of the inhabitants would have declared themselves Church of England, since they were baptized, married and buried as such, in adult life they rarely went to Church between the baptisms of their offspring. Only the children went there in any numbers, after Sunday school, while about a dozen of the older people were regular attenders:

> the rest stayed at home, the women cooking and nursing, and the men, after an elaborate Sunday toilet, which included shaving and cutting each other's hair and much puffing and splashing with buckets of water, . . . spent the rest of the day eating, sleeping, reading the newspaper, and strolling round to see how their neighbours' pigs and gardens were looking.[268]

A number of clergymen found this unresponsiveness desperately discouraging. Among them was the rector of Hulcott, Buckinghamshire, who noted sadly in June 1914 that he found the ministry in his small parish of 114 inhabitants more difficult than that among the larger population whom he had served in London: 'If it was not for the sympathy of our farmers it would break any man's heart who cared for souls. Most of our labourers think of only what they can get in the way of gifts & money. They do not value spiritual things.'[21]

Still worse was the plight of those incumbents who faced outright opposition from their parishioners. This occurred during the agricultural trade union movement of the 1870s when, all too often, the Church sided with the employers, thereby earning the dislike and suspicion of labouring people. Admittedly some clerics, like the Bishop of Manchester and the incumbents of Harbury and Stoneleigh in Warwickshire, sympathized with the men, but they were outnumbered by the critics. The fact that most of the union leaders, including Joseph Arch himself, were active Nonconformists, added to the problem by reinforcing the underlying religious prejudices of both sides. In 1874 the union newspaper, the *Labourers' Union Chronicle*, assumed the sub-title of 'an independent Advocate of the British Toiler's Rights to Free Land, Freedom from Priestcraft, and from the Tyranny of Capital', and a number of speakers at branch meetings pressed for Church disestablishment, alongside demands more relevant to the economic aspirations of their members. In Norfolk alone, 243 of the 463 branch officials were Methodists (205 being Primitives); in Lincolnshire, the relevant figure was 98 Methodists out of the 306 officials.[250] Methodist organization also provided a model for much of the union framework and strategy, with the Methodist circuits in many areas corresponding roughly to the groups of villages which were subsequently incorporated into union districts.

Alienation from the Church of England reached a peak in the 1870s, when the union movement itself was at its height. More than one incumbent doubtless agreed with the Oxfordshire parson who complained of falling church attendance 'in consequence of a spirit of insubordination and disaffection towards employers and clergy being roused by inflammatory speeches & publications' of the union.

Matters reached fever pitch in 1876–78, when there was the so-called 'battle of the vestries', as unionists in many villages and country towns sought to get their candidate elected as the people's warden, so as to have a say in the running of parish affairs and the distribution of the charities. At East Dereham, Norfolk, the vicar expressed apprehension at the outcome of his annual vestry meeting in April 1877. In the end the issue was resolved amicably, though at first 'the atmosphere was very threatening . . . I stated that I was glad to see the labourers taking an interest in these matters (I suspect that they were all paid their day's wages by the Union), and that they would be treated with the same courtesy and consideration as other people'. Apparently, in proverbial fashion, this soft answer turned away wrath, for despite his fears, both the wardens selected proved acceptable to him and to the church people in general.[121]

Even when the union movement weakened in the late 1870s and beyond, these anti-Church sentiments did not entirely disappear. As late as 1884 the incumbent of Fringford in Oxfordshire was blaming the fact that the labourers had been 'largely influenced by Union' for decreased church attendance in his parish. Three years earlier another Oxfordshire incumbent from Westcote Barton had similarly blamed the 'influence of Dissent in the neighbouring Parish – and the hostility of the Labourers Union' for the failure of his congregation to increase.[21]

However, as relations slowly recovered from the disruptive influences of the union movement and its associated political campaigns, a new threat was posed to the Church. This came from the growth of anti-tithe agitation among farmers hit by the agricultural depression. Feelings ran particularly high in Essex, where grain prices had fallen so sharply, and among hard-hit hop producers in Kent and Sussex, as well as among farmers of all kinds in Wales. In 1886 the right of clergy to collect new tithes on hops, fruit and market garden produce was abolished, but whilst this assisted agriculturists in counties like Kent, it did nothing for farmers in the principality. It was there that the anti-tithe movement was to reach maximum strength.

Unrest over tithes first appeared in Wales in the small and remote parish of Llanarmon-yn-Iâl in Denbighshire when some farmers formed a deputation to the rector to demand a 25 per cent rebate on the payments due from them. He refused, and although negotiations were subsequently reopened, a number of the farmers refused to co-operate. Under the law, an incumbent was entitled to give ten days' notice and then to distrain goods (usually livestock) to the value of the tithes due, and to arrange for them to be auctioned. At Llanarmon this process was delayed because no local auctioneer would agree to undertake the work, but by the end of August the first sales had been successfully carried through, amid scenes of some violence. Soon unrest spread to neighbouring parishes, and by early September an Anti-Tithe League had been formed, to encourage and support all those prepared to resist payment.[149]

The movement was quickly taken up in other parts of the principality. Thus a sale at Whitford, Flint, in December 1886 attracted a crowd of between 1,000 and 1,500. The deputy chief constable of the county attended with eighty policemen to try and protect the auctioneer and his assistants. The police were pelted with rotten eggs and other missiles, and an effort was made to force the distraining party into a nearby horsepond.

As the months passed, and the dispute remained unresolved, hostility between farmers and the Anglican clergy intensified. At one forced auction at Llanhowell near St David's, Pembrokeshire in September 1890 the incumbent's effigy, dressed in seafaring garb, was carried aloft by the crowd. Upon its breast was the slogan in Welsh: 'Under the law and not under grace'. Missiles were again thrown at the auctioneers and amid scenes of considerable anger the sale had to be abandoned. Often during these years, when a clergyman met one of his Nonconformist parishioners during the course of daily business, he would be greeted with a scowl, 'and these Welshmen, hitherto kindly and courteous declined even "to tell the road" and passed on with a muttered oath'.[151] Elsewhere parsonage doors were coated with tar, church property was attacked, and hostile crowds gathered outside rectories and vicarages.

The financial position of the clergy in the disaffected areas was, in the meantime, becoming more and more desperate, since most depended upon the tithe rent-charge for a major part of their stipend. In one parish in 1888, where £200 should have been paid at the tithe audit, a mere £8 was actually received; in another village, where £124 was due, the sum received was £6.[234] Some men were able to carry on only by selling their books and other property, or withdrawing their children from private schools, or stinting their diet. One hard-pressed cleric would scarcely venture into the village because he felt so acutely his debts at the local shops; another sold a carpet to raise some cash.

By now the persistent anti-tithe agitation in Wales was attracting attention in England, too. The matter was raised in Parliament, and the government decided that legislation was needed. After several fruitless efforts, in March 1891 the Tithe Rent-Charge Recovery and Redemption Act at length reached the statute book. One of its most important provisions was that landlords alone were now responsible for tithe payments. If they chose to pass on the charge to their tenants, they could do so only by incorporating it into the rent. Consequently, tenants could not refuse to pay the tithe without also refusing to pay the rent, and thus laying themselves open to eviction from their holding. Many of the larger landowners, in England as well as in Wales, decided not to pass on the extra sums to their tenants, and so the tithe agitation among tenant farmers died down. Of course, small *owner-occupiers*, of whom there were a number in such counties as Pembrokeshire and Cardigan, were not helped by the measure, and some of them continued sporadic resistance to tithes for months after the 1891 Act was implemented. At the same time the agitation focused attention on the grievances of the Welsh in religious affairs, and helped to lead to the disestablishment of the Anglican Church in Wales in 1920.

But as we saw in Chapter 2, even where the clergy were not faced with the bitter opposition experienced by their more unfortunate brethren in Wales, the financial plight of many became desperate as tithe incomes plummeted as a result of agricultural depression, and glebes became well-nigh impossible to let. At Kencott in Oxfordshire, the incumbent noted in 1896 that as a result of the depression the value of his living had been reduced from £370 to £103 10s., 'less than the stipend of a first curacy'; when all outgoings had been taken into account, he put the net income of the benefice at a mere £68 18s. 3d.[21] In the Peterborough diocese, where glebe land was particularly common (averaging 129 acres per benefice), rents had been cut by about 25 per cent as early as 1881, and in the years that followed tenants became ever more difficult to find.[235] Strict economy became the order of the day in all those parsonages where the incumbent had no comfortable private income. And although most clergymen, even in reduced circumstances, normally secured more than the £120 or so earned annually by dissenting ministers in country areas, their outgoings were usually heavier. Not only had they large houses to run, but there were also many calls upon their purse to help support village schools, clothing clubs and other charities. In 1887 Rowland Prothero described the sad process of their decline. First they reduced their outdoor establishment by dismissing the gardeners and selling the horse and carriage:

> Servant after servant is discharged till not one is left; then follows the careful husbanding of fuel, the severest practice of domestic economy, even the disposal of books, furniture, and apparel. Sons are withdrawn from school or college, daughters are obliged to go out as governesses; life insurances are sold, pledged, or allowed to drop. Sometimes an effort is made to obtain pupils. . . . The Church services must be maintained. . . . No one will give more than the parson, and the clergy are still obliged to head subscriptions to schools and local objects; the wants of the sick poor have still to be met by soups and jellies and clothing . . . he cannot, like the squire, shut up his house and leave the neighbourhood.[235]

By 1887, more than one-third of the 13,000 beneficed clergy were securing less than £200 a year. It was in these circumstances that the custom of an Easter offering, used as a gift to the parson, spread rapidly through country parishes. Prior to the mid-1880s it had been a rare occurrence but by 1905 nearly half of all parishes were said to give such an offering to their incumbent.[136]

Perhaps most painful of all to many clergymen, faced with diminished incomes and the general decline in village life, was their deep sense of loneliness and isolation. The hunting, shooting and fishing parsons of earlier years had largely disappeared. Now such frivolities were deemed unsuitable for the new, more sober, religious orthodoxy. In many parishes, the clergyman was 'the only man of education or refinement' resident, and there were few opportunities for interesting intellectual discussions or even for visits with fellow-clerics. In these circumstances, a number turned their attention to antiquarian pursuits or the study of natural history as interesting but inexpensive hobbies. Others, like the Revd J. C. Atkinson of Danby, Yorkshire, concentrated on the investigation of folklore traditions and dialects.

Significantly, too, as Atkinson's researches demonstrated, despite the apparently widespread acceptance of Christianity, vestiges of the old superstitions continued to flourish in many country communities, to the clergy's distress. In more remote areas, there was still a fear of witchcraft and the power of the 'evil eye'. In 1879 at East Deringham in Norfolk a farmer was heavily fined for assaulting the daughter of an old woman who, he claimed, had 'charmed' him by the use of a 'walking toad', which was her familiar. Four years earlier, at Long Compton in Warwickshire, an old woman was beaten to death by a labourer who claimed she had bewitched him. He was eventually found guilty of manslaughter and sent to Warwick gaol, where he remained until his death. According to a report in the *Oxford Times*, which appeared in July 1899, in the months that followed this case 'Women as well as men became bitten by the crave for witch-finding; and the little out-of-the-world villages along the romantic Vale of the Red Horse were in a state of great unrest, each native or resident suspecting the other of possessing the dangerous gift of the evil eye.' As late as June 1905 the Oxfordshire historian Percy Manning claimed that many country people were 'absolutely pagan, or at least . . . covered with a thin veneer of Christianity'.[48]

More logically, at a time when formal medical knowledge was limited, there was also a resort to folklore remedies to cure illnesses, with charms considered of major importance. Rheumatism, for example, could be guarded against by carrying a stolen potato in the pocket, while cramp in the leg could be prevented by tying a piece of stolen tar-cord around the affected limb. Unusual events, like a cock crowing at midnight or a fruit tree flowering out of season, were regarded as portents of death and disaster.[153]

It is significant that this superstitious darker side of village life survived at a time when newspapers, bicycles and railways excursions were breaking down much of the old isolation of country living. Such practices continued to offer an unobtrusive yet resilient challenge to the Christian tradition up to the end of the period, as the more perceptive clergymen recognized.

Nevertheless, as the rural community became more open to outside influences, support for these ancient beliefs undoubtedly waned. Much the same was true of the festivals and celebrations which had been held in villages for centuries past but which were now falling into disuse. Yet even in the 1900s most communities still had their May-day festivities, when children went round from house to house carrying garlands, singing songs, and begging for pennies. St Valentine's Day, too, was, widely observed, while mummers' plays were regularly performed at Christmas. In Oxfordshire the morris dancers continued to follow their traditional rituals, and in the midlands and the north Plough Monday was widely celebrated by the farm lads. But perhaps most important of all these survivals of earlier days was the feast of the local friendly society. This was regarded as the real fête of the labourers, and was often held around Whitsuntide. On the chosen day, all work in the village ceased. Stalls and sideshows were erected, and society members marched in procession, wearing coloured sashes, and with banners waving and band playing, to attend a special church service. Even the larger affiliated societies like the Ancient Order of Foresters and the Oddfellows, which were gradually replacing the small village clubs in much of the north and the midlands, decided to adopt these traditional trappings.

But, of course, the friendly society was more than a mere excuse for annual jollifications. It had an important economic and social function, providing members with a degree of protection against the hardships of life by way of sickness benefits, medical treatment, pensions in old age and funeral payments. One such organization existed at Dinton, Buckinghamshire, in the early 1870s, when it had about one hundred members and paid a sickness benefit of 8s. a week and a death grant of £3. Contributions amounted to 1s. 2d. a month. Unlike many societies elsewhere, it had no contract with a local doctor to give medical treatment to members. Another weakness was that it operated on a seven-year cycle, at the end of which it broke up and re-formed, with the funds divided among the erstwhile members.[75] This system was very popular in Buckinghamshire, but it clearly prevented a society from building up reserves to cope with a serious spell of epidemic disease or other misfortune. It also gave societies the opportunity to exclude from membership those who were in poor health or were growing old, and were thus more likely to be a charge on the funds. In this fashion, many of the apparent benefits of mutual aid were lost.

A further flaw in the friendly society movement was the fact that in some villages there were several competing clubs. Waddesdon in Buckinghamshire was a case in point, with no fewer than six different organizations in the early 1870s. Four were based on the seven-year 'sharing-out' principle, one was organized and patronized by the local farmers, and the other catered on a more permanent basis for a general mixture of villagers. There were only 350 members in the six clubs, the largest of which had about 90 members. Elsewhere it was common to have three or four clubs per village, with most of them originating in the different beer shops or public houses within the community. Since their club nights were normally held in the latter, the landlords had an obvious commercial interest in encouraging their proliferation. Yet such small bodies as these, operating without regard to actuarial principles, were extremely unstable and likely to collapse without warning, leaving their members stranded. Many even failed to register with the Registrar of Friendly Societies, and so had no official check on their activities.

The difficulties of the smaller clubs intensified during the later nineteenth century when the younger men left the villages for work elsewhere, and when the effects of agricultural depression reduced the voluntary contributions of farmers, landowners and others to their funds. Buckland Dinham in Somerset provides an example of this. In 1868 the payments made to members over seventy had been raised from 4s. to 5s. per week, while sickness benefits to younger members were also increased. Then in 1887 a reverse trend set in, with the old age benefit removed altogether and the maximum age of entry reduced from thirty-five to twenty-five. The society was obviously suffering from a preponderance of older members, and in 1912 it had to be wound up.[165]

It was to meet the deficiencies of the village clubs that county societies were established in a number of areas, under the patronage of local gentry and clergy, and with the objective of providing members with fixed and reliable benefits. Unfortunately, the fact that they did not have feast days and that their rates of contribution were higher than those of the smaller bodies made them unpopular among the labourers. The lack of a celebratory aspect was particularly important. To the agricultural labourer a club from which, so long as he was in health, he received absolutely nothing, 'no beer, no feast, no fire', was too much for human nature to bear, and so he preferred the village club, with all its weaknesses.[75]

Rather more hopeful was the expansion of the larger affiliated societies. Although in the south of England their rates of contribution were often too high for farm labourers, in the midlands and the north, where wages were better, they made considerable progress. Even in the south, as real wages improved in the final quarter of the century, rural recruitment increased. This was especially true of the Foresters, whose membership in Somerset alone rose from 1,267 in 1862, divided among twenty-two branches, to 11,981 and eighty-five branches in 1896. In five counties in the south-west in 1873 the allocation of branches of the affiliated orders and of local societies was as follows:[165]

	Branches of Orders	Local Societies
Somerset	84	62
Gloucestershire	142	108
Wiltshire	51	37
Dorset	49	36
Devon	112	109

When the Liberal government passed the 1911 National Insurance Act, these larger organizations were given further encouragement by the fact that they became 'approved societies' for the purpose of administering that legislation. By contrast, the small village clubs were unable to meet the conditions laid down for participation, and inevitably suffered in consequence. At Filkins in Oxfordshire the once flourishing village friendly society broke up in 1911–12, when the new benefit scheme came into operation.[31] Many others followed along the same path.

Yet, with all their weaknesses, these village clubs had fulfilled an important role. They had kept members from total dependence on a harsh Poor Law system, and had given to many a sense of self-reliance and communal pride. Their club nights were significant social events, offering men the opportunity to meet and discuss their problems and their hopes for the future. Even the discipline they imposed through their rules of conduct at meetings, and the fines they levied for bad behaviour and non-attendance, helped to give an ordered framework to day-to-day relationships within the community.

Only in the far north of England did friendly societies fail to penetrate rural life in any numbers. There their progress was hampered by the fact that labourers were normally hired by the year or half-year, and were thus cared for by their employer if they became ill within that period. In this part of the country burial societies alone flourished, designed to meet the funeral expenses of a member and his family.[75] But by their very nature they lacked the community spirit and wider social obligations of the genuine friendly society. As such, they failed to provide two of the major functions of a village club.

7
Rural Politics

Within the Victorian and Edwardian countryside the exercise of political power, like that of social leadership, remained largely in the hands of the aristocracy and gentry, despite their economic difficulties and the attempts by Parliament to weaken their control through a variety of reform measures. In many respects, the political history of these years is of a powerful élite waging a vigorous and mainly successful rearguard action against those who wished to deprive them of their erstwhile dominance. At the same time, there were growing pressures from both farmers and agricultural labourers to have a greater say in the running of affairs. Each of these groups formed unions whose aims, at least in part, were political. Thus the National Farmers' Union (established in 1908), although anxious to keep 'absolutely free from party politics', nevertheless soon evinced a desire to sponsor its own MPS. As one of its leaders pointed out in January 1911, many industrial trade unions already had members in the Commons; the farmers should follow that example: 'They wanted a member who could serve their interests alone, and who would go into the Cabinet and become Minister of Agriculture as soon as possible.'[45] To this end a special parliamentary fund was established, and in 1913 it was decided to appoint a 'lobbyist' whose duty it was to liaise between the Union and the Commons. At that date NFU membership stood at just below 20,000.

Equally, from the first appearance of their national union in 1872, the agricultural labourers lost no opportunity of demanding that the vote be extended to them – a right which they eventually secured in 1884. Prior to this, at many union meetings, franchise songs were sung in which the workers' feelings were made very clear:

But the County Member, I'm much afraid,
  Has but little care for us.
So we ought to vote, deny it who can,
  'Tis the right of an honest Englishman.[120]

And when, in 1906, just a decade after the collapse of the old National Agricultural Labourers' Union (NALU), a new organization was set up in Norfolk under the leadership of George Edwards, it is notable that three local Liberal politicians were among its sponsors. Significantly, during both the general elections held in 1910, Edwards and the union's full-time organizer were given leave from their official duties so that they might give full attention to electoral matters – in the Liberal interest.

Yet, despite this growing political activity, landowners were able to withstand most of the challenges to their authority with ease. More indicative of future decline was the fact that whereas in the 1850s and 1860s they had contributed roughly two-thirds of the House of Commons, between 1885 and 1905 that proportion had dropped to roughly a third; on the eve of the First World War it was about a quarter.[216] In 1885, for the first time, the number of commercial men and manufacturers in the House of Commons exceeded those from a landed background, though it was not until the Liberal Cabinet of 1906 that the aristocracy and gentry ceased to form a majority in the highest rank of government. Landowners like Lord Willoughby de Broke might rail against the 'formidable symptoms of industrialism, and the untoward manifestations of the thing called democracy' which were 'destined to disturb the peace of mind' of the landed classes, and 'to react so hideously upon the nation at large'.[282] But, before 1914, these fears proved largely illusory.

Nowhere were landowners' efforts to preserve the political *status quo* more successful than in the sphere of local government in England, although in Wales the story was rather different. Those who had seen the 1888 Local Government Act, establishing county councils, as a far-reaching reform which would force the magistracy to drop its dual role of judge and administrator in favour of 'representative democracy' were to be sadly disappointed. Up to the time of the First World War, most county councils were dominated by the same kind of people as those who had controlled the old non-elective system. As late as 1911, over one-fifth of the county councillors and aldermen in the forty-seven English county councils were listed in the exclusive pages of *Walford's County Families* for that year.[230] Only in a few cases was resentment against the magistracy sufficiently powerful to influence the overall complexion of councils, and in many cases candidates were returned unopposed. In Berkshire in 1889 there was no contest in twenty-six of the county's thirty-nine rural divisions. According to the *Hampshire Chronicle*, of these unchallenged candidates 'the large majority' were justices of the peace; and in England and Wales as a whole, only 54 per cent of county council seats were fought at these first elections. In subsequent years the percentage was lower still, with a mere 24 per cent disputed in 1892.[66] In the early days there was what the *Hampshire Chronicle* called a 'prevailing tendency to select county justices and other gentlemen' who had 'substantial interests in their respective localities'. Often, as in Northumberland, it was customary to bring defeated magistrates on to the council as aldermen.[101]

The larger magnates also frequently had a major say in the selection of candidates. In Bedfordshire, where the Duke of Bedford was chairman of the county council, his relative, Lord Ampthill, and his agent-in-chief, Rowland Prothero, both became councillors. In addition, the agent for the Woburn Abbey estate, Charles Hall, took an active part in electioneering, compiling a list showing the way electors intended to vote and lending carriages to convey friendly electors to the poll on election day. In 1889 he also sent the Duke a list of councillors elected from the fourteen districts in which his employer had interests; five of the fourteen were his tenants. In Woburn itself, the Duke's influence was 'regarded as decisive, and his wishes were respected'. Before the county council election of 1898 the sitting member, James Crouch, who owed his position to Bedford's support, even offered 'to retire in favour of anyone His Grace might prefer'. The Duke, for his part, made clear his wish 'to have early information' should opposition be attempted against his chosen candidate.[230]

One of the relatively few areas which did not follow this trend wus Holland in Lincolnshire, where the new Council was dominated by farmers and shopkeepers. Their success was attributed partly to a strong Liberal organization in the division, 'but mainly [to] a reaction against years of rule by a small, unrepresentative, and predominantly tory bench of magistrates'.[221] Norfolk, too, had ten JPs defeated at the election, but this still left twenty-six of the fifty-three councillors drawn from the ranks of the magistracy; in Essex, where nine JPs were defeated, twenty-five of the councillors were drawn from that sector out of a total of sixty-five.

So whilst landowners like Lord Harrowby could comment

gloomily: 'Our rural society here is convulsed by the County Council business: we shall all have to live in the county for the next 3 years to keep things straight', and Lord Stanmore could express apprehension that the rural gentry of England would follow those in France and 'have no influence' in village administration, in practice their anxieties proved unfounded.[30] Although some land-owners withdrew from the conduct of county affairs when their leadership role was challenged, most stayed on. And once the new institutions had settled down, the changes made in the running of county business proved largely cosmetic, whilst the cost of secur-ing election, plus the fact that the duties were unpaid, ensured that very few working men candidates of any kind were successful. As one critic put it, the county council was 'almost as out of reach of the agricultural labourer as the House of Lords'.[170]

Only in Wales, with its multiplicity of small peasant farmers, was the strength of anti-landlord, anti-Tory feeling sufficiently powerful to secure substantial alterations. Here the Liberals won control of every county save Brecknockshire when the first elec-tions were held in 1889. In North Wales 175 out of 260 councillors were Liberal, and in South Wales and Monmouthshire, 215 out of 330. As Kenneth Morgan has written, 'the age-long ascendancy of landowners on the magistrates' bench, self-perpetuating governors of the countryside, was abruptly terminated'.[218] The *Western Mail* attributed this change of fortune to the growing alienation between landlords and the 'humbler folk' of the countryside, with the former inclined to adopt attitudes of 'pretentious condescen-sion in their fitful intercourse with their "inferiors"' that had come 'to be keenly resented'. But Wales proved a notable exception to the general rule of county government under the new regime.

Much the same was true of the parish and district councils which were set up under the Local Government Act of 1894. The Liberals, who had brought forward the measure and had seen it emasculated by the House of Lords, were particularly disappoin-ted at its failure to give working men a major say in the running of local affairs. Prior to its introduction, parish business had been in the hands of virtually moribund vestries, in which the parson and the churchwardens played a leading role – a fact which aroused the hostility of many Nonconformists. As the President of the Local Government Board put it, the vestries were 'decrepit survivals of former days. . . . They have the form but not the power of local government; . . . and they are in the main useless and obstructive'. Even the hours at which they met were inconvenient, with meetings frequently held in the daytime, when labouring people were unable to attend. They were also discouraged from taking an active part in affairs if they did attend.

It was to counter these petty frustrations that the parish councils were established. To Joseph Arch, they were 'going to revolutionise' village life by giving England back 'her vanished peasantry'.[120] In view of the restricted powers which they possessed and the strict limits placed on their spending power (normally the proceeds of a 3d. rate only), this was most unlikely. The reality proved a good deal more sobering. Admittedly working men were elected in a number of parishes when the first polls were held in December 1894. In Norfolk, Suffolk and Oxfordshire, for example, they achieved considerable success. In Dorset, too, 'political feeling' ran 'very high', according to the *Hampshire Chronicle*, with labourers displaying 'great activity' in the elections, even defeating their employers at the poll in several places, while at Cranborne, a country seat of Lord Salisbury, the village postman defeated the vicar of the parish. But elsewhere the power of the landed interest and the success of its candidates were apparent at both parish and district council level. In Bedfordshire Charles Hall analysed a list of those elected in areas of the county where the Duke had property, and expressed satisfaction at the findings. The *Wilts and Gloucestershire Standard* of Cirencester, reflecting the views of the influential Bathurst family, declared that the 1894 elections had been a triumph for the traditional rulers of the countryside over those who had tried to teach the agricultural workers 'to look upon the parson and the squire and the farmer as their natural and mortal enemies . . . The elections show, either that "Tory tyranny" existed only in the heated imagination of party grievance-manufacturers, or else that the down-trodden electors hug their chains with provoking complacency'.[230]

Even such limited progress as the labourers and their supporters had achieved in 1894 was not sustained when the time for fresh elections came in 1897. Perhaps through indifference, or through a fear of reprisals should they appear over-zealous in the wrong cause, they tended to take little part in the proceedings. This was especially true of men living in tied housing. Possibly, too, the almost complete demise of rural trade unions by this date was of significance, since with their disappearance was lost any opportunity of making an organized attempt to capture the parish councils. The main beneficiaries from the new bodies were farmers, smallholders and village tradespeople. The farmers in particular were in no mood, in the mid-1890s when wheat had dropped to its lowest price of the century, 'to tolerate social as well as economic extinction'.[170]

It is, therefore, against a background of continuing dominance of local affairs by the traditional sectors of society that the detailed course of parliamentary politics in the countryside has to be examined. 'Democracy' had not effected any dramatic change in the conduct of county and parish business. What was its impact in the arena of the parliamentary constituency?

It was in 1872 that Parliament took the first step to meet the complaints of those electors who claimed that the existing system of 'open' contests was subject to abuse by landowners, who were able to put pressure on tenants to vote along a particular 'estate' line. By this date, cases of open intimidation in England were comparatively rare, but more subtle influences, such as the giving of favours to those who adopted the correct stance, were still exercised. Nevertheless it was in Wales that discontent on the issue reached a peak after the 1868 general election, when several hundred farmers who had voted Liberal in defiance of their landlords were evicted from their holdings. Almost thirty years later the bitter memory of those days remained fresh in the minds of rural electors in the principality. As a Cardiganshire witness told the Royal Commission on Land in Wales in 1896: 'The terrorism (*sic*) occasioned as the result of the evictions of 1869 can hardly be said to have quite subsided to this day, the old dread still lurks in the county.' The Royal Commission itself admitted that those events exerted 'so potent an influence as to cause tenants in many districts to put insecurity of tensure as the foremost of their grievances'.[89]

So it was that the 1872 Secret Ballot Act was passed, to end open voting once and for all. Unfortunately, the hopes that it would also eliminate all the abuses associated with the old system were soon dashed. One of the principal difficulties, as Henry Pelling points out, was that the confidentiality of the poll depended upon the integrity of the officials who were organizing it. Each ballot paper bore a number, and it was always possible for an unscrupulous official to trace the paper of a particular elector. Equally, it was easy for a landowner or a major employer to gain an impression of how a particular village or district had voted, and to react accordingly. Pelling writes of the 'very real fear of intimidation or "the screw" as it was called' which was found in rural districts. He quotes the example of the Marquess of Hastings, who was said to have evicted a farmer after the 1900 election by coldly informing him: 'I am anxious to have a tenant who would act on more friendly terms with his landlord, and also one not so hostile to the clergy and everything connected with the Church of England.'[228] Four years later, when Lord Wimborne changed his politics, the tenants on his Dorset estate were expected to do the same.

These problems of undue influence became more acute when the agricultural labourers obtained the vote in 1884, for then pressure was exerted by employers as well. According to one Norfolk farm worker, when election time came round, the 'Master would go to the man and say, "Wich way are you goen to vote John?" If the answer did not please him he would tell the man wich way he must vote, and John did it, or the Master made a spare man of him'.[178] In East Dorset as late as 1910 the Liberal candidate, Captain Guest, was unseated after a lengthy trial, on the grounds that he had infringed the regulations on election expenditure. But the judge also 'commented severely on some points in the conduct of the contest, especially the action of the agent of one of the Wimborne estates in standing before a polling station with a notebook', presumably recording the names of those who went to vote. Guest was the son of Lady Wimborne.[34] It was to guard against such veiled intimidation that a County Voters' Protection Society was set up in 1890, with the aim of giving rural workers 'something like genuine independence' by prosecuting those who sought to exert unfair influence. Not surprisingly, given the nature of such cases, it did not have much success.

These electoral misdoings were, however, not all confined to one side. Occasionally, especially before the passage of the 1883 Corrupt and Illegal Practices Prevention Act, those who gave their franchise to a candidate also expected a reward for it. In Essex during the 1870s the land agent and farmer J. Oxley Parker an enthusiastic Conservative, regularly encouraged supporters with the distribution of refreshments. According to his son, each Christmas day the farmyard was filled with freeman voters from Maldon who had come to wish him a happy Christmas 'and to drink his health and receive 2/6 each, and probably some food besides'. At election times, both then and later, Oxley Parker's waggons were loaded with voters, and the horses drawing them were adorned with blue rosettes. Each man going to the poll was given a blue rosette, and a large blue flag was fixed to the waggon.[223]

But there were far more direct demands for favours than this. In Buckinghamshire, after a by-election in 1876 caused by Benjamin Disraeli's elevation to the peerage, the successful Conservative candidate, Thomas Fremantle, was approached to secure a post office appointment for one voter. Another man was even more explicit:

> I have taken the Libearty (*sic*) of writing to you to ask you a favour for a Presant (*sic*) of a bit of *Game* for *Christmas* as i went down to Long Crendon Polling Place to Vote for you wich i done with Pleasure and i thought it nothing but right to ask you for a little *Game* as it put me to a great expence and ill convenience.[10]

This was endorsed by Fremantle: 'Answd. 18 Dec: to send a present in consideration of voting might render me liable to a petition', that is, to an attempt to unseat him.

In Wiltshire, Francis Kilvert similarly recorded the anger of a disappointed Chippenham elector whom he met. The man had voted for the successful candidate at the general election of 1874, but had received no share of the 'gift of coal etc.' subsequently distributed by the successful candidate's agent. Kilvert then added sadly: 'So much for electioneering, and the efficacy of the bribery bill. It is all corruption, corruption, corruption.'[232]

Even after 1883 something approaching bribery could still apply. In 1898 Henry Chaplin, as President of the Local Government Board, appointed one of his leading constituency supporters in Lincolnshire to the post of Poor Law auditor for the county, at a salary of about £1,000 per annum.[221]

A less materialistic way in which landed aristocrats could reward influential supporters was by securing for them appointment to the magistracy. In March 1892 the Marquess of Salisbury's eldest son,

Lord Cranborne, was advised by the election agent in his Darwen constituency to submit the names of certain political supporters to the chancellor of the Duchy of Lancaster: 'As this is the last time we, possibly, may be able to do the job, would you have any objections to my sending up the names of Pilkington Shinock. . . . If appointed it would do good and bend the whole Shinock interest to us.'[230]

Not until the early twentieth century were efforts made to widen the source of recruitment to the bench. First, in 1906, came the abolition of all property qualifications for magistrates, followed, four years later, by the appointment of a Royal Commission to examine the selection of successful candidates. The Commission, in its report, referred disapprovingly to the fact that 'in many districts the selection of even competent Justices of the Peace' was regarded 'as the result of party success, and the Justices themselves . . . regarded as the representatives of a political party or of a social class'. This imperilled the respect in which they were held, and 'without which the due and effective administration of the law is unattainable'.[79] It was in accordance with the Royal Commission's recommendations that in 1911 the sole power of the lord lieutenant to recommend the appointment of JPs was abolished. Instead, in an effort to break the aristocratic and Conservative Party hold on these appointments, advisory committees were to be established within the counties and boroughs. But the process of change was slow, and in 1913 some advisory committee members had still not been appointed. Inevitably the lord lieutenant continued to exercise many discretionary powers.

Appointment as a magistrate, or even as a Poor Law auditor, was a reward available to political supporters in the upper ranks of county society only. But those lower down the scale were not averse to receiving less prestigious gifts, along the lines of those requested of Thomas Fremantle. As late as 1895 Rider Haggard, who contested East Norfolk as a Conservative, recalled the pressures to which he had been subjected by an importunate electorate:

From the moment a candidate appears in the field he is fair game and every man's hand is in his pocket. Demands for 'your patronage and support' fall on him, thick as leaves in Vallombrosa. I remember that I was even pestered to supply voters with wooden legs! Why should an election in a county division cost, as this one did, something over £2,000 in all?[176]

When he arrived at meetings he would speak for about half an hour, often to a hostile audience of agricultural labourers who were supporters of his opponent. They were 'wont to express their active dislike of me and my opinions by making hideous noises resembling those of the lower animals in pain. . . . When the meeting was over my wife and I . . . used to emerge and face the booing without, which sometimes was accompanied by hustling and stone-throwing'. In the event he lost by only just under two hundred votes, but the experience was so distasteful that he refused to repeat it.

With the widening of the franchise in 1884, many county members and candidates found the burden of campaigning especially arduous, at a time when most local journeys had still to be undertaken laboriously by horse-drawn vehicles. For as J. W. Lowther wrote to Sir Stafford Northcote in that year, it was no longer possible for MPs to confine their attention to a few important meetings; now 'every petty hamlet expects its member or members to pay annual visits in person'.[221]

Of course, a large proportion of the electors who followed the lead of landlords or employers did so neither as a result of intimidation nor of bribery. Some conformed because of genuine loyalty to the family concerned or because of a belief that the traditional leaders of society were those best fitted to lead. Others took the view that it was 'safer' to follow the landlord's line. As an Oxfordshire cottager firmly informed one canvasser who was seeking his vote in defiance of the landlord's known opinions: 'No, Sir, excuse me . . . I don't want to lose my coals at Christmas.' Even on the Ardington and Lockinge estate of the enlightened Lord Wantage in Berkshire, a journalist was told in the early 1890s: 'Oh, yes . . . they all votes Lord Wantage's way. . . . It wouldn't do for 'em to go again 'im.'[213]

But many took their landlord's opinion from a simple desire to please or from personal diffidence at expressing an independent view on political questions. Only when something happened to upset this quiescence, as in 1885, when the agricultural labourers exercised their franchises for the first time, or in 1906, when the free trade versus tariff protection battle raged, did they follow their own initiative. It was in these circumstances that Henry Pelling could write of the rural divisions of central England between 1885 and 1910:

> the most Liberal constituency was that with the greatest Liberal landlord (Mid-Northamptonshire – Lord Spencer); and the most Unionist constituency was that with the most influential Unionist family (Mid-Buckinghamshire – the Rothschilds). The swing from Liberalism to Unionism between 1885 and 1892, which was especially noticeable north of the Thames . . . was apparently primarily due to the transference of the allegiance of former Liberal landlords – the Dukes of Bedford and Grafton as well as the Rothschilds and a good many lesser figures. There were some remarkable Liberal successes in 1906, which showed that the big landlords did not have it quite all their own way. But by 1910 things reverted to 'normal' and 'normality' meant that traditional county influences were still of decisive importance in this part of England.[228]

In West Derbyshire the role of the Duke of Devonshire was similarly paramount. Throughout the period of 1885 to 1910 the successful candidate was always a member of the Cavendish family, and when the Devonshire allegiance was switched from Liberal to Unionist following the former Party's Home Rule split in 1886, the voters obediently followed suit.

In the Wisbech division of Cambridgeshire, the accession of the politically committed 11th Duke of Bedford in 1893 led to the establishment of a Unionist Association on his Thorney estate at the end of May 1895, shortly before the general election of that year. The Duke himself acted as president, and membership quickly reached over one hundred. On 4 July it was decided to suspend the Association for the duration of the election, but when polling took place on 17 July the Unionist candidate was successful, capturing the seat from his Liberal opponent.[2] The Bedford connection had seemingly helped to bring that change about.

Flora Thompson, in *Lark Rise to Candleford*, perhaps summarized most clearly the strange mixture of enthusiasm and diffidence which characterized many humbler electors at that time. At her native Juniper Hill they took their new responsibility as voters seriously, and often discussed the questions of the day in the public house:

A mild Liberalism prevailed, a Liberalism that would be regarded as hide-bound Toryism now, but was daring enough in
those days. One man who had been to work in Northampton
proclaimed himself a Radical; but he was cancelled out by the
landlord, who called himself a 'true blue'. With the collabora-
tion of this Left and Right, questions of the moment were
thrashed out and settled to the satisfaction of the majority. . . .
Sometimes a speech by Gladstone, or some other leader would
be read aloud from a newspaper and punctuated by the fervent
'Hear! Hear' of the company. Or Sam, the man with advanced
opinions, would relate with reverent pride the story of his
meeting and shaking hands with Joseph Arch, the farm worker's
champion. 'Joseph Arch!' he would cry. 'Joseph Arch is the man
for the farm labourer!' and knock on the table and wave aloft
his pewter mug, very carefully, for every drop was precious.

Then the landlord, standing back to the fireplace . . . would
say with the authority of one in his own house, 'It's no good you
chaps think'n you're goin' against the gentry. They've got the
land, and they've got the money, *an'* they'll keep it. Where'd
you be without them to give you work an' pay your wages, I'd
like to know?' and this, as yet, unanswerable question would
cast a chill over the company until some one conjured it away
with the name of Gladstone. Gladstone! The Grand Old Man!
The People's William! Their faith in his power was touching.[268]

If the elimination of unfair electoral 'influence' was one major
issue tackled in county constituencies in the mid-Victorian period,
a second, still more serious grievance for country people was the
franchise question itself. Although the urban householder had
received the vote in 1867, in rural districts a limited franchise
continued to apply. Only those working men who lived within the
area of a borough constituency or who, like the agricultural trade
union leader Joseph Arch owned their own cottage, were able to
exercise this basic democratic right. Inevitably, the rural unions
gave the matter their attention from early days and in this they
received the support of many non-labourer friends including
Joseph Chamberlain, Jesse Collings, and Sir George Trevelyan.
These men, all active Liberals, saw the enfranchisement of the
labourers as a possible way of 'dishing' the Conservatives in their
traditional rural strongholds.

In the event, the county householder was given the vote only in 1884, when the union movement had long passed its peak. But it is clear that the unionists' earlier efforts to secure reform had been influential in bringing that change about. Even the *Economist*, never an enthusiastic supporter of agricultural trade unionism, recognized their contribution in 1877, in an article entitled 'A Positive Argument for Extending the County Franchise'. In this it claimed that the 'existence and spread of labourers' unions' supplied 'a prima facie reason for giving the labourers votes. It is evidence that the class has, and it is conscious that it has, desires and interests peculiar to itself, and that it can no longer be treated as a mere appendage to some other class.' The NALU newspaper naturally made much the same point, declaring in 1884 that but for the union's struggles, the 'settlement of the county franchise question' would have been as remote as it appeared to be in 1872, when it began its agitation.[43] But perhaps the most powerful expression of this view was put forward by the Countess of Warwick in an introduction to the autobiography of Joseph Arch, which she edited: 'The supreme achievement of the Union, its culminating point as it were', she wrote, 'was the franchise for the agricultural labourer. When that was obtained the Union was no longer politically necessary, and it died a natural death.'[120]

Certainly, the NALU spared no effort in promoting the cause of franchise reform, and it is noticeable that recruitment to its ranks showed a temporary improvement during the months in which the 1884 Bill was winding its way through Parliament. Membership rose to about 18,000 in that year, as compared to approximately 15,000 recorded in 1883 and 10,700 in 1885. When the measure finally reached the statute book, immediate steps were taken to advise labourers on the action they must take to register as voters. Information was given on the mechanics of voting itself, with mock polls held by many union branches. In these both Liberal and Conservative 'candidates' were put forward though, not surprisingly, the former always emerged victorious, as at Alderton in Suffolk, where of eighty ballot papers distributed, seventy-eight were completed in favour of the Liberal.

The first general election under the new arrangements took place in the winter of 1885, following a redistribution of constituency seats, and in the weeks that led up to it the NALU newspaper strove hard to persuade the labourers to follow a Liberal line.

Joseph Arch, the union president, who was himself to be that party's candidate in North-West Norfolk, addressed countless meetings at which he hammered home the same message. As early as February 1885 he had issued an appeal to the new electors of his native Warwickshire, calling upon them 'to return a good sound Liberal reformer for every seat' in what he described as that 'Tory-ridden' county. Later he reassured the labourers about the secrecy of the ballot, and suggested that on polling day, 'all the working men of the village meet together, and march to the polling booth, with one of your best men at the head'. The advice was designed to counter any timidity or diffidence which the individual labourer might feel, especially if he saw his employer or his landlord's agent in the vicinity of the polling booth and knew he was going to vote contrary to their wishes.[185] Landlords made their own arrangements, too. In South Bedfordshire, the Duke of Bedford's agent noted that instructions had been 'received that the Duke's workmen and Labourers were to attend the Polls . . . in their own time after working hours'.[2] It is unlikely that many of them ignored this advice.

The parties were aware that the new voters now formed a majority of the rural electorate, and naturally turned their attention towards them. Political clubs were formed in the larger villages, usually branches of the Conservative Primrose League or member clubs of the National Liberal Federation, and many evening meetings were organized. Joseph Chamberlain, in his so-called 'unauthorized programme', brought forward a series of propositions particularly designed to appeal to the newly enfranchised farm workers and to swing them behind the Liberals in the vital county constituencies. Among these proposals were free elementary education; manhood suffrage, with payment of MPs; and land law reform, to give the labourer 'a stake in the soil', through the granting of allotments and smallholdings. By Conservative opponents, the latter scheme was derisorily dubbed 'three acres and a cow', but it did the Liberals no harm in the eyes of many rural voters, who hankered after smallholder status.

This flurry of interest in the welfare of the new voters naturally caused some resentment among the farmers, who found themselved neglected. As the *Mark Lane Express*, writing on their behalf, sourly declared: 'we have been astonished at the almost exclusive regard paid to the new voters by party leaders on both sides, as if the old voters counted for nothing'. It then added ominously: 'We have on more than one occasion declared our opinion to the effect that the farmers would carry a large proportion of their workmen with them, and we have protested against the cynical manner in which party leaders have ignored, or nearly ignored, the interests of those agricultural electors who, on previous occasions, have been considered as the arbiters of the county contests.' Indeed, as one Norfolk labourer pointed out, the farmers were so bitter against their workers having the vote precisely because they knew that if the men went to the poll in a body and voted for a single candidate, they would carry their choice and defeat the farmers' favoured candidate. These feelings of resentment on the part of agriculturists were to be expressed in later elections, as in 1892, when a 'North Lincoln Farmer' wrote to the *Mark Lane Express* to protest that of 'all the three classes whose interests are bound up with the soil, the farmer is the most neglected both by politicians and others'. It was the labourers who were receiving the lion's share of attention.

Nevertheless, from the Liberals' point of view this careful courting of the labourer brought its reward in 1885, when despite losses in the towns, where there were defections among some industrial workers and Irish electors, their success in the counties enabled them to emerge once more as the governing party. The final state of the poll was 334 Liberal MPs, 250 Conservatives, and 86 Irish Nationalists. Of those Liberal seats 133 had been won in the counties, as compared to only fifty-four county seats held in 1880. In Shropshire, for example, three of the four county divisions went Liberal on the only occasion in the county's history when the Conservatives' share of the vote was exceeded by that of the Liberals. Here, as elsewhere, men tramped through dark lanes to attend meetings in order to 'stick up for Gladstone', and their partisanship led to a serious riot at Market Drayton.[128]

For the workers, the election was their first opportunity to show their independence of landlords and farmers by voting against those whom their traditional masters normally supported. But apart from this spirit of 'rebellion' religious factors played a part, too, in some constituencies. In districts where Nonconformity was strong, support for the Liberal Party was at its greatest, for the Church of England was often seen as 'the Tory Party at prayer'. This applied particularly in Wales, where Nonconformist ministers were accused by their opponents of being 'devoted adherents' of the Liberal cause, whose 'influence sways the elections from one end of the Principality to the other'.[49] In the Richmond division of Yorkshire, too, it was claimed that 'any little dissenting chapel at election time' because 'a committee room for the Radicals'.[228] Both in 1885 and later, the proximity of industrial employment, or the existence of industrial workers in a rural constituency, operated in the same direction. In the south-west of England the mid-Cornwall or St Austell division was considered the safest Liberal seat in the region, primarily because of the loyalty of the china-clay workers. In Northumberland, in 1891, the *Times* mourned the decline of 'territorial influence' in 'forming and educating political opinion'. The reason lay in the growth of industry, particularly mining: 'The real secret of the radicalism of rural Northumbria', it declared, 'is to be found in the propinquity of the miners. The hind is well paid, but the underground miner is paid much better.'

However, although the Liberals were returned in 1885 as the largest political party and the landowning monopoly of the county representation was at last undermined, parliamentary affairs were soon in a state of flux. From the beginning of the new session the Irish Nationalists held the balance of power. Inevitably, Irish affairs came to overshadow proceedings until they led, in the summer of 1886, to a split in the Liberal Party, as Joseph Chamberlain, Lord Hartington, and a number of other leading figures refused to accept Gladstone's Home Rule proposals.

Meanwhile, given their preoccupation with Irish matters, the Liberals failed to act on any of the reform measures listed in Chamberlain's 'unauthorized programme'. Although understandable in the circumstances, the omission caused much disappointment to rural voters. At the same time the Conservatives redoubled their efforts to win back former strongholds. Branches of the Primrose League were formed, and candidates were encouraged to 'nurse' their constituencies. As the *Wiltshire County Mirror* pointed out, the successful candidate was likely to be the one who visited the village feasts, chatted in village schoolrooms, and took part in 'pleasant friendly musical evenings in the winter'.

Apart from disillusionment with the Liberals' peformance and, in some cases, a fear of intimidation if they supported the 'wrong' candidate, a third factor undermining labourer support for the Party in the general election of 1886 (which arose from the Home

Rule split) was the fact that it took place at the haymaking season, when the men were busily engaged in the fields. Many could not spare the time to vote, especially if they knew that their employer disapproved of their politics, and was likely to dismiss them if they simply walked off the job. Even the agricultural trade union leader, Joseph Arch, was defeated in North-West Norfolk. He attributed the rebuff to a lack of carriages to convey his supporters to the polling stations and to 'great territorial influence', but he also noted that some of his supporters shouted to him that they had begun work 'at 3 a.m. in order to have plenty of time in which to walk to the poll'. Not all potential voters were prepared to rise at that hour in order to give themselves a good start to the day's tasks.[185] Overall, the Conservatives and Unionists emerged victorious from the contest, with the Liberals taking only 83 county seats as opposed to the 133 secured six months earlier. With a few variations, this relatively poor showing in the counties continued to apply to the Liberal Party until 1906. There were occasional upsets – Walter Long, a leading Conservative, was defeated in the Devizes division of Wiltshire in 1892, for example – but in general the elections of 1886, 1892, 1895 and 1900 were all remarkable for the high level of non-voting in county constituencies. This may have been partly due to the fact that all four elections took place during the busy haymaking and harvest period. But there was, too, fear of intimidation 'when the landlords were so united on one side in politics'. In Pelling's view, even the success of Joseph Arch between 1892 and 1900 was due more to the exceptional tolerance of the major landlords in Norfolk North-West (namely the Prince of Wales on the Sandringham estate and the Earl of Leicester at Holkham) than to any 'inherent independence of the labourers'.[228] Emigration, also, may have weakened the Liberal ranks, in that the most determined and independent men were those likely to seek their fortune elsewhere. Finally, there was the fact that in a number of rural seats the successful candidate was returned unopposed. In Shropshire, although there were eight general elections between 1885 and 1918, only in 1885, 1906 and January 1910 were all of the seats contested. From 1886 to 1900 the five members were Conservatives or their allies, and in 1895 and 1900 only *one* seat was contested against them, on both occasions unsuccessfully.[128] Given arrangements such as these, labourers anxious to support the Radical cause must have felt frustration and despair at their inability to change the existing order. Even when an opportunity to vote was offered them, many doubtless felt that it was just a waste of time to go to the polls. On a broader basis, too, attempts were made in 1892–93 to combine the political interests of landowner, farmer and labourer in a National Agricultural Union, under the leadership of Lord Winchilsea. Its programme proposed that the movement of rents and wages should be linked to the price of corn, but in the event the labourers regarded it with much suspicion. The farmers, too, were sceptical and within a few months the whole organization was virtually dead.

Not until 1906 was the inertia of the countryside again seriously disturbed, when a section of the Conservative Party turned to tariff reform and protectionism. Although this was a cause dear to the heart of some landowners and farmers hit by the competition of cheap foreign food, their labourers took a different line, remembering the misery which their forefathers had endured in the days before the Corn Laws were repealed in 1846. Even among farmers, opinions were divided. Milk producers, benefiting from cheap imported animal fodder, continued to support free trade; grain producers, although in favour of protectionism in general, had little enthusiasm for the cause of imperial preference, which was also a part of the tariff reformers' programme. After all, it was from Canada, India, Australia and New Zealand that a major portion of food imports was coming. In addition, a number of agriculturists considered tariffs on imported food to be outside the realms of practical politics, given the importance of the large urban electorate. In support of their pessimistic view they could point to the imposition of a revenue duty of 3d. per hundredweight on imported corn and 5d. per hundredweight on imported flour which had been included in the 1902 Budget, at the end of the Boer War. Opposition from consumers had been immediate and powerful, the measure had failed to help the farmers, and in 1903 it had been hastily repealed. It was difficult to see any more far-reaching proposals being implemented in these circumstances.

So the protectionist cause foundered both in the towns and in the countryside. The *Annual Register* of 1906 commented on the 'remarkable Unionist defeats' at this election, and noted that 'in the agricultural districts . . . the fear of the "little loaf" was perhaps reinforced by the traditions of Corn Law days'. Liberal satisfaction was immense. George Sturt, himself a Radical, noted in his diary on 16 January 1906 that the celebrations of the Farnham Liberals 'jubilating over the downfall of some other supporter of Balfour' could be heard more than a mile and a half away. A few days later he also reported that various attempts had been made to persuade working people to vote Conservative, but without success. At Waverley Abbey all the men had to wear Tory colours and were taken to the polls, but amongst themselves they said of the Conservative candidate, 'he's the feller as wants to interfere with our grub', and they voted against him. In Warwickshire that committed Tory supporter, Lord Willoughby de Broke, described the shock experienced by the country gentlemen when the results of the election were announced. For the Liberals now had 429 seats, compared to the Conservatives' 158; they thus held a substantial overall majority in the Commons, independent of the Irish Nationalists. The proportion of landowners among MPS dropped to one-fifth, and in Willoughby de Broke's view the Conservative Party now 'had nothing to fall back upon except the House of Lords'.[282] It is to an examination of the implications for rural politics of the Lords versus Commons battles which now ensued that we must turn.

A growing alarm over the long-term effects of a wider franchise, combined with a deep-seated anger and frustration at the impact of agricultural depression and of government taxation policies, had been present among the more conservative elements of the landed classes well before the 1906 Liberal landslide. Rowland Prothero, later to be chief agent to the Duke of Bedford, had warned in 1888 of the dangers of land confiscation, and had complained that when the air was filled with 'vague threats, the attitude of ministers remained studiously neutral'.[233] Eleven years later the Earl of Meath suggested that the growing population of Britain would create a poor and hungry stratum which, 'driven to desperation and beguiled by the honeyed words of Socialists and Anarchists', would seek 'to improve their miserable lot by the general destruction of society'. To the Duke of Northumberland, there had never been a period 'when masses of men . . . have been persuaded that it is good that they should be compelled to work for a daily wage while others should not. Our ancestors were wise enough to see this, and kept the political power of the State in the hands of those who had property.'[230]

Within society at large, meanwhile, there was disquiet over the great inequalities of land ownership which existed in Britain, with some reformers demanding outright nationalization of this most basic asset, as Prothero had feared. Among them was the Socialist writer Robert Blatchford, who boldly asserted: 'You will find that the original title to all the land possessed by private owners is the title of conquest or theft. . . . You may say, of course, that the law of the land has confirmed the old nobility in the possession of their stolen property. That is quite true. But it is equally true that the law was made by the landowners themselves.'[180] Much the same approach was adopted by Alfred R. Wallace in his *Land Nationalisation*, which was first published in 1892 and had run into five editions by 1909. He also linked state ownership to a widening of access to land occupation, arguing that by this means alone, 'every man, from the labourer upwards' might procure a suitable property for his personal occupation, 'and, unless this is done, fully half the benefits of a good land-system will be lost'.[277] In 1889 the newly established Land Nationalization Society embarked upon a propaganda campaign in the rural areas, sending out yellow-painted vans to tour the countryside. It was a practice they continued up to the time of the First World War.

Among the most persuasive critics was the American reformer Henry George, whose book *Progress and Poverty* first became widely available in the United Kingdom in 1881. By the end of the decade, more than a hundred thousand copies of it had been sold there. George Edwards, later to be the founding father of the National Union of Agricultural and Allied Workers, read the book at around this time and asserted that Henry George's ideas had done 'more to mould my thought on social questions than those of any other writer'.[152] George believed that the true remedy for the poverty which had accompanied industrialization and economic progress was to 'make land common property', not by direct confiscation as the nationalizers envisaged, but by confiscation of the rent which the land yielded. 'We already take some rent in taxation', he declared. 'We have only to make some changes in our modes of taxation to take it all.' George's British supporters translated these proposals into a demand for a reimposition of the land tax. And in 1883 an organization subsequently christened the

English Land Restoration League was formed to campaign for the acceptance of George's proposals. In 1891 it extended its activities by embarking upon a largely unsuccessful series of propaganda tours into the rural districts, in which it sought to persuade farm workers and other country people of the need to end the existing system of land tenure.[126] In several counties it also supported some short-lived agricultural trade unions. Unlike those of its Land Nationalization Society counterparts, however, these tours were ended in 1897.

Debates over landownership had, therefore, already brought the subject to the forefront of national politics by the 1880s. But the real debate was joined following the Liberal government's 1909 Budget. The particular point at issue was its proposal to introduce a new land tax to help pay for its social reform programme. Although this did not affect *agricultural* land as such, but only the unearned increment secured on development land, it was seen as a thin end of an undesirable wedge by many apprehensive owners. Their anxieties were reinforced by a further proposal to carry out a national enquiry into land values and ownership. The increasingly radical speeches of the Chancellor of the Exchequer, David Lloyd George, also seemed to confirm their fears, as did those of other ministers, including the leading Scottish politician and lawyer Alexander Ure. He declared 'he would not be satisfied till he got land taxed at 20s. in the £'.[87] In a speech at Limehouse in July 1909, Lloyd George spelt out his philosophy:

> We mean to value all the land in the kingdom. . . . And if land goes up in future by hundreds and thousands an acre through the efforts of the community, the community will get 20 per cent of that increment. . . . Take the very well-known case of the Duke of Northumberland, when a county council wanted to buy a small plot of land as a site for a school to train the children who in due course would become the men labouring on his property. The rent was quite an insignificant thing; his contribution to the rates I think was on the basis of 30s. an acre. What did he demand for a school? £900 an acre. All we say is this – if it is worth £900, let him pay taxes on £900.[174]

And in October of the same year, in tones reminiscent of Robert Blatchford, he asked a Newcastle audience: 'Who ordained that a few should have the land of Britain as a perquisite? Who made ten thousand people owners of the soil, and the rest of us trespassers in the land of our birth?' Popular songs were composed to the effect that 'God gave the land to the people'.

So it was that many 'backwoods' peers, already embittered by declining rent rolls, decided to make a stand on the emotive issue of land taxation. In all, about thirty per cent of the 350 peers who entered the Unionist lobby to reject the 1909 Budget were recruited from those who normally attended the House fewer than ten times per Parliamentary session.[230] But even active members of the Upper House felt it necessary to make their hostility clear. Lord Stanmore was one who reluctantly came to that decision:

> If we assent to the hardly veiled 'tacking' involved in the first part of the Bill, we shall proclaim our utter impotence and incompetence to play the part of a second chamber . . . and we shall be swept away as mere cumberers of the ground with the common assent of all parties.
>
> On the other hand there is no doubt danger in taking a bolder course. Revolutionary agitators may succeed in stirring up among the mass of ignorant voters a really honest indignation against what they are told are 'Lordly usurpations' and 'unconstitutional tyranny' and the common sense of the more thoughtful part of the community may be thus overborne. But at the worst we should end with dignity, and not be branded by future generations as a set of mean spirited cowards who deserved our fate.[30]

Despite this opposition, the Budget was eventually approved, after a fresh general election, in April 1910. But the issue, coming in the wake of several previous examples of Lords hostility to the legislation of the Liberal government, raised grave constitutional questions. The upshot was that the Liberals determined to curb the powers of the Upper House by introducing a Parliament Bill, which would end that House's power to veto financial legislation and would allow it to delay other measures for no longer than three years.

The official policy of the leaders of the Unionist Party, faced with a Liberal threat to create enough peers to pass the Bill, was to abstain from voting on the measure. But to a small group of 112 members of the Lords, this lukewarm response was not enough. Among the leaders of the 'diehards' was Lord Willoughby de

Broke. However, it is wrong to see the opposition they offered as merely the last desperate throe of reactionary 'backwoodsmen' against the new order. Many of them were regular attenders at Parliament, who were prepared to see reform on such issues as tariff duties, the introduction of national military service, and allied matters. Only on certain issues were they resistant to change, and among these was the constitutional question.

Yet, if most of them were not 'backwoodsmen' in the accepted sense, their personal commitment to rural life and to the traditional power of the landed classes was considerable. Many expressed opposition to political change in language more reminiscent of the hunting field than the debating chamber. Willoughby de Broke, for example, supported the hereditary principle by comparing it with his experience of country life: 'I have been brought up in the midst of stock-breeding of all kinds all my life, and I am prepared to defend the hereditary principle . . . whether the principle is applied to Peers or . . . to foxhounds.'[230] Similarly, when he was reproached for his opposition to Lord Lansdowne, the Unionist leader in the Upper House, who had adopted a temporizing stance, he replied defiantly: 'As master of hounds, I don't like killing a fox without my huntsmen, but it is better than losing my hounds.' Those who supported his views on the Parliament Bill were referred to as the 'bag'.[282]

In the end the fight of the 'diehards' against the new legislation proved abortive, but that outcome was achieved only at the expense of engendering great bitterness between themselves and their party leaders, as well as with the Liberals.

Even after this struggle the land question did not disappear from the parliamentary scene. For although owners were able to undermine the efforts of the land valuation survey be delaying the submission of their returns, so that by the autumn of 1913 only two-thirds of it had been completed, Lloyd George refused to let the matter rest. He persuaded fellow-Cabinet members of the need to tackle allied social questions, such as providing agricultural labourers with a living wage (a cause dear to the heart of the farm workers' union, which had pressed for the provision of statutory wages machinery since 1910), as well as fair hours of work, improved housing and increased access to smallholdings and allotments. He also proposed that greater powers of compensation should be given to tenant farmers to meet the cost of damage caused to their crops by game and to meet expenditure on improvements which they had carried out to their holdings. But most controversial of all was his demand that the state be 'granted far greater powers both to acquire land and to prevent land monopoly'.[245] Later that year he announced that the government had decided to set up a Ministry of Lands which would incorporate the existing powers of the Board of Agriculture, but would also deal with such matters as land valuation, the control and supervision of smallholdings, land development, the resolution of disputes between landlords and tenants, and similar matters. In this fashion, 'the State would have far greater control over the management of land than it had ever had before'. His interventionist ideas were reinforced by the Land Enquiry Committee which the Liberal Party had set up in 1912; a year later its report argued that insecurity of tenure was preventing tenants from investing their own capital in more intensive farming. It recommended that government-appointed Land Courts should be given powers, on appeal by either party to a lease, to fix fair rents, decide compensation payable at the end of a lease, and to fix the price to be paid upon compulsory acquisition of land by public bodies. In support of this policy it pointed to the success of the Land Court system in Scotland.[204] It was in these circumstances that the *Economist* of 25 October 1913 warned that once the questions of Home Rule and the disestablishment of the Church in Wales had been carried through, land reform would be the next major issue before the country.

However, by now problems in Ireland and the threat of World War were looming larger, and the land campaign petered out. Even the establishment of a legal minimum wage for agricultural workers was delayed until May 1918. Yet the early years of the twentieth century saw, for the first time, the issue of landownership brought into the central arena of national affairs. In those feverish pre-War years the rights and powers of the landed interest assumed a major constitutional importance which they were never to achieve again.

As for the owners themselves, many decided to take advantage of an upturn in the market to dispose of parts of their property. Among the reasons put forward was their apprehension as to the probably tendency of future legislation and taxation in regard to land. The Duke of Bedford disposed of nearly half his estates in these years, and in 1912 alone nineteen noblemen were listed as selling large properties. In 1913 the number of the nobility in the land market was even greater, and the half-season of 1914, interrupted by the War, brought the dispersal during the previous five years to a value of about £20m., or perhaps 800,000 acres.[266]

To blame a radical government for the changes was a convenient ploy brought forward by many who were disposing of major family inheritances at this time. But, in reality, of greater importance was the fact that after years of agricultural depression, the ownership of land was losing much of its former lustre. The bigger landlords were anxious to diversify their capital holdings, perhaps by investing in the Colonies or South America or – most unwisely – in Russia.[87] One such case was that of the leading Conservative Walter Long, who announced a major land sale in 1910, on the grounds that government policy towards the larger owners had compelled 'all of us . . . to most carefully consider our position'. In fact he had begun to dispose of his property several years earlier, well before the 1909 Finance Bill was brought forward. The latter had become merely a convenient scapegoat for later sales. He was not alone in adopting that approach.

After the War land sales increased yet again, and in the four years 1918–21 inclusive it is estimated that a quarter of England and Wales changed hands. Only with the collapse of agriculture in 1921, together with the general recession in business, did the hectic activity at last die away.[266] It is to an examination of agricultural conditions in the period immediately before and during the First World War that we shall now turn.

8

The End of an Era: 1900–18

When Rider Haggard carried out his survey of rural England in
1901/2, much of the pessimism he expressed about the immediate
prospects of British agriculture was already out of date. He
envisaged a future in which the highest standards of farming would
be abandoned by agriculturists driven to the edge of financial
disaster by years of low prices, and predicted a countryside
denuded of its most intelligent and active labourers.[177] Yet as
early as the mid-1890s the downward movement of grain prices,
one of the major symbols of the depression, had been arrested, as
world demand for corn at last caught up with the vast increase in
supply which had taken place in the final quarter of the nineteenth
century. Beef prices, too, moved upwards from the summer of
1908, as falls in cattle sales from American ranches reduced the
volume of meat available for export. Farmers who had survived
the agricultural depression by cutting costs to meet falling prices
now found themselves with the unfamiliar task of holding down
their expenditure at a time of rising prices and increased labour
costs.

The upturn in prices was the most obvious, and for farmers and
landowners the most welcome, sign of changing times, but it was
not the sole indicator. Foreign produce still took a major share of
the British home market, and agriculturists had to come to terms
with the fact that in the early twentieth century, even with the aid
of imported feeding stuffs, they were able to supply only about
two-fifths of the beef, mutton and lamb, and less than a quarter of
the wheat and cheese consumed in this country. Fewer people
were fed from home resources in 1909–13 than in 1870, and the
tillage area of England and Wales had fallen by 3¼ m. acres, as
corn land was laid down to grass.[154] Yet, by changing products and
improving methods, agriculturists had gradually adjusted to the
new circumstances. In particular, sales of liquid milk became the
principal source of revenue of dairy farmers, with more than 80
per cent of total milk output disposed of in this fashion, principally

211

to the towns – especially London. Only in certain parts of Wales, the West Country, and a few other districts out of the reach of the railways was farmhouse butter still being sold. Many larger farmers, despite their traditional contempt for 'cow-keeping', grew to welcome their regular milk cheques.

Elsewhere, sales of fruit and vegetables or of eggs and poultry – traditionally the preserves of the farmers' wives – helped to restore prosperity. Even in the eastern counties, where the dryness of the climate precluded the introduction of dairying on any scale, the more perceptive and flexible farmers seized their opportunity to meet the changing tastes of urban consumers by producing fruit and vegetables. On many farms the growing of fodder crops and hay for urban horses also provided a valuable income, while in return dung was brought back from the towns to fertilize the soil.

Potato growing, too, expanded, especially on the silt and warp soils of Lincolnshire and Yorkshire and the light land of West Lancashire and Cheshire, where it became a money-making crop. And in the lowlands along the north-east coast of England, where a vast industrial complex was interspersed with family farms and part-time holdings, farmers were able to make a comfortable living by providing milk, pork, mutton and lamb, poultry and eggs, potatoes and other vegetables for local consumers. In Durham the mining villages situated at some distance from a port were particularly valuable outlets, since foreign produce brought to them had to incur local transport costs, which made it less competitive against food grown near at hand. Colliery companies, too, farmed considerable tracts in this area, partly to prevent expensive compensation claims when fields above coal mines sank into them, and partly to provide grazing, hay and oats for the horses they used. They also offered land to their employees for allotments and paddocks, so that they could grow vegetables, or keep pigs, poultry, and even greyhounds, whippets and pigeons for their leisure hours.[280]

In the maritime south of England, the expansion of the holiday trade along the Channel coast offered important seasonal markets for the output of many small farms and market gardens. In West Devon and Cornwall, the normal kinds of pastoral farming were supplemented by specialist products like clotted cream, early potatoes, strawberries and poultry, as well as the provision of holiday accommodation for summer visitors. Many farms in

Devon made and sold their own cider and, with the aid of these various sidelines, occupiers saw the profitability of their holdings rising once more in the new century.

Alongside this, as Maude Davies discovered at Corsley, Wiltshire, during 1905–06, farmers continued to adopt the traditional method of dealing with economic difficulties by taking on a second occupation. Of thirty-four farmers listed in Corsley, twelve had a secondary source of income, including five who held over 100 acres of land, and four between fifty and 100 acres. Indeed, the second largest farmer in the parish, cultivating 327 acres, also kept a public house. Other secondary occupations included hauling coal, postal work, a carrier's business, and running a small bakery.[146] In industrial areas, employment on the land might be coupled with even more varied jobs. Ellis Rhodes, who farmed at Shelley in Yorkshire, combined this with carting coals for the local gas works, a local brewery, and the Shelley Urban District Council. He also acted as a refuse collector for the local authority and later became the deputy manager of a colliery. He was killed in an accident there in 1907, the year in which his family relinquished the farm.[9]

The changing emphasis within agriculture in the late Victorian and Edwardian era was shown clearly in a summary of the industry's output produced for the 1908 census of production. At that date about two-thirds of total output comprised livestock and livestock products, while a high proportion of the crops were grown for animal fodder, including oats for horses and cattle, tail corn for poultry and pigs, and poorer quality barley which was destined for feed either on the farm where it was grown or through the millers. The figures in Table 10 ignore crops consumed on the farm where they were grown as animal fodder, and they also omit the produce of plots under one acre:[59]

Yet it would be idle to pretend that all farmers responded to the changed conditions with understanding and efficiency. Even the conversion to grassland, which by 1914 covered two-thirds of the cultivated area of England and Wales, was often carried through imperfectly, with the land scantily manured, unlimed and poorly drained. Daniel Hall, who followed in Rider Haggard's footsteps about a decade later, was one who, whilst welcoming the improved profitability of farming, none the less pinpointed a number of weaknesses. Among the most important of them was the poor

Table 10   Output of British Agriculture in 1908

Produce	Value	% of total value of output
Farm crops	£46.6m.	30.9
Fruit and flowers	£4.6m.	3.1
Timber	£0.6m.	0.4
Livestock	£61.4m.	40.7
Wool	£2.6m.	1.7
Milk and dairy produce	£30.0m.	19.9
Poultry and eggs	£5.0m.	3.3
	£150.8m.	100.0

standard of education among agriculturists and the extent to which this led them to neglect many of the opportunities available to them. One aspect which met his disapproval was the slowness to adopt labour-saving machinery, with farmers frequently allowing their men to go on working by hand rather than taking the trouble to teach them new ways. 'Five men may be found receiving 15s. a week when the ideal to be aimed at should be two men earning 30s. each and doing the same work with the help of machines', he declared firmly. 'It is less, not more, labour we want on most of our farms, but then the labour should be of the best and paid at rates competing with the wages of the artisan.'[179] Paradoxically, though, other critics advised farmers even in 1914 to pause before substituting machines 'when men are available and wages are not too high', in the interests of work creation and social harmony.

Hall's comments about the labour situation are particularly significant when it is recalled that in 1900 one-fifth of the British corn harvest was still being cut by non-mechanical means. Not until the First World War was full mechanization achieved. In addition, at the 1911 Census, for the first time since the 1860s, the number of men employed on farms showed an increase over the previous decade. Even the total of farmers rose a little, as landowners found it easier to let holdings and were able to reduce the amount of property in hand. The 224.3 thousand farmers and graziers recorded in 1901 had risen to 228.8 thousand ten years later. But it was among the workers (shepherds, stockmen and general labourers) that the greatest advance was made, from 621.1

thousand males and females so employed at the earlier date to
656.3 thousand at the later, an increase of around 5½per cent.
Part of the explanation for this doubtless lay in the unusually low
figures recorded in 1901 during the Boer War, when men were
engaged in the armed forces or in urban industry, but there is no
doubt that the greater prosperity of agriculture had a role to play,
too. Farmers no longer felt impelled to economize on their labour
forces as stringently as in earlier years, while the expansion of
dairying and horticulture, both labour-intensive activities using
little machinery, reinforced the trend. Interestingly, too, it was
among men in the most active age group of twenty-five to fifty-five
that the increase took place; the proportion of men *over* 55 fell
from 19.1 per cent of farm workers in 1901 to 18.2 per cent a
decade later.

As regards the wider question of education, Hall considered
that what the farmer needed was not so much extra technical
knowledge as 'the more flexible habit of mind that comes with
reading, the susceptibility to ideas that is acquired from acquaint-
ance with a different atmosphere than the one in which he
ordinarily lives'.[179] In some cases, the greater use of co-operative
selling methods might be appropriate, for example in the disposal
of fruit and vegetables. Even in the prosperous Vale of Evesham,
little headway had been made either with joint enterprises like jam
factories or with large-scale arrangements for collective buying
and selling. Instead the majority of the growers were 'fierce
individualists, keenly on the look-out for some special private
market'. Nor was there any effective organization to negotiate for
improved terms with wholesalers or with the railway companies
who carried the produce to its principal markets in the Black
Country, Birmingham and South Wales.

The lack of flexibility on the part of less progressive farmers was
also demonstrated by the failure of men in North Wales to take
advantage of the seasonal markets provided by local seaside
resorts. Instead they concentrated on their traditional stock-
raising and butter-making activities at a time when there were
shortages of liquid milk and cream in the district. The growing of
vegetables and fruit was likewise neglected. Hall noted that on his
tour he had seen no market gardening near to the resorts. Instead
the vegetables and fruit consumed were brought in via Liverpool
and Manchester. Even potatoes were imported, 'though we saw

some excellent breadths of main crop potatoes and one or two earlies . . . not a single field of cabbages, cauliflowers, marrows, or peas did we see, all crops which might yield from a single acre pretty nearly the whole rental of the usual North Wales farm'. Even when the holiday season was over, markets were to hand in the nearby slate-quarrying areas and in the manufacturing districts of Lancashire, the Potteries and the Black Country. 'But', commented Hall ironically, 'we were informed that the Welsh farmer would scorn to grow a cabbage lest he should derogate from his social status as a farmer.'

The fact that family farms still predominated in the principality, and that most of the labour was provided by relatives or resident farm servants, doubtless contributed to this conservatism. Only in the vicinity of the Glamorgan coalfields were some of the old attitudes breaking down, with a sharpening of class feelings between masters and men.[60]

But for the majority of farmers and their landlords, the final decade before the First World War clearly provided a welcome break from the penny-pinching experiences of the last quarter of the previous century. A. G. Street, whose father occupied more than six hundred acres of land in Wiltshire (four hundred of it arable), recalled the tennis parties, shooting parties, and meetings of the local hunt attended by the larger tenant farmers as well as by the gentry.[258] Landlords, for their part, could better afford to follow their favourite field sports and they not only invited tenants who co-operated with them in this respect to join shooting parties but treated them generously as regards repairs and improvements. 'Looking back on those day', Street declared, 'it seems to me that the shooting was more important than the farming.'

To Daniel Hall, however, there was a damaging lack of agrarian leadership among the landlord class compared to the situation a century earlier. 'There is nowadays no one to set beside Coke of Norfolk or the landowners who did pioneering work in the second quarter of the nineteenth century. . . . The great opportunities of leadership they might exercise in the way of drawing their tenants into co-operative marketing and purchase, or improved methods of farming, are rarely or never exercised.' At their worst, landlords had degenerated into mere rent receivers, and it was left to the agricultural colleges, Rothamsted experimental station, and similar institutions to carry out the work of research and development. The Board of Agriculture (established in 1889;) also encouraged experimentation, as in 1911, when it sponsored work at seven centres in England to assess the potentialities of sugar beet as a field crop in this country. But it was all on a small scale.

Rentals, meanwhile, had begun to move upwards once more. On the Savernake and Wilton estates in Wiltshire and on Lord Sidmouth's Devon estate, increases of 10 per cent were recorded in these years, though on the Duke of Northumberland's extensive properties they remained unchanged.[266] But farmers were now able to meet the increases without too much difficulty. As A. G. Street noted, in good seasons they expected to prosper and in bad ones to get by. Only in rare instances, mostly arising out of drink, gambling, or other character defects, did they run into serious financial difficulties. It was all very different from the situation two decades earlier.

Only the farm worker failed to benefit, as wage rates lagged behind the upsurge in prices. In 1913, when B. Seebohm Rowntree and his assistant, May Kendall, investigated labourers' living conditions, they concluded that whilst the cost of living had risen by 10 per cent between 1900 and 1910, the wages of ordinary labourers in England and Wales had risen by an average of only 3 per cent. Prices had increased a further 5 per cent between 1910 and 1912, 'with the result that *the real wages of agricultural labourers have actually diminished since 1900*'. A detailed examination of the circumstances of forty-two families in different parts of the country was carried out and on the strength of this, and of such national agricultural wage statistics as were available, Rowntree and Kendall concluded that except for the five northern counties of Northumberland, Durham, Westmorland, Lancashire and Derbyshire, where alternative employment opportunities had maintained wages at a higher level, the average earnings of ordinary farm labourers 'in every county of England and Wales' were below those needed to maintain full physical efficiency. They admitted that gardens and allotments, or the earnings of other members of the family, could bring levels above that standard, but this did not detract from the fact that '*the wage paid by farmers to agricultural labourers is, in the vast majority of cases, insufficient to maintain a family of average size in a state of merely physical efficiency*'.[246]

Critics could point out that Rowntree's sample was too small to give a true picture, and that he paid insufficient attention to regional differences in wage rates, save for his comments about the north of England, as well as to differences associated with the age and efficiency of individual workers. In addition, the position of stockmen was ignored, although in 1911 almost a quarter of a million workers were concerned with sheep, cattle and horses, i.e. 222.9 thousand, or just over a third of the total farm labour force. But it must also be remembered that stockmen had to work longer hours than their day labourer counterparts, and the small amount of extra cash they earned hardly compensated for the extra time they had to devote to caring for the animals. During the winter months, too, when the hours of daylight were shorter, it was common for farmers, even in the early twentieth century, to pay lower rates than in the summer, whilst during bad weather day men might be laid off without any pay. In 1913 the report of the Liberal Land Enquiry Committee suggested that of 1,922 parishes investigated, 47 per cent contained cases where workers' money wages had been reduced through loss of time in wet or frosty weather; in the south midlands and eastern counties alone, the proportion of parishes thus affected was 67.5 per cent.[204]

Rowntree's researches indicated that a family of five persons, i.e. husband, wife, and three children, paying a rent of 2s. per week, required an average weekly income of at least 20s. 6d. if they were to be above the poverty line. Yet the government's own statistics suggested that the weekly earnings of ordinary agricultural labourers in England averaged only 17s. 6d. in 1907; or 18s. 4d. if stockmen were included. Of this latter figure 3s., or nearly one-sixth, represented payment in kind and extra earnings at harvest, etc. In Wales, the weekly earnings of all classes of farm workers averaged 18s., and the extra payments and income in kind in this case amounted to the equivalent of 4s. 3d. per week. But within that 'average' were hidden the regional differences referred to earlier. In 1907, the average of 14s. 11d. earned in Oxfordshire could be compared to 20s. 10d. secured in Derbyshire, and 22s. 6d. and 21s. 6d. earned by stockmen in Durham and Northumberland respectively. When all factors had been taken into account, Rowntree estimated that only 9.5 per cent of agricultural labourers of all classes lived in counties where the 'average' wage figure was 20s. or above; 44.1 per cent lived in counties where it ranged between 18s. and 20s.; and the remainder secured less than 18s. a week. In addition, in calculating the 'minimum' income needed, no account had been taken of expenditure on tobacco, beer, newspapers, railways fares, amusements, or luxuries of any kind.[246] On the eve of the First World War, therefore, the real income of most farm workers had fallen below that of their late Victorian counterparts, who had benefited so greatly from the sharp fall in prices in the final quarter of the nineteenth century. Just as wage rates had proved 'sticky' in a downward direction when prices were falling, so in the Edwardian era they responded sluggishly to the reverse trend. The modest prosperity secured by labourers in the 1890s had been inexorably eroded.

Despite this, as we have seen, the number of men employed on the land as labourers, stockmen and shepherds was increasing as against the position in 1901 – even if it remained well below the 780.7 thousand male and female workers recorded in 1891, let alone the figures for earlier years. Clearly a proportion of country-men preferred to work on farms when they had the opportunity to do so, rather than seek their fortunes in the towns. Unfortunately it was the men with initiative who were most likely to move away, leaving behind those with less drive or, in some cases, with a deeper and more genuine love of the countryside. For the worker's attachment to the land and its changing seasons should never be underestimated. It was present among many of the inarticulate, hardworking men who went quietly about their daily tasks. The young Yorkshire farm servant Fred Kitchen recalled the pride he and his fellows took in their work:

> I . . . soon found ploughing the pleasantest job on the farm . . . and by the way most plough lads sing and whistle you can bet they are enjoying the work. There is artistry in drawing a clean straight furrow. Simple as it looks it's not every Tom, Dick, and Harry that can do it. . . . Every Sunday morning a group of farm chaps could be seen examining each other's ploughing, . . . and the plough lads took great pride in showing off their best.[204]

The depth of this affection for the soil – this sense of place – is brought out clearly by A. G. Street in his novel *The Gentleman of the Party*. In it the hero, George Simmons, an expert dairyman, not only clung tenaciously to his occupation, despite opportunities to earn higher wages elsewhere during the First World War, but felt himself at peace only when he had settled in the Wiltshire village of his birth. For a time he worked twelve miles away, in the Dorset vale country, and Street described his sense of desolation as he left his native village, walking behind the farm waggon which carried his scanty possessions to their new destination:

> As he walked George watched the familiar curve of the distant downs to the left of the road, and continually looked back at his old friend, Wexbury Hill, until some five miles along the road when the round clump of firs on its summit was lost to sight. This saddened him, for he felt that now in truth he was journeying into a foreign country. . . . Suddenly the downs disappeared, and they were descending into the Blackmore Vale, a flat land of rich pastures, small hedged fields, and stout timber. Wealthy-looking country, and obviously good dairying land, but with no downs, no hills of any kind – just a flat green chessboard divided into squares by dark-green, almost black hedgerows. Another strangeness, too, was that nearly all the country was in grass, there being only an occasional small patch of ploughland. George looked back towards the vanished downs with dismay.[290]

It would be incorrect to suggest that the majority of labourers were thus far committed to the landscape of their birth. The scale on which they migrated to the towns and overseas, as well as to agricultural work in other parishes in this country, proves that. But for a minority such feelings were obviously important in helping to decide whether or not they remained on the land.

If the number of labourers in 1911 had risen from the low level of ten years before, more of them were now prepared to show dissatisfaction with their conditions of employment than had been the case at the end of the Victorian era. George Edwards's Eastern Counties Agricultural Labourers' and Small Holders' Union, later renamed the National Union of Agricultural Labourers and Rural Workers, increased its membership from 1,600 at the end of 1906, shortly after its foundation, to 15,000 by the middle of 1914. At that date it had 360 branches in England and Wales, and 8,000 new members had joined during 1913 alone. Alongside this the Workers' Union, an organization primarily concerned with general labourers in the towns, also intensified its recruitment of farm workers from the autumn of 1912. Its main area of activity was the midlands, though it campaigned in East Anglia, Yorkshire and

Shropshire. By the early months of 1913 it claimed to have established some 150 agricultural branches and to have 'a foothold in at least fourteen counties'.[194] Although most of the nation's farm workers remained aloof from both organizations, a number of strikes and disputes did occur. The Workers' Union, for example, claimed to have won wage advances in Herefordshire, Gloucestershire and Wiltshire through militant action. And the *Mark Lane Express*, mouthpiece of the National Farmers' Union, referred gloomily in June 1913 to the unrest in the industry: 'it only wants the match to start the smouldering fire of discontent in many places into a blaze'.

One of the largest and most successful strikes in this period occurred in South-West Lancashire, an area where the men were already relatively well-paid but where anxiety over rising prices had led to pressure for wage advances. By May 1913 Edwards's union had recruited over 2,500 members in the area, divided amongst almost thirty branches, and felt confident enough to put forward demands for a Saturday half-holiday, a minimum wage of 24s. a week, 6d. an hour overtime, and recognition of the union by the farmers. The latter responded by discharging a number of the men, and by 20 June the dispute had so spread that about 1,000 workers were either on strike or locked out. Cash help flowed in from nearby towns, and the picketing of Irish boats arriving at Liverpool docks by members of the dockers' and stewards' unions hindered farmers' attempts to recruit Irishmen as replacements for the striking labourers. According to the *Mark Lane Express* on 30 June, pickets were also out in force preventing carts of farm produce from reaching their destination in Liverpool, though special permits were issued by the strike committee to allow sales by those farmers who had recognized their organization.

An important factor was that the dispute had broken out at a time when both hay and early potatoes were ready for gathering, and the farmers were thus under some pressure. Eventually matters came to a head early in July, when members of the National Union of Railwaymen declared that if the dispute were not ended in forty-eight hours they would refuse to handle any produce from the strike district. That proved decisive. Four days later the conflict was over, with the men receiving their Saturday half-holiday, their 6d. an hour overtime, and union recognition. Although they did not get the 24s. a week minimum wage

demanded, most employers raised pay by amounts ranging from
1s. to 3s. a week on the existing basic rate of around 20s. a
week.[294] The workers' success was undoubtedly due in part to the
perishable nature of the produce their employers were selling –
market gardeners and dairy farmers could not afford to miss
deliveries of vegetables and milk. But it owed something, too, to
the availability of alternative employment in the area, and to the
support of the dockers and railwaymen.

Where the men lacked these bargaining advantages, they were
not so successful. At St Faith's near Norwich a dispute broke out
early in 1910, when workers demanded a Saturday half-holiday
and a rise of 1s. a week in pay. The employers responded with a
firm refusal and, when the men gave notice of a strike from the end
of May, they were able to recruit sufficient non-unionists to fill
their places. These latter were housed in specially constructed
huts, and were moved around the farms in carts guarded by the
police.[175] The conflict dragged on for eight months, amid growing
bitterness, before the union leaders called it off early in January
1911. They were alarmed at the drain on union funds and the
apparent impossibility of persuading farmers to concede the wage
demand of 14s. a week. For the strikers, it was total defeat. Of
seventy-five men still out when the dispute ended, only thirty-
three were taken back immediately, on pre-strike conditions. The
remaining forty-two were left dependent on union dispute pay. A
month later, on 24 February, there were still thirty-two men and
boys supported by union funds, of whom twenty-three were
normally in regular employment. On that date it was decided that
strike pay would cease after a further week, with 'all hard cases'
dealt with individually thereafter. The last of the strike benefit was
handed over on 18 March, but a month later Edwards reported
that several men were still out of work, although most had
managed to obtain fresh employment.[8]

This failure at St Faith's did not discourage unionists elsewhere
from taking action, and in 1914 even the Norfolk workers received
a boost when the king's agent at Sandringham agreed to meet one
of the union leaders to discuss general conditions. As a result,
labourers on the king's own farms were paid 16s. a week, with
Saturday half-holiday. The agent also promised to recommend all
the king's farmer tenants to let the cottages they held on a six
months' tenancy, so as to remove one source of insecurity for their

workers. 'The King's Pay and the King's Conditions' became the slogan among Norfolk labourers, and although some employers resisted these pressures, in most cases basic wages throughout the county were raised to 15s. a week.[175]

On a wider front the public was becoming more aware of the unsatisfactory living conditions which many farm workers still experienced. This arose partly out of the Liberal Party's land campaign and of the findings of its Land Enquiry Committee, which blamed bad housing for the spread of epidemic diseases like diphtheria and scarlet fever, and claimed that many country cottages were unfit for human habitation. In its view at least 120,000 new dwellings were required in England and Wales, and these should be provided, if necessary, by rural district councils, under powers already given to them by the Housing and Town Planning Act of 1909.[204] Elsewhere, a growing number of books, articles and pamphlets on labouring life made their appearance. They ranged from classic historical studies, like W. Hasbach's *A History of the English Agricultural Labourer*, first published in English in 1908, and J. L. and B. Hammond's *The Village Labourer*, published in 1911, to such surveys as D. C. Pedder's *Where Men Decay* (1908), O. Jocelyn Dunlop's *The Farm Labourer: The History of a Modern Problem* (1913), B. Seebohm Rowntree and May Kendall's *How the Labourer Lives*, which also appeared in 1913, and F. E. Green's *The Awakening of England*, written about the same time. Government surveys of wages and conditions of employment in agriculture added to the flood of information, and helped to make the population at large more conscious both of the problems faced by rural workers and of the action needed to remedy them.

By 1914, there was a clear upsurge of interest in country life, and this applied not merely to economic affairs but to cultural attitudes as well. An increasing number of townspeople longed to return to what were felt to be the simpler verities of the country-side – what Ruskin, in the previous century, had defined as the true satisfactions of human existence: 'To watch the corn grow, and the blossoms set; to draw hard breath over ploughshare or spade; to read, to think, to have, to hope, to pray.'[281] In *Notes from Nowhere*, published in 1890, William Morris developed further this view of a society in which men were freed from the thrall of the machine and could dwell amid pastoral scenes where they could work with their hands at what they enjoyed doing. The anti-industrial views of Morris and his disciples were spread even more widely by Robert Blatchford's *Merrie England* (1894), which within a few years had sold a million copies in Great Britain. Blatchford identified socialism with rural life and saw agriculture as supplying the essential basis of any healthy national existence.

Significantly, this philosophical commitment to the simple life was almost always expressed by those who were comparatively well-off, and who were not themselves forced to engage in the backbreaking toil which farm work, and some handicrafts, required. Their romantic view of country life exerted its influence on the reading public, where it was symbolized by the appearance of the successful magazine *Country Life* at the end of the 1890s. It was started, appropriately enough, by a 'country-loving businessman'.[281]

The growth of these attitudes led to many comfortably placed middle-class people seeking the tranquillity of the rural world. The cheapening of railway fares and the spread of the rail network made possible the growth of suburbs and commuter belts. By the early twentieth century complaints were heard of the 'great run on cottages for week-end purposes for golfers' in the Chiltern district of Buckinghamshire, and of the demands of 'riverside' weekenders in the vicinity of the Thames.[60] Housing developments sprang up on the fringes of most of the larger towns and conurbations, and between 1901 and 1911 Kent, Sussex, Surrey and Hampshire all registered increases in their populations living in rural areas. Significantly, all were residential counties linked with London.[249]

Flora Thompson, working at the post office at Grayshott in Hampshire, commented on the new fashions in dress and ways of living which accompanied the influx in that part of the country.[267] George Sturt, writing of The Bourne, near Farnham, in Surrey, noted similar changes, and in his case with some ill grace. For the newcomers did not fit in with the old way of life. Instead they wished to impose their own standards and interests. Sturt commented scathingly on the new buildings and raw new roads which were under construction and the way the final shabby patches of heathland were disappearing. The hamlet had ceased to be a country place, and had been turned instead into 'a suburb of the town in the next valley, . . . the once quiet high-road is noisy with the motor-cars of the richer residents and all the town traffic that waits upon the less wealthy'.[261] During the day, as the labourer worked in his garden, he could see and hear the invasion of the new people, so alien to his own way of life. The 'sounds of piano-playing come to him, or of the affected excitement of a tennis-party; or the braying of a motor-car informs him that the rich who are his masters are on the road'.

Yet, however much Sturt and his fellows might dislike these changes, they were powerless to stop them. The growth of suburbia was destined to continue inexorably.

Far less successful in merging the life and work of town and country were the attempts of William Morris and his supporters to revive handicraft industries in the rural districts. The newly established arts and crafts movement, for example, sought to concentrate its activities in the countryside, away from the influence of urbanization and of machine production. In 1902 its principal body, the Guild of Handicraft, moved from London to Chipping Campden in Gloucestershire, where a group of skilled craftsmen divided their time between following their trade and cultivating seventy-seven acres of land which they had acquired. Filled with missionary zeal, they also established art classes, social clubs, and even swimming associations for the local people. But the movement gradually lost momentum in that remote location and in 1914 it was wound up.[281] At Haslemere in Surrey a second venture, the Peasant Arts Society, attempted to encourage cottage handweaving, while at Woolhampton in Berkshire there was a scheme to establish an art pottery industry. Neither prospered. Clearly these efforts to return to the 'simple life' struck few chords of sympathy with local inhabitants, who knew from bitter experience just how arduous that could be.

But where the idealism of the arts and crafts movement failed to penetrate the heart of village life, the same could not be said of the harsher realities of the manufacturing, mining and quarrying industries. As in D. H. Lawrence's childhood home at Eastwood in Nottinghamshire, so in parts of Derbyshire, Leicestershire, Yorkshire and South Wales, agriculture was forced to retreat in the face of an expanding coal industry. During these years there was a wholesale alteration in the economic and social character of many communities as they moved from farming to mining. In Cornwall the china clay works, tinmining, and quarrying had a similar result, while in Flint in North Wales the main engines of change were the quarries.[60]

Already by 1914, therefore, many traditional distinctions between town and country had been blurred, as former urban dwellers moved into new villas in the suburbs, and as industry itself, particularly mining, extended its tentacles over a widening area. These changes had been under way since the beginning of the industrial revolution, but they received fresh impetus during the early twentieth century. The First World War was to intensify the trends further and was largely to shatter such of the old ways as had managed to survive. It is that period of war we must now consider.

Following the declaration of hostilities on 4 August 1914, there was a great upsurge of patriotic feeling within all classes in rural England. Amongst the first to be called to the colours were the reservists, who were quickly joined by a number of volunteers, members of the Territorial Army or the local yeomanry. Some were sent overseas almost immediately; others, like George Sherston, the hero of Siegfried Sassoon's autobiographical novel *The Complete Memoirs of George Sherston*, spent the first weeks of hostilities training at hastily established camps dotted about the countryside. 'The flavour and significance of life were around me in the homely smells of the thriving farm where we were quartered', wrote Sassoon; 'my own abounding health responded zestfully to the outdoor world, to the apple-scented orchards, and all those fertilities which the harassed farmer was gathering in while stupendous events were developing across the Channel.'[289] Not until the following year was Sherston himself to face the bitter realities of the battle-front.

In countless villages, meanwhile, recruitment meetings were held and women's knitting and sewing parties organized, to provide 'comforts' for the fighting men. A growing number of landowners felt it their duty to encourage the youthful members of their own families to enlist and to put pressure on younger, unmarried estate workers to follow suit. This was especially the case once the harvest of 1914 had been safely gathered in. On the Earl of Ancaster's estates in Lincolnshire and Rutland a circular was issued to employees, promising that if they joined up their situations would be kept open for them, and their families cared for. 'Those desirous of enlisting should send their names to the head of their department, or the Agent . . . as early as possible. All travelling expenses to the nearest recruitment station will be allowed.' In addition a bonus of £5 was to paid by the Earl to each man who joined up. The Duke of Rutland put forward much the same proposals, save that in his case no bonus was offered. The policy proved successful, for early in September twenty-two young men from the villages of Empingham and Normanton in Lincolnshire were taken in motor-cars lent by the Ancaster family to enlist at the Stamford recruitment centre. Three days later the fourteen who had passed their medical examination were on their way to barracks in Lincoln, taking with them a pipe, tobacco and cigarettes supplied by the Countess of Ancaster and the local clergyman.[50]

There were some exceptions to this approach. On the Duke of Bedford's estate his agent, Rowland Prothero (later Lord Ernle and from 1916 President of the Board of Agriculture) refused to hold recruitment meetings because he was 'coward enough to shrink from trying to influence my friends and neighbours'.[156] But that kind of sensitivity was rarely displayed in the heady early days of the War. Even the Agricultural Shows played their part. At the Bath and West Show of 1915, the only one held by that Society during the War, the secretary reported the recruiting sergeants 'busy in all directions. . . . Those who were told off for this duty were admitted free and provision was made in the yard for the medical examination of likely candidates for military service. Many placards appealed to all who could to join the ranks of the King's Army, and the officers and men engaged appeared to be well satisfied with the results of their efforts'.[192]

Often workers enlisted who had little idea what they were fighting for. F. E. Green wrote of a cowman, whom he knew, asking whether Belgium belonged to Britain, while an old man whose son had been sent to Egypt anxiously enquired whether India was 'this side or t'other of Egypt'.[170] Others, especially married men, were attracted by the fact that with their various allowances they could earn more for themselves and their families in the forces than on the land, and cases were quoted by farmers where 25 or even 50 per cent of their men had enlisted.[17]

Overall, a Board of Trade return suggested that by January 1915 approximately 15.6 per cent of the farm labourers of England and

Wales had joined up, or had been recruited by the government for civilian work. The number of male labourers actually employed on the land, however, had dropped by only 12.4 per cent below the January 1914 figure.[211] This was because farmers were able to recruit from other sources a considerable number of replacements. In some cases elderly or retired workers returned to employment; more often, men wounded out of the services or youths too young to enlist were secured. The percentage of enlistments varied widely, too, between districts. In the south-west it had reached 18 per cent of the labour force, whereas in some northern areas, where labourers were engaged by the half-year or year, it was only about half that figure. In the Driffield area of Yorkshire, farmers complained of the problems created by a local Waggoners' Reserve of the Army Service Corps. Before the War the men had received £1 a year to be registered as waggoners, and when hostilities broke out about a thousand of them were called up. One farmer grumbled that on the four holdings around him, twenty servants had been enrolled and had left at short notice by October 1914.[45] In subsequent years the outflow continued, and by January 1917 the War Cabinet estimated that about 240,000 permanent male workers had been lost to the industry in Britain as a whole. Modern writers, including P. E. Dewey, have argued that this was an exaggeration, but even Dewey's own figures suggest a loss of more than a quarter of all regularly hired male workers over eighteen during the course of the War, plus about one-sixth of the farmers' sons in the same age category.[98] The loss of such a large group of active, experienced men inevitably affected both farming standards and the nature of community life.

One way of meeting the labour shortage was to persuade village women to take up land work again. In the early stages of the War neither they nor the farmers were enthusiastic about this solution, for women were rarely experienced in taking on jobs connected with horses, sheep or beef cattle, and most lacked the physical strength to lug heavy sacks of seed about for the drills, or of grain for the threshers. In addition, those whose husbands were in the armed forces were able to manage comfortably on the allowances they received. In October 1914 the wife of a private or corporal with two children was paid 17s. 6d. a week, excluding the man's own personal allowance. Not until 1916 did attitudes change, with volunteers now assured that 'every woman who helps in agriculture during the war is as truly serving her country as the man who is fighting in the trenches or on the sea'. Some were even issued with certificates and armbands to show that they had registered for agricultural work.[119]

As a result of these efforts, by the end of 1917 perhaps 270,000 women were employed in farm work of one sort or another. Most were village women, although a small contribution was made from the beginning of that year by the new Women's Land Army. At the end of 1917 it had approximately 5,700 recruits working on the farms. Clad in long, mud-proof boots, brown knee breeches, jerseys and mackintoshes, the land girls, often from non-agricultural, middle-class backgrounds, were viewed with suspicion by farmers and their wives, as well as by the village women. In Essex it was said that these latter were so jealous of them that they sometimes refused to work alongside them.[60] But in the long run most of the barriers were broken down and their contribution, particularly for milking and general field work, was welcomed. Normally they were given a special short course of training on a farm or at an agricultural college before they were sent to their employer. The aim was to equip them with the skills to milk five or six cows twice a day, to feed calves and pigs, clean out barns and carry out rough field work.[26]

In the main, however, the women's contribution was an intensification of the part-time work they had performed at the busy seasons in pre-war days. Late in 1918 it was reported from Northumberland that, in places where it had been customary for a man and wife to be engaged as a 'double-hind', the women were carrying on the work alone, while in Cheshire about one-third of the total agricultural labour force was now female. In parts of Lincolnshire, too, there was an increased use of the gang system, and in Worcestershire, Oxfordshire and Staffordshire, women were similarly taking a major role.[60] To wives and mothers left at home waiting for news of loved ones, the opportunity to play a useful part on the farms was no doubt welcome. An added incentive was, perhaps, that military allowances were now failing to keep pace with inflation, and on economic grounds many women in the latter stages of the War found they had to work. Inevitably, their employment disrupted family life. In Holland, Lincolnshire, young girls were given exemption from school, so that they could stay at home to carry out domestic chores and look after still younger brothers and sisters whilst their mothers worked on the farms.

The children, too, were drawn into the fray. Although child employment in agriculture had been on the wane for some years before 1914, immediately hostilities broke out education authorities were inundated with appeals from farmers for a relaxation of attendance bye-laws to permit young children to work. From then on numbers quickly increased. During the period 1 February to 30 April 1915, in the nation as a whole, 3,705 boys and 106 girls were given exemption from school attendance for farm work, even though they were below the official school leaving age. One Yorkshire member of the National Farmers' Union had even suggested jokingly in October 1914 that the best thing would be to close the schools, so that all the lads could go on the farms, and 'all the teachers . . . to the front'.[45] Certainly, the number of youngsters recruited rose sharply, and by 31 May 1916 14,441 boys and 1,312 girls were so employed, of whom 493 boys and fifty-three girls were under twelve.[85] The deleterious effect this had upon the school routine, and the pressures it placed on the children concerned, are easy to envisage. In some cases the hours of school attendance were also adjusted to fit in with the children's work plans. At Little Brickhill, Buckinghamshire, in the spring of 1916, the school day commenced at 8 a.m.; the 'luncheon' break was taken between 10.30 a.m. and 11.30 a.m.; and the day ended at 1.40 p.m.[28] The children were then free to spend the afternoon at work. It was on grounds such as these that F. E. Green wrote bitterly of the way in which children had been robbed of their education whilst 'their natural protector was away fighting our battles in the trenches. Nothing is meaner in our war annals than this exploitation of children'. The Chief Medical Officer to the Board of Education also expressed concern in 1916 at the way in which young children were being used for farm work. But his words fell on deaf ears, and youngsters continued to be employed until the end of hostilities. By that time there may have been as many as 50,000 at work.[293]

Nor was this all. About half the counties made special bye-laws, lowering the standard of compulsory attendance that had been required before the War, whilst from August 1917 country children were recruited on a part-time basis to collect horse chestnuts and blackberries, the former to be used to replace grain in certain unspecified industrial processes 'essential to the prosecution of the war', and the latter to be sent to central depots to be made into jam for the armed forces. Both campaigns were enthusiastically adopted. At the tiny Calverton Church School in Buckinghamshire, with little more than thirty scholars on the books, a total of 333½ lb of blackberries were collected between 24 September and 29 October 1917, and at Little Brickhill school over the same period the amount gathered almost reached 600 lb.[28] During the same year encouragement was given to schools to cultivate gardens, where extra vegetables, especially potatoes, could be grown. Countless log books contain references to youngsters working on the so-called 'Victory Plots', digging, planting, and harvesting the crops. These schemes were continued with equal vigour during the 1918 season, the aim being to inculcate into the children a sense of personal and national commitment, 'a keener sense of common sacrifice and common duty', and the desire to participate as far as they were able in the great struggle.[69]

The recruitment of men from the farms for the armed services and their partial replacement by women and children were among the most obvious effects of the War upon agricultural life, but they were certainly not the only ones. Horses and fodder, too, were requisitioned for military purposes, whilst rising prices and reduced supplies of imported animal feed and fertilizers hampered food production. Farmers also complained of the way in which stacks of oats, hay, or straw were requisitioned by the Army and were then left for months in the stackyard because of a miscalculation of local needs. The farmer was unable to use the stacks himself, or the space they occupied for the next season's crop; neither could he obtain payment until the War Office took physical possession of the supplies. Not until July 1915 did the War Office listen to agriculturists' complaints on this score and set up forage appeals committees, one for the north and one for the south of the country, to hear charges of excessive purchases or inadequate prices. Shortly afterwards, agricultural sub-committees were also set up by county councils to act as links between the farmer and the Board of Agriculture over such matters as the supply of labour, the provision of fertilizers, and similar issues. At the same time, encouragement was given to agriculturists to grow more wheat, oats, potatoes, and other essential food stuffs, but as no guarantees over prices were offered, the response of farmers was disappointing. They had bitter memories of the disasters faced by grain farmers thirty years before, and were chary of embarking upon any major 'plough up' campaign without a degree of government financial commitment being put forward.[17]

Production was disrupted, too, by the conversion of thousands of acres of formerly cultivated land into army camps and training centres, and later into aerodromes. Munitions factories also sprang up in rural areas and soon recruited local labour, especially women. The Chilterns was one district affected in this fashion, and as early as 19 September 1914 the *Bucks Herald* was reporting the transformation of the normally sleepy little town of Tring by the billeting of 1,600 soldiers, with another thousand in nearby villages. Firing ranges were constructed upon former farm land, and gunfire disturbed the usually peaceful countryside. Early in February 1915 the headmaster of nearby Ivinghoe school described the large numbers of soldiers who were passing through the village, 'drums beating, and the men singing disturbs, somewhat, the work, & excites the children, but they see the true meaning of discipline'.[28]

The advent of an army camp inevitably disrupted the entire agricultural routine of a neighbourhood, with the fields and lanes of the affected district often becoming a sea of mud, especially during the wet winter and spring of 1914–15. A Sussex farmer complained at a meeting of the National Farmers' Union that the military had commandeered 100 acres of formerly enclosed pasture land around his house. Roads had been driven across it, the land was covered with huts, and his farmyard was a muddy morass. Rifle ranges had been set up across part of his arable land and the soldiers had entrenched thirty acres at the south end of his farm. He himself had no control over developments but was entirely in the hands of the War Office. In the meantime, he could see his life's work being destroyed around him. Sussex was, of course, one of the counties worst affected by these developments. 'Every town you visit is a garrison town swarming with soldiers in the making and everywhere possible big camps are in existence', wrote the headmaster of Fletching school in February 1915. 'In Lewes . . . there are more soldiers than inhabitants.'[27]

Farm workers were engaged to help build the camps, and many discovered that the pay offered by contractors was considerably better than that provided by the farmers. They hastily left the land

for the new employment. Horses, too, were temporarily commandeered for the same purpose. On one farm at Tarrant Launceston,
Dorset, where a naval camp was under construction, the farmer
had to hire out seven of his horses and three of his waggons to help
with building work during the last weeks of 1914. The normal
hiring fee was £1 10s. a day for three horses and a waggon, and £1
for one horse and waggon, but that was small compensation when
work was being held back on his farm.[9]

A. G. Street's family holding in Wiltshire faced similar uphea-
vals. From the spring of 1915, the military authorities started to
build camps all round the neighbourhood: 'This altered the labour
market with a vengeance. Boys who were not yet of military age,
were at a premium, and could get three times as much money as
their fathers, by working for the contractors who were constructing the new camps. At that period the farms in our neighbourhood would have been denuded of almost all labour', wrote Street,
'but for the fact that the married men lived in the farm
cottages. . . . Young carters being especially in demand for camp-
hauling, we were hard put to it to man our six two-horse single-
furrow plough teams.'[258] Even when the camps were completed
there were many other jobs for local labourers to carry out, and
the farmers, for their part, although benefiting from the higher
prices paid for food, managed to continue in business only by
adopting labour-saving methods and by allowing the standard of
husbandry to deteriorate. Banks were left untrimmed, ditches
uncleaned and, towards the end of the War, excessive cropping of
corn and fertilizer shortages caused the soil to lose fertility.

In the initial stages of the War, the government took little action
to regulate either recruitment for the armed services or the pattern
of agricultural production, so as to ensure that a larger proportion
of the population could be fed from home resources. Throughout
these years there was, indeed, a conflict of aim between the Board
of Agriculture, which was anxious to maximize food production,
and the War Office, which was concerned to maintain military
strength. Thus, under arrangements made in August 1915 for the
registration of all males aged between fifteen and sixty-five who
were not already serving with the forces, skilled men working as
bailiffs, shepherds, stockmen, horsemen, thatchers, and workers
on threshing machines and steam ploughs were to be 'starred' for
exemption. Yet recruiting officers continued to accept such men as

volunteers, provided that they could pass their medical examination. Not until the autumn of 1915 did the War Office allow tribunals composed of representatives of county and borough councils, farmers, and other employers to hear appeals by agriculturists against the enlistment of men judged indispensable for civilian production.[280] But that, too, was only partially effective, and when conscription was introduced in the spring of 1916 agricultural workers were given no blanket exemption, although periodically special restrictions on their recruitment were promulgated, only to be set aside as the exigencies of war increased. Farmers alone were certified as exempt under the terms of the Military Service Acts.

The confusions of this indecisive policy are exemplified by events at the very end of the War, when the Cabinet decided early in 1918 that another 30,000 men must be recruited from agriculture for military service before 30 June, if the German spring offensive were to be countered. By the middle of June, however, it became clear that it would be impossible to find 30,000 Grade I agriculturists for service unless a major part of the year's harvest were to be sacrificed. On 26 June, therefore, the War Cabinet decided that no more calling up notices were to be proceeded with. The number of men already posted to the colours under this scheme was just over 22,000. The fortunate remainder were never called up, as the military situation then eased.

Partly to compensate for these demands upon farm labour, the War Office offered temporary soldier help, recruited from home-based troops. The first initiatives along these lines came in the summer of 1915, when soldiers who wished for it were given two weeks' furlough to help with the haymaking. The finding of employment and the rate of remuneration were left to private negotiation between the individual soldier and the farmer. This scheme was expanded in the autumn, when official rates of pay were specified, and it was stipulated that soldiers would be supplied only if it could be proved that a shortage of civilian labour existed.[99] From the farmer's point of view the bargain was not particularly attractive. Not only had he to provide transport to and from the railway station for the soldiers, or else accommodate them on his farm, but he had to pay them the substantial daily wage of 4s. 6d. for a working day restricted to nine or ten hours, instead of the twelve or thirteen customarily worked on farms at harvest time.[280] But under pressure of labour shortage many farmers accepted the conditions, and soldiers were supplied for every harvest of the War.

Another problem was that the men provided under the schemes were often townsmen, who knew little of agricultural employment. This was a particular difficulty where workers were required for ploughing. Early in March 1917 12,500 men were released from the home defence force on furlough to assist with the ploughing; they were supplemented by 11,500 men of the CIII category, who were physically unfitted for active service in the Army and were to be formed into agricultural companies to work on the land for the rest of the War. But when these 24,000 men arrived on the farms, it was discovered that only an eighth of them had any actual experience of ploughing. The authorities then had to order all skilled soldier ploughmen in the United Kingdom to report to their depots on agricultural furlough until 30 April. By the first week of April, 40,000 men from these three different classes of recruit were working on the farms. But military needs again supervened, and before the tillage programme had been completed 18,000 of the skilled ploughmen belonging to Category A were recalled in readiness for a fresh offensive in France and Flanders.[155] In the case of the remaining men, the furlough was extended to July 25. It was in this piecemeal, disorganized, hand-to-mouth fashion that the system continued to the end of the War. By January 1918 a total of 41,361 soldiers were at work on Britain's farms.

From the beginning of 1917 the labour of prisoners of war was also utilized on the land, initially on a minimal scale, but by 1 January 1918 numbers had risen to 5,934. During the next month a number of German prisoners who were skilled ploughmen were transferred to this country from camps in France, and by June numbers had increased to 11,794. They were accommodated either in 190 special camps set up for the purpose, or in lodgings provided on the farms.[155] In Oxfordshire five such camps were established, each accommodating about forty men, and by the beginning of March 1918 the military authorities were informing farmers within a five-mile radius of them that they could hire gangs of five men, with a British soldier agricultural worker as guard, on a day rate basis. Horses, tractors, and other implements were also available for hire under a system of piecework payments.[47] In addition, during the corn and potato harvests of 1918, sixteen mobile gangs of ten prisoners operated in different parts of the county, travelling from farm to farm. 'In two instances only were the prisoners unemployed' on account of 'prejudice on the part of farmers in the neighbourhood', the *Oxford Chronicle* reported in November 1918. Similar schemes operated elsewhere, and by the end of 1918 the joint contribution of soldiers and prisoners of war to the farm labour force had risen sharply, to 72,247 and 30,405 men, respectively.

Despite the low productivity of many of the prisoners in the early days, attributable in part to bad feeding (for farmers were not allowed to feed those brought in from camps) and partly to poor supervision, they provided welcome additional labour for hard-pressed farmers.[293] And when the latter were permitted to provide them with extra food and drink (such as boiled potatoes and coffee) their output rose sharply. They continued to be employed for some months after the War had ended, as efforts were made to adjust to peacetime production, and as late as September 1919 there were around 25,000 of them still at work. Not until December of that year was the repatriation programme finally carried through.

From February 1917, a small use was also made of newly recruited National Service volunteers. In a circular issued early in the year the National Service Department called on men aged between eighteen and sixty-one to enrol: 'Professional men, clerks, shop-keepers, all who are country-born and country-bred, who had perhaps some knowledge of gardening and feel they would be useful on the land should enrol'.[18] In practice, very few proved suitable for the work.

A wider employment of the Women's Land Army, with 11,529 women engaged on farms under its auspices by the end of 1918, and the increased use of imported tractors – the government supplying 1,600 of these by early 1918 – were other ways in which the authorities sought to compensate for the problems created by their military recruitment drives in country districts. But although more machinery was in use, a major programme of mechanization was held back by the fact that most *native* agricultural implement makers were concentrating on munitions work. There was also a damaging shortage of blacksmiths, wheelwrights and harness-makers, who were needed to repair the agricultural implements and machinery. Blacksmiths' and wheelwrights' shops were closed, or seriously understaffed, in many counties.[155]

However, despite the often contradictory policies pursued for military recruitment, the overall quantity of labour on the land was well maintained by the employment of various substitute workers, though in quality terms these rarely matched the men they were replacing. Even in the worst year, 1916, one estimate suggests a shortfall of only about 7 per cent in the total compared to the pre-War situation.[99] It was by these efforts that the output of the industry was sustained, and that, thanks to judicious changes in product patterns and to food *economy* measures, including rationing, by the end of the War, British agriculture was feeding the population for an equivalent of 155 days in the year, compared to only 125 days at its outbreak.

That achievement had been made all the more difficult by the fact that initially the government had been just as unwilling to interfere with the pattern of food production as it had been to organize the nation's agricultural manpower on a systematic basis. The Board of Agriculture throughout had sought to encourage farmers to grow more grain, but had not been prepared to back this up by a system of guaranteed prices in the early stages. Even the recommendations in July 1915 of the Milner Committee in favour of guarantees failed to bring about a change. So, despite official exhortations, in 1916 the wheat acreage actually fell, and the total arable area dropped below the level of 1913. The harvest for that year was also poor.

Under this *laissez-faire* policy, the principal beneficiaries were the farmers, who were free to concentrate on producing those items most profitable to them. They also gained from the fact that whereas over the period 1914 to 1916 the cost of living rose by 46 per cent, the prices they secured for their products increased on average by around 59 per cent. Rents, by contrast, remained virtually static, except when farms changed hands, and agricultural wage rates rose by less than 20 per cent over the same period. With income running so comfortably ahead of outgoings it was small wonder that one official observer could claim: 'On most farms 1916 was *the* good year for farmers'.[58] Subsequently A. G. Street noted of the War period as a whole: 'It was impossible to lose money at farming just then'.

But if 1916, with its high prices and shortages, proved advantageous to farmers, for the rest of the nation it was a time of grave difficulty. To add to the problems of the poor harvest there was the menace of a determined German submarine campaign, which hampered attempts to import food from the United States. In these dire circumstances, in December 1916 a new Cabinet at last resolved to intervene directly to stimulate the home supply of grain and potatoes through a guaranteed pricing system. The use of price controls, first introduced for milk in November 1916, was also to be extended to a wider range of food in order to safeguard the consumer. The guarantees for wheat and oats were subsequently incorporated in the 1917 Corn Production Act, while a separate arrangement for potatoes was put in hand. In addition, in an unprecedented interference with private property rights, the Corn Production Act not only prohibited increases in farm rentals but also empowered the Board of Agriculture to enforce the proper cultivation of the land. If an occupier were unable or unwilling to reform, his holding could be taken in hand and farmed under the auspices of the special War Agricultural Executive Committees, which were now to be established in every county. In practice, this part of the legislation had no great impact. Only about 24,000 acres had to be taken in hand; Essex, with 2,500 acres and Kent, with 1,900, headed the list.[211] Where such drastic action was needed, the Executive Committees wisely entrusted the management of these near-derelict holdings to some skilful local farmer, who took a pride in restoring the land to fertility.

Alongside these initiatives went a new bread control policy, designed to ensure that milling ratios were raised and that as much of the grain as possible was used for breadmaking purposes. Inevitably this reduced the cereal residues available for animal fodder and, coupled with the restrictions on the imports of animal feeding stuffs, added to the difficulties of livestock producers. In 1918, for the only time during the War, farmers' real profitability actually diminished as compared to the preceding twelve months, although it remained well above the pre-War level.

Finally, for farm workers the Corn Production Act established a system of Wages Boards, designed to fix a minimum wage for the industry. This was something for which the agricultural trade union movement had been pressing for almost a decade, and by 1918, when the scheme came into operation, rates of 30s. a week and more were being fixed.[175] Prior to this the wages of labourers had lagged behind prices, so that in January 1917 real wages were on average 13 per cent below the pre-War level. A Commission of

Inquiry into Industrial Unrest in that year concluded that in the south-west, the fact that labourers in Somerset, Gloucestershire, and Wiltshire were still being paid at the rate of 18s. or 20s. per week was one cause of discontent in that area.[77] Not until after 1918 were the men's real wages restored to the pre-War standard.

Meanwhile, the trade unions were drawn into the wage fixing machinery and in these conditions of official recognition and labour shortage, membership of both major organizations in the industry soared. By October 1919 Edwards's National Union claimed 170,749 members, divided among 2,583 branches; the Workers' Union indicated that it had over 100,000 members in its agricultural section. In the early 1920s, under the pressure of renewed agricultural depression, this new wages machinery was swept aside. But its demise proved only temporary. In 1924 Wages Boards were re-established, and in this respect, as with the general interventionist stance of the government towards agriculture, the War marked a turning point. It was a final retreat from pre-War policies of *laissez-faire*. Even the withdrawal by the state of its system of guaranteed minimum prices for cereal products in 1921 proved only temporary. By the 1930s price guarantees and production quotas for agricultural products were widely accepted.

It was, then, under conditions of greater state control than had ever existed before that the War at last came to an end with the signing of the Armistice in November 1918. But despite the ostensible return to normality, village life was never to be the same again. Apart from the residual effects of government intervention and the increased mechanization of agriculture, there was the human cost to be counted. The War Memorials which still dot the landscape bear mute witness to that. At Waddesdon in Buckinghamshire, where in 1911 the population stood at around 1,500, there are sixty names recorded. At Sutton Courtenay, then in Berkshire, of 159 men listed as serving in the armed forces, thirty-one had died or were missing and twenty-three had been wounded by the time hostilities ended. About one in three of all those who joined up were thus killed or injured. This takes no account of the mental anguish and the spiritual scars which may have been endured by many of the survivors.

Perhaps the clearest indication of the toll exacted is given by a sergeant from Odiham in Hampshire, who served with the Royal

Hampshire Regiment at the battle of Passchendaele. 'My platoon was all Hampshire men,' he wrote, 'they came from villages I knew, and as they got knocked off I said to myself, "There goes Hartley Wintney or there goes Old Basing." It was like wiping those places off the map . . . some of them I'd even been to school with and I said to myself, "Hampshire's getting a good old doing".'[285]

Meanwhile, for the wives and mothers who remained behind, waiting for news, there were months of constant, gnawing anxiety. The *Mark Lane Express* in September 1914 described one woman waiting at her cottage door as the local carrier came on his regular journey from town. She wanted to ask if he had seen the latest edition of the newspaper and if there were anything fresh to report, for she had two sons at the front. Similarly, at the small Cotswold town of Burford, the third soldier to be killed, a young man named William Kite, was the only surviving son of an elderly labouring couple whose five other children had all died from tuberculosis. To his parents, who had never been farther than five miles from home, 'war' meant little. All they knew was that throughout their lives, Fate had taken away whatever it gave, and their son was no exception. In all, thirty-six men from Burford lost their lives in the War.

The landed classes, too, with their long military traditions, suffered grievously from the slaughter of the battlefield – *pro rata* perhaps more than any other group. By the end of 1914 the dead already included three peers, fifty-two sons of peers, sixteen baronets and eighty-two sons of baronets, in addition to six knights and eighty-four knights' sons. Winchester, typical of the public schools, sent none of its boys to Oxford in 1915, and of those who had left school immediately prior to the outbreak of war, the vast majority had joined up before conscription was brought in.

Heavier death duties also forced many land sales, especially if the owner's death was quickly followed by that of the heir, killed at the front. Often, family mansions were converted into temporary hospitals or convalescent homes, while the daughters of the house undertook nursing or canteen work. Life-styles were changed radically as a result of higher taxes, general shortages, and a lack of domestic servants. Field sports were drastically curtailed, and fox-hunting was largely at an end by 1917. Shooting, too, was much reduced. At Gorhambury, the gamekeeping staff was so diminished by 1918 that virtually no rabbits were shot in that season.[266]

For most country people, though, it was the all-pervading anxiety of the long struggle which was hardest to bear. This was identified by the headmaster of the village school at Fletching in Sussex, when he described his emotions as the armistice was signed in November 1918:

I am afraid [the War] has aged us more than the 4½ years warrant as regards time, and this is especially true with those whose friends were fighting, or in positions of danger. . . . As I look back over the last 4½ years I can see so many tragedies in families I know well, & I can see so many of my old boys who are dead or wounded, or dying of consumption & recall them as boys at school where I used to urge on them the duty of patriotism, so that at present, it doesn't seem right that those who have escaped shall give themselves up to Joy days.[27]

It is, then, on a sombre note that we must conclude this account of the changing countryside between 1870 and the First World War. The self-confidence and prosperity of the mid-Victorian era – at least as far as landowners and farmers were concerned – had already given way to doubts and difficulties in the years of agricultural recession. Then came a measure of revival in the early twentieth century, before the onslaught of the War itself ended once and for all the old deferential character of rural society. After 1918, class differences were to be sharpened and the sense of community to be eroded still further. Agriculture, too, after an immediate post-War boom, entered upon years of depression in the 1920s and 1930s, its share of national income falling from over 6 per cent in the War years to 4.2 per cent in 1924 and 3.9 per cent eleven years later.[147] Especially hard-hit were those former tenants who had purchased their farms in the great land sales upsurge of 1918–21, but now found themselves burdened by large debts which they were unable to repay and the interest upon which provided a serious drain on their already scanty resources. By 1921, about 20 per cent of the land in England and Wales was owned by those who occupied it, compared to only 11 per cent in that category in 1914.

But the break-up of so many landed estates had important social effects beyond its influence on the farming community. No longer were major owners available to provide the cohesive cement of village life in the way they had often done, or to provide entertainment or charitable help for cottagers. No longer were large domestic and garden staffs recruited to work in mansion house and grounds, as even those owners who survived cut back on their expenditure. Often the mansion itself was sold, and as early as May 1920 the *Times* was regretting that many properties were being turned into schools or institutions or were being purchased by war profiteers.

It was in ways such as these that the 1914–18 War proved a major landmark in the story of the English countryside. After 1918, farming itself became more of an industry and less a way of life. Rural trades shrivelled further under competition from the mass-produced goods of urban manufacturers and from the output of factories which were being erected in formerly rural or semi-rural towns like Oxford, or Dunstable, or Slough. Even the landscape itself, under the pressure of renewed agricultural depression, assumed an abandoned and derelict appearance by the end of the 1930s. It was in this context that A. G. Street wrote of the years after 1918 as a 'waning of the glory', a casting aside of the old ways and a tentative and cautious search for a new kind of world.

Appendix

(*a*) *The rental and outgoings at three different periods of an estate in South Norfolk*

	1875	1885	1894
Rental	£4,139	£2,725	£1,796
Outgoings	£1,122	£1,166	£1,216
Percentage of rent absorbed by outgoings	27.1	42.8	67.7
Net receipts	£3,017	£1,559	£580

N.B. On this estate 'outgoings' increased between 1875 and 1894, despite the fall in rental.
From: *Final Report of the Royal Commission on Agricultural Depression*, P.P.1897 Vol. XV, p.29.

(*b*) *Estate accounts presented to the Royal Commission on Agricultural Depression – England*

(1878 a peak rent year)

	Year	Acreage	Rent actually received	Average rent per acre £ s d	% reduction in rent per acre
North Devon: Hon. Mark	1878	23,626	£20,778	17 7	
Rolle's estate	1892	22,670	£19,318	17 0	3.31
Cheshire: Duke of Westmin-	1883	14,565	£25,050	1 14 9	
ster's Eaton estate (only from 1883)	1892	14,318	£23,769	1 13 2	4.55
East Devon: Hon. Mark	1878	15,520	£24,614	1 11 8	
Rolle's estate	1892	15,520	£22,980	1 9 7	6.57
An Estate in Cheshire	1878	15,922	£34,345	2 3 2	
	1892	15,922	£32,022	2 0 2	6.94
Estates in Devon, Cornwall	1878	24,368	£36,362	1 9 10	
and Dorset	1892	24,792	£34,408	1 7 9	6.98

	Year	Acreage	Rent actually received	Average rent per acre			% reduction in rent per acre
				£	s	d	
Derbyshire: Duke of Devonshire's	1878	35,116	£43,655	1	4	10	9.73
estates	1892	34,430	£38,712	1	2	6	
Sussex: Goodwood estate	1878	14,247	£18,550	1	6	0	10.89
	1892	11,948	£13,878	1	3	2	
Yorkshire: Earl of Harewood's	1878	28,102	£37,627	1	6	2	13.69
estate	1892	28,193	£31,792	1	2	7	
Estates in Nottinghamshire,	1881	45,000	£32,492		14	5	16.76
Derbyshire, Lincolnshire and	1892	45,803	£28,504		12	0	
Worcester, from 1881 only							
Estate in Northumberland	1878	10,745	£9,034		16	9	17.41
	1892	11,180	£7,780		13	10	
Suffolk: Hon. W. F. D. Smith's	1878	4,654	£6,116	1	6	3	17.46
estate	1892	3,391	£3,677	1	1	8	
Gloucester: Berkeley estate	1878	17,547	£37,422	2	2	7	17.80
	1892	17,720	£30,996	1	14	11	
Westmorland: Underley estate	1878	20,394	£23,163	1	2	8	18.75
	1892	22,443	£20,650		18	5	
Lincoln and Rutland: Earl of	1878	53,049	£85,850	1	12	4	21.13
Ancaster's estate	1892	46,648	£59,467	1	5	6	
Yorkshire: West Riding, Bolton	1880	14,321	£11,873		16	6	23.73
Abbey Estate (from 1880)	1892	13,861	£8,742		12	7	
Norfolk: Earl of Leicester's	1878	44,571	£59,455	1	6	8	26.56
Holkham estate	1892	45,096	£44,305		19	7	
Suffolk: Orwell Estate	1878	15,287	£20,656	1	7	0	33.33
	1892	11,770	£10,615		18	0	
Cambridgeshire, Northampton-	1878	23,188	£44,296	1	18	2	36.02
shire and Huntingdonshire	1892	22,845	£27,963	1	4	5	
estates							

Extracted from George Lambert's *Minority Report to the Royal Commission on Agricultural Depression,* P.P.1897, Vol. XV, p.207.
N.B. Lambert noted that '20 or 22 per cent is about the average reduction in the rental value of land generally'.

Bibliography

Manuscript collections

1. Amos, George, blacksmith's accounts at Gloucestershire Record Office.
2. Bedford estate records at Bedford Estate Office, London.
3. Census of Population, Returns for 1871, at the Public Record Office.
4. Christ Church Estate Records at Christ Church Library, Oxford.
5. Crop Returns of the Counties at the Public Record Office.
6. Dashwood Papers at the Bodleian Library, Oxford.
7. Dew, George J., Diaries of, at the Bodleian Library, Oxford.
8. Eastern Counties Agricultural Labourers and Small Holders Union (later the National Agricultural Labourers' and Rural Workers' Union), records of, at the Museum of English Rural Life, Reading.
9. Farm Records in the Library of the University of Reading.
10. Fremantle MSS. at Buckinghamshire Record Office.
11. Ford, James, Reminiscences and Diary of a Police Superintendent, at the Museum of English Rural Life, Reading.
12. Hackwood Estate MSS. at Hampshire Record Office.
13. Harcourt Estate Papers at the Bodleian Library, Oxford.
14. Hiring Fairs, material on, at the Museum of English Rural Life, Reading.
15. Manning MSS. at the Bodleian Library, Oxford.
16. Mentmore Estate MSS. at Buckinghamshire Record Office.
17. National Farmers' Union, Records of, at the Museum of English Rural Life, Reading.
18. National Service Records at Hampshire Record Office.
19. National Union of Teachers, Records of, at Union Headquarters, London.
20. Norfolk Federal Union, Rules of, at the Public Record Office.

21. Oxford Diocese: Clergy Visitation Returns at the Bodleian Library, Oxford.
22. Oxley Parker Papers at Essex Record Office.
23. Petre Estate Papers at Essex Record Office.
24. Poor Law Union Minute Books at relevant County Record Offices.
25. Poor Law Inspectors, Reports of, at the Public Record Office.
26. Roscoe, Theodora, 'The Call of the Land', MS. at Buckinghamshire Record Office.
27. Saunders, Robert, Letters of, at Imperial War Museum, London.
28. School Log Books at relevant County Record Offices.
29. Smith, Margaret E., 'A Study of Scottish Settlers in Essex in the late Nineteenth Century', typescript at Essex Record Office.
30. Stanmore Papers at the British Library.
31. Swinford, George, 'History of Filkins', typescript at the Bodleian Library, Oxford.
32. Wake Papers at Northamptonshire Record Office.
33. War Committee: General Survey of War Conditions, at the Public Record Office.

Newspapers and journals

34. *Annual Register*
35. *Bucks Herald*
36. *Country Life*
37. *Dorset County Chronicle*
38. *Economist*
39. *English Labourers' Chronicle*
40. *Essex Weekly News*
41. *Hampshire Chronicle*
42. *Haverfordwest and Milford Haven Telegraph*
43. *Labourers' Union Chronicle*
44. Land Agents' Society, Journal of
45. *Mark Lane Express*
46. *Norfolk News*
47. *Oxford Chronicle*
48. *Oxford Times*

49. *Pembrokeshire Herald*
50. *Stamford Mercury*
51. *Times*, The
52. Yearbooks of the National Farmers' Union

Official reports and publications
(PP = Parliamentary Papers)

53. Aged Poor, Royal Commission on, PP 1895, Vol. XV.
54. Agricultural Depression: Final Report on, PP 1897, Vol. XV; Reports of Assistant Commissioners, PP 1894, Vol. XVI, Pt. 1; Minutes of Evidence, PP 1895, Vol. XVI.
55. Agricultural Interest, Royal Commission on, PP 1882, Vol. XV.
56. Agricultural Population, Report on the Decline of, in Great Britain 1881–1906, PP 1906, Vol. XCVI.
57. Agricultural Returns for Great Britain for 1890, PP 1890, Vol. LXXIX.
58. Agricultural Wages Board: Report of Committee Appointed to Enquire into the Financial Results of the Occupation of Agricultural Land and the Cost of Living of Rural Workers, PP 1919, Vol. VIII.
59. Agricultural Output of Great Britain in 1908, Report on, PP 1912–13, Vol. X.
60. Agriculture and Fisheries, Board of: Report on Wages and Conditions of Employment of Agricultural Labourers, PP 1919, Vol. IX.
61. Agriculture, Reports of the Royal Commission on the Employment of Children, Young Persons and Women in, First Report, PP 1867–68, Vol. XVII; Second Report, PP 1868–69, Vol. XIII; Third Report, PP 1870, Vol. XIII.
62. Attendance at Continuation Schools, Report of the Consultative Committee on, PP 1909, Vol. XVII.
63. Censuses of Population, Reports of, for 1871 to 1911.
64. Century of Agricultural Statistics: Great Britain, 1866–1966 (1968).
65. Children's Employment Commission, Second, Fourth and Sixth Reports of, PP 1864, Vol. XXII; 1865, Vol. XX; and 1867, Vol. XVI.

66. County Council Elections, Return Relating to the Cost &c. of, PP 1892, Vol. LXVIII.
67. Earnings, Returns of Agricultural Labourers', for 1869, PP 1868–69, Vol. L.
68. Education, Reports of the Committee of the Privy Council on, annually to 1899.
69. Education, Reports of the Board of, annually from 1900.
70. Elementary Education Acts, Final Report of the Commissioners on, PP 1888, Vol. XXXV.
71. Employment of School Children, Report of the Inter-Departmental Committee on, PP 1902, Vol. XXV.
72. Factory and Workshops Commission, Reports of, PP 1876, Vol. XXIX.
73. Factory Inspectors, Reports of.
74. Fisheries, Report by Inspectors of, into Disturbances in Radnorshire, PP 1881, Vol. XXIII.
75. Friendly and Benefit Building Societies, Report of Royal Commission on, PP 1874, Vol. XXIII, Pts. 1 and 2.
76. Game Laws, Select Committee on, PP 1873, Vol. XIII.
77. Industrial Unrest, Commission of Inquiry into, PP 1917–18, Vol. XV.
78. Judicial Statistics, Annual Returns of.
79. Justices of the Peace, Report of Royal Commission on the Selection of, PP 1910, Vol. XXXVII.
80. Labour, Royal Commission on: The Agricultural Labourer, England, PP 1893–94, Vol. XXXV. Wales, PP 1893–94, Vol. XXXVI.
81. Local Government Board, Annual Reports of.
82. Parliamentary and Municipal Elections, Select Committee on, PP 1868–69, Vol. VIII.
83. Physical Deterioration, Report of Inter-Departmental Committee on, PP 1904, Vol. XXXII.
84. School Attendance, Report of the Inter-Departmental Committee on Partial Exemption from, PP 1909, Vol. XVII.
85. School Attendance and Employment in Agriculture, PP 1916, Vol. XXII.
86. Secondary Education, Royal Commission on, Reports of Assistant Commissioners, PP 1895, Vol. XLVIII.
87. Tenant Farmers, Report of the Departmental Committee on, PP 1912–13, Vol. XLVII.

88. Tithe Rent-charge in Wales, Report of an Inquiry as to Disturbances in Connection with, PP 1887, Vol. XXXVIII.
89. Wales and Monmouthshire, Report of the Royal Commission on Land in, PP 1894, Vol. XXXVII; 1895, Vol. XL and XLI; 1896, Vol. XXIV.
90. *Hansard.*

Periodicals

Abbreviations:

Ag. Hist. Rev.	*Agricultural History Review*
Econ. Hist. Rev.	*Economic History Review*
Hist. Jour	*Historical Journal*
JRASE	*Journal of the Royal Agricultural Society of England*
Land Mag.	*Land Magazine*
Loc. Hist.	*Local Historian*
P.P.	*Past and Present*

91. Arnold, Rollo, 'The "Revolt of the Field" in Kent, 1872–1879' in *P.P.*, No. 64 (1974).
92. Armstrong, W. A., 'The Influence of Demographic Factors on the Position of the Agricultural Labourer in England and Wales, c.1750–1914' in *Ag. Hist. Rev.*, Vol. 29, Pt. 2 (1981).
93. Cannadine, David, 'Aristocratic Indebtedness in the Nineteenth Century: The Case Re-opened' in *Econ. Hist. Rev.*, 2nd Series, Vol. 30, No. 4 (1977).
94. Cannadine, David, 'The Landowner as Millionaire: The Finances of the Dukes of Devonshire, c.1800–c.1926' in *Ag. Hist. Rev.*, Vol. 25, Pt. 2 (1977).
95. Cochrane, Constance, 'Labourers' Cottages' in *Land Mag.*, Vol. 4 (1900).
96. Collins, E. J. T. and Jones, E. L., 'Sectoral Advance in English Agriculture 1850–80' in *Ag. Hist. Rev.*, Vol. 15, Pt. 2 (1967).
97. Collins, E. J. T., 'Migrant Labour in British Agriculture in the Nineteenth Century' in *Econ. Hist. Rev.* 2nd Series, Vol. 29, No. 1 (1976).
98. Dewey P. E., 'Agricultural Labour Supply in England and

Wales during the First World War' in *Econ. Hist. Rev.*, 2nd Series, Vol. 28, No. 1 (1975).

99. Dewey, P. E., 'Government Provision of Farm Labour in England and Wales, 1914–18' in *Ag. Hist. Rev.*, Vol. 27, Pt. 2 (1979).

100. Dunbabin, J. P. D., 'The "Revolt of the Field": The Agricultural Labourers' Movement in the 1870s' in *P.P.*, No. 26 (1963).

101. Dunbabin, J. P. D., 'Expectations of the New County Councils, and their Realization' in *Hist. Jour.*, Vol. 8, No. 3 (1965).

102. Fisher, J. R., 'The Farmers' Alliance: An Agricultural Protest Movement of the 1880's in *Ag. Hist. Rev.*, Vol. 26, Pt. 1 (1978).

103. Fox, A. Wilson, 'Agricultural Wages in England and Wales During the Last Half Century' in *Journal of the Royal Statistical Society*, Vol. 66 (1903).

104. Heath, Richard, 'The Rural Revolution' in *Contemporary Review* (1895).

105. Horn, Pamela, 'The Dorset Dairy System' in *Ag. Hist. Rev.*, Vol. 26, Pt. 2 (1978).

106. Horn, Pamela, 'Agricultural Trade Unionism and Emigration, 1872–1881' in *Hist. Jour.*, Vol. 15, No. 1 (1972).

107. Horn, Pamela, 'Rural Unionism in the 1890s: The Berkshire Agricultural and General Workers' Union' in *Loc. Hist.*, Vol. 13, No. 6 (1979).

108. Jones, David, 'The Second Rebecca Riots: A Study of Poaching on the River Wye' in *Llafur*, Vol. 2, No. 1 (1976).

109. Jones, David, 'The Poacher: A Study in Victorian Crime and Protest' in *Hist. Jour.*, Vol. 22, No. 4 (1979).

110. McConnell, Primrose, 'Experiences of a Scotsman on the Essex Clays' in *JRASE*, 3rd Series, Vol. 2, Pt. 2 (1891).

111. McQuiston, Julian R., 'Tenant Right: Farmer against Landlord in Victorian England, 1847–1883' in *Agricultural History*, Vol. 47, No. 2 (1973).

112. Mutch, Alistair, 'Farmers' Organizations and Agricultural Depression in Lancashire, 1890–1900' in *Ag. Hist. Rev.*, Vol. 31, Pt. 1 (1983).

113. Orwin, C. S., 'The History of Tenant Right' in *Agricultural Progress*, Vol. 15, Pt. 3 (1938).

114. Rose, Michael E., 'The Allowance System under the new Poor Law' in *Econ. Hist. Rev.*, 2nd Series, Vol. 19, No. 3 (1966).
115. Smith, T. Carrington, 'Fifty Years of Staffordshire Farming' in *Land Mag.*, Vol. 4 (1900).
116. Smith, T. Carrington, 'The English Farmer and his Critics' in *Land Mag.*, Vol. 1 (1897).
117. Taylor, Arnold D., 'Hodge and his Parson' in *Nineteenth Century*, Vol. 31 (1892).
117. Taylor, Arnold D., 'Hodge and his Parson' in *Nineteenth Century*, Vol. 31 (1892).
118. Wilson, H. M., 'Cottage Sanitation' in *JRASE*, 3rd Series, Vol. 3, Pt. 4 (1892).

Printed books and pamphlets (excluding novels)

119. Andrews, Irene O. and Hobbs, Margarett A., *Economic Effects of the War Upon Women and Children in Great Britain* (1918).
120. Arch, Joseph, *The Story of His Life Told by Himself* (1898).
121. Armstrong, H. B. J., ed., *A Norfolk Diary* (1949).
122. Ashby, Arthur W., *Allotments and Small Holdings in Oxfordshire* (1917).
123. Ashby, M. K. *Joseph Ashby of Tysoe 1859–1919* (1961).
124. Atkinson, Revd J. C., *Forty Years in a Moorland Parish* (1891).
125. Bagehot, Walter, *The English Constitution* (n.d. probably c.1872 ed.).
126. Barry, E. Eldon, *Nationalization in British Politics* (1965).
127. Bath, Marchioness of, *Before the Sunset Fades* (1967 ed.).
128. Baugh, G. C., ed., *Victoria History of the County of Shropshire*, Vol. 3 (1979).
129. Beastall, T. W., *A North Country Estate* (1975).
130. Beck, G. A., *The English Catholics 1850–1950* (1950).
131. Bedford, Duke of, *The Story of a Great Agricultural Estate* (1897).
132. 'Bourne, George', see Sturt, George.
133. Brodrick, Hon. George C., *English Land and English Landlords* (1881).

134. Caird, James, *Our Daily Food* (1868)
135 Caird, James, *The Landed Interest and the Supply of Food* (1878).
136. Chadwick, Owen, *The Victorian Church* (1972 ed.).
137. Chambers, J. D. and Mingay, G. E., *The Agricultural Revolution 1750–1880* (1966).
138. Clifford, Frederick, *The Agricultural Lock-out of 1874* (1875).
139. Colloms, Brenda, *Victorian Country Parsons* (1977).
140. Cornish, James G., *Reminiscences of Country Life* (1939).
141. Court, Lewis H., *The Romance of a Country Circuit* (1921).
142. Crittall, E., ed., *Victoria History of the County of Wiltshire*, Vol. 4 (1959).
143. Cuttle, George, *The Legacy of the Rural Guardians* (1934).
144. Darby H. C., ed., *A New Historical Geography of England after 1600* (1976).
145. Davies, Margaret Llewellyn, ed., *Life As We Have Known It* (1977 ed.).
146. Davies, Maude F., *Life in an English Village* (1909).
147. Deane, Phyllis & Cole, W. A., *British Economic Growth 1688–1959* (1962).
148. Donald, Joyce, ed., *The Letters of Thomas Hayton* (1979).
149. Dunbabin, J. P. D., *Rural Discontent in Nineteenth Century Britain* (1974).
150. Dunlop, O. Jocelyn, *The Farm Labourer: The History of a Modern Problem* (1913).
151. Edwards, Alfred G., *Memories* (1927).
152. Edwards, George, *From Crow-Scaring to Westminster* 1957 ed.).
153. Elworth, Frederick T., *The Evil Eye* (1895).
154. Ernle, Lord (see also Prothero, Rowland E.), *English Farming Past and Present* (2nd ed. 1917 and 6th ed. 1961).
155. Ernle, Lord, *The Land and Its People* (n.d. c.1925).
156. Ernle, Lord, *Whippingham to Westminster* (1938).
157. Evans, Eric J., *The Contentious Tithe* (1976).
158. Evans, George Ewart, *Ask the Fellows Who Cut the Hay* (1965 ed.).
159. Evans, George Ewart, *The Horse in the Furrow* (1965 ed.).
160. Evans, George Ewart, *The Farm and the Village* (1969).
161. Evans, George Ewart, *Where Beards Wag All* (1970).
162. Fisher, J. R., *Clare Sewell Read, 1826–1905* (1975).

163. Fitzrandolph, Helen and Hay, M. D., *The Rural Industries of England and Wales*, Vol. 1 (1926); Vol. 3 (1927).
164. Fox, H. S. A. and Butlin, R. A., eds., *Change in the Countryside* (1979).
165. Fuller, Margaret, *West Country Friendly Societies* (1964).
166. Gavin, Sir William, *Ninety Years of Family Farming* (1967).
167. Girouard, Mark, *The Victorian Country House* (1971).
168. Grace, D. R. and Phillips, D. C., *Ransomes of Ipswich* (1975).
169. Graves, Robert, *Goodbye to All That* (1960 ed.).
170. Green, F. E., *A History of the English Agricultural Labourer* (1920).
171. Green, J. L., *The Rural Industries of England* (n.d. c.1894).
172. Grey, Edwin, *Cottage Life in a Hertfordshire Village* (1977 ed.).
173. Grigg, John, *The Young Lloyd George* (1973).
174. Grigg, John, *Lloyd George: The People's Champion 1902–1911* (1978).
175. Groves, Reg, *Sharpen the Sickle!* (1959).
176. Haggard, H. Rider, *The Days of My Life* (1926).
177. Haggard, H. Rider, *Rural England* (1902).
178. Haggard, Lilias Rider, ed., *I Walked by Night by the 'King of the Norfolk Poachers'* (1974 ed.).
179. Hall, A. D., *A Pilgrimage of British Farming 1910–1912* (1913).
180. Hardy, Dennis, *Alternative Communities in Nineteenth Century England* (1979).
181. Hasbach, W., *A History of the English Agricultural Labourer* (1966 ed.).
182. Havinden, Michael, *Estate Villages* (1966).
183. 'Home, Michael' (Bush C. C.), *Autumn Fields* (1946).
184. 'Home, Michael' (Bush C. C.), *Winter Harvest* (1967).
185. Horn, Pamela, *Joseph Arch* (1971).
186. Horn, Pamela, *Education in Rural England, 1800–1914* (1978).
187. Horn, Pamela, *Labouring Life in the Victorian Countryside* (1976).
188. Horn, Pamela, *Oxfordshire Village Life: The Diaries of George James Dew (1846–1928), Relieving Officer* (1983).
189. Horn, Pamela, *The Rural World: 1780–1850* (1980).

190. Horn, Pamela, *The Rise and Fall of the Victorian Servant* (1975).
191. Howell, David W., *Land and People in Nineteenth Century Wales* (1978).
192. Hudson, Kenneth, *The Bath and West* (1976).
193. Hunt, E. H., *Regional Wage Variations in Britain 1850–1914* (1973).
194. Hyman, Richard, *The Workers' Union* (1971).
195. James, Revd Herbert, *The Country Clergyman and His Work* (1890).
196. Jefferies, Richard, *Hodge and His Masters* (1966 ed.).
197. Jefferies, Richard, *Field and Farm* (1957).
198. Jessopp, Augustus, *Arcady for Better for Worse* (1887).
199. Johnson, Revd Theodore, ed., *The Parish Guide* (1887).
200. Kebbel, T. E., *The Old and the New Country Life* (1891).
201. Kendall, S. G., *Farming Memoirs of a West Country Yeoman* (1944).
202. Kent, John, *Holding the Fort* (1978).
203. Kerr, Barbara, *Bound to the Soil* (1968).
204. Kitchen, Fred, *Brother to the Ox* (1963 ed.).
204. *Land, The: The Report of the Land Enquiry Committee*, Vol. 1, *Rural* (1913).
205. Lewis, Mary, ed., *Old Days in the Kent Hop Gardens* (1962).
206. Mackerness, E. D., ed., *The Journals of George Sturt 1890–1927* (1967).
207. Martin, E. W., *The Shearers and the Shorn* (1965).
208. Martins, S. Wade, *A Great Estate at Work* (1980).
209. Matthews, A. H. H., *Fifty Years of Agricultural Politics* (1915).
210. Mead, Isaac, *The Life Story of an Essex Lad* (1923).
211. Middleton, Thomas H., *Food Production in War* (1923).
212. Millerson, Geoffrey, *The Qualifying Associations* (1964).
213. [Millin, George,] *Life in Our Villages by the Special Commissioner of the 'Daily News'* (1891).
214. Mills, Dennis R., *Lord and Peasant in Nineteenth Century Britain* (1980).
215. Minchinton, W. E., ed., *Essays in Agrarian History* (1968).
216. Mingay, G. E. ed., *The Victorian Countryside* (1981).
217. Morgan, David H., *Harvesters and Harvesting 1840–1900* (1982).

218. Morgan, Kenneth O., *Wales in British Politics 1868–1922* (1980 ed.).
219. Nevill, Ralph, ed., *The Reminiscences of Lady Dorothy Nevill* (n.d. c.1906).
220. Ogilvie, Vivian, *The English Public School* (1957).
221. Olney, R. J., *Rural Society and County Government in Nineteenth Century Lincolnshire* (1979).
222. Orwin, Christabel S. and Whetham, Edith H., *History of British Agriculture 1846–1914* (1964).
223. Oxley Parker, J., *The Oxley Parker Papers* (1964).
224. Page, Wm., ed., *The Victoria History of the County of Hertford*, Vol. 2 (1908).
225. Page, Wm. and Round, J. Horace, eds., *The Victoria History of the County of Essex*, Vol. 2 (1907).
226. Page, Wm., ed., *The Victoria History of the County of Durham*, Vol. 2 (1907).
227. Page, Wm., ed., *The Victoria History of the County of Kent*, Vol. 1 (1908).
228. Pelling, Henry, *Social Geography of British Elections 1885–1910* (1967).
229. Perry, P. J., ed., *British Agriculture 1875–1914* (1973).
230. Phillips, Gregory D., *The Diehards* (1979).
231. Platts, A. and Hainton, G. H., *Education in Gloucestershire* (1954).
232. Plomer, William, ed., *Kilvert's Diary* (1977 ed.).
233. Prothero, Rowland E. (see also Ernle, Lord), *The Pioneers and Progress of English Farming* (1888).
234. Prothero, Rowland E., *The Anti-Tithe Agitation in Wales* (1888).
235. Prothero, Rowland E., *The Agricultural Depression and the Sufferings of the Clergy* (1887).
236. Randell, Arthur, *Sixty Years a Fenman*, ed. Enid Porter (1966).
237. *Rebecca Riots in Radnorshire* by an 'Occasional Correspondent' (Reprinted from the *Hereford Times*) (1879).
238. Redlich, J. and Hirst, F. W., *Local Government in England* (1903).
239. Robin, Jean, *Elmdon: Continuity and Change in a North-West Essex Village 1861–1964* (1980).
240. Rolt, L. T. C., *Waterloo Ironworks* (1969).

241. Rose, Kenneth, *The Later Cecils* (1975).
242. Rose, Walter, *The Village Carpenter* (1937).
243. Rose, Walter, *Good Neighbours* (1969 ed.).
244. Rowse, A. L., *The Churchills* (1970 ed.).
245. Rowland, Peter, *Lloyd George* (1975).
246. Rowntree, B. Seebohm and Kendall, May, *How the Labourer Lives* (2nd ed.) (n.d. c.1918).
247. Rubinstein, W. D., *Men of Property* (1981).
248. Russell, Rex C., *A History of Schools and Education in Lindsey, Lincolnshire 1800–1914* (Pt. 1, 1965) (Pt. 3, 1966).
249. Saville, John, *Rural Depopulation in England and Wales 1851–1951* (1957).
250. Scotland, Nigel, *Methodism and the Revolt of the Field* (1981).
251. Sellman, Roger R., *Devon Village Schools in the Nineteenth Century* (1967).
252. Smith, E. Lorrain, *Go East for a Farm* (1932).
253. Sneyd-Kynnersley, E. M., *HMI – Some Passages in the Life of One of H.M. Inspectors of Schools* (2nd ed.) (1910).
254. Spring, David, *The English Landed Estate in the Nineteenth Century: Its Administration* (1963).
255. Springall, L. Marion, *Labouring Life in Norfolk Villages 1834–1914* (1936).
256. Stovin, Jean, ed., *Journals of a Methodist Farmer 1871–1875* (1982).
257. Streatfeild, Noel, ed., *The Day Before Yesterday* (1956).
258. Street, A. G., *Farmer's Glory* (1959 ed.).
259. Street, A. G., *Wessex Wins* (1941).
260. Stubbs, Charles W., *The Church in the Villages* (1893).
261. Sturt, George ('Bourne, George') *Change in the Village* (1966 ed.).
262. Sturt, George, *The Wheelwright's Shop* (1963 ed.).
263. Taylor, Audrey M., *Gilletts: Bankers at Banbury and Oxford* (1964).
264. Thirsk, Joan and Imray, J., *Suffolk Farming in the Nineteenth Century* (1958).
265. Thirsk, Joan, *English Peasant Farming* (1957).
266. Thompson, F. M. L., *English Landed Society in the Nineteenth Century* (1963).
267. Thompson, Flora, *A Country Calendar and other Writings* (1979).

268. Thompson, Flora, *Lark Rise to Candleford* (1963 ed.).
269. Thompson, Thea, *Edwardian Childhoods* (1981).
270. *Tithe War, The* (issued by Clwyd Record Office, 1978).
271. Tollemache, Lionel A., *Old and Odd Memories* (1908).
272. Tubbs, Colin R., *The New Forest* (1968).
273. Turner, Barry, *Free Trade and Protection* (1971).
274. Vaughan, Herbert M., *The South Wales Squires* (1926).
275. Venn, J. A., *The Foundations of Agricultural Economics* (2nd ed.) (1933).
276. Vincent, J. E., *The Land Question in North Wales* (1896).
277. Wallace, Alfred R., *Land Nationalization* (1909 ed.).
278. *Wantage, Lord, V.C., K.C.B., A Memoir by his Wife* (1907).
279. Wearmouth, R. F., *Methodism and the Struggles of the Working Classes 1850–1900* (1954).
280. Whetham, Edith H., *The Agrarian History of England and Wales*, Vol. 8, *1914–1939* (1978).
281. Wiener, Martin J., *English Culture and the Decline of the Industrial Spirit 1850–1980* (1981).
282. Willoughby de Broke, Lord, *The Passing Years* (1924).
283. Winstanley, Michael, *Life in Kent at the Turn of the Century* (1978).
284. Woods, K. S., *The Rural Industries Round Oxford* (1921).
285. Wykes, Alan, *The Royal Hampshire Regiment* (1968).

Novels

286. Hardy, Thomas, *The Woodlanders* (1978 ed.).
287. Hardy. Thomas, *Far from the Madding Crowd* (1927 ed.).
288. Hardy, Thomas, *Tess of the D'Urbervilles* (1963 ed.).
289. Sassoon, Siegfried, *The Complete Memoirs of George Shers-ton* (1949 ed.).
290. Street, A. G., *The Gentleman of the Party* (1944 ed.).
291. Uttley, Alison, *The Country Child* (1976 ed.).

Theses

292. Baker, Caroline, 'Homedwellers and Foreigners: The Seasonal Labour Force in Kentish Agriculture, with particular Reference to Hop Picking' (University of Kent M.Phil. thesis, 1979).

293. Dewey, P. E., 'Farm Labour in Wartime: The Relationship Between the Agricultural Labour Supply and Food Production in Great Britain During 1914–1918' (University of Reading Ph.D. thesis, 1978).

294. Madden, Michael, 'The National Union of Agricultural Workers 1906–1956' (Oxford University B. Litt. thesis, 1956).

295. Mutch, Alistair, 'Rural Society in Lancashire 1840–1914' (Manchester University Ph.D. thesis, 1980).

296. Reid, Fergus M., 'Economic and Social Aspects of Landownership in the Nineteenth Century' (Oxford University B. Litt. thesis, 1956).

297. Thompson, F. M. L., 'The Economic and Social Background of the English Landed Interest, 1840–70, with particular reference to the Estates of the Dukes of Northumberland' (Oxford University D. Phil. thesis, 1956).

Index

259

Index

261